# Light and quantum
# BIOPHYSICS
# in the 21st century

## Globalisation, Extinction and Cultures that revere and sustainably harvest sunlight

by Anne Whittingham

www.nefertitigarden.com

Dedication:
This book is dedicated to the living creatures of planet Earth who are born in the 21st century.

Acknowledgements
Dr John Tyman, Aysha Sun, Irene Brown, Professor Robert Pope, Sandra van Woesik, John Whittingham, Manna Hart, Jude Fanton, Dede Callichy, Jain, Helena Norberg-Hodge, George Williams.

First Edition November 2019

Copyright 2019 Anne Whittingham.

All rights reserved. The material contained within this book is protected by copyright law. No part may be copied, reproduced, presented, stored, communicated or transmitted in any form by any means without prior written permission. All enquiries should be directed to the author.

Light and Quantum Biophysics in the 21st century: Globalisation, Extinction and Cultures that revere and sustainably harvest sunlight. by Anne Whittingham

1st ed.
Paperback ISBN 978-0-6487308-0-4

Self published by Anne Whittingham
PO Box 349, Billinudgel NSW 2483
Email: info@nefertitigarden.com

Printed in Australia by Heaneys Performers in Print

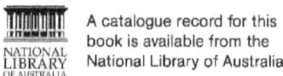
A catalogue record for this book is available from the National Library of Australia

For further information about orders:
www.nerfertitigarden.com and https://www.amazon.com/

Disclaimer: The material in this publication is of the nature of general comment only, and does not represent professional advice. It is not intended to provide specific guidance for particular circumstances and it should not be relied on as the basis for any decision to take action or not take action on any matter which it covers. Readers should obtain professional advice where appropriate, before making any such decision. To the maximum extent permitted by law, the author and publisher disclaim all responsibility and liability to any person, arising directly or indirectly from any person taking or not taking action based on the information in this publication.

# Table of Contents

1 Introduction

2 South East Asia

3 North Asia and Fengshui

4 Islamic

5 Africa

6 India and Bangladesh

7 Europe

8 South and Central America

9 North America

10 The 21$^{st}$ Century

References and Image credits

# 1 Introduction – table of contents

| | |
|---|---|
| Prelude | 6 |
| Ten components of the Light Garden | 7 |
| Scope of the book | 9 |
| Replicating Ripples: a metaphor for quantum biophysics | 10 |
| The Laws of Nature | 12 |
| Light Gardens | 13 |
| Expanded Consciousness of Light | 14 |
| Cause leads to Effect | 15 |
| Plans, Movement and Spirals | 16 |
| What are these energy flows? | 17 |
| Ten components of the Light Garden | 18 |
| Biofields and Biophysics | 19 |
| Biophotons | 20 |
| Physics and Biology in Western culture | 21 |
| Light, Atoms and Growth | 22 |
| From the Small to the Large | 24 |
| I am the Light | 25 |
| Were to from Here ? | 26 |

# Prelude

This book is dedicated to the living creatures of planet Earth who are born in the 21st century. It is intended for readers interested in light, the beauty of nature, quantum biophysics and the interaction between the spiritual and practical dimensions of life, as humanity seeks to manage climate change in the 21st century. The potential for that combination of interests to make a positive, cooperative contribution to Life in the 21st century is what prompted me to write this book, in the context that photonics are to the 21st century what electronics was to the 20th century.

The book aims to articulate and promote an expanded consciousness of light at two scales, based around the *'Light Garden'* model that is developed. The first scale is one that can be usefully applied to both the theory and the practice of farming and gardening. The second is at the global scale regeneration of the natural living systems of Earth, during our current era of the Anthropocene. (1)

Examples of how different cultures on each continent are working at these two scales in both practical and spiritual terms are considered in each chapter. For example, Chapter 4 considers the pervasive symbology of light in Islamic countries and how this is reflected in the approach to gardening and environmental management, in both the historical and contemporary contexts. Whilst it is interesting to compare one culture with another in terms of the *'Light Gardens'* that have been created, there is space in this book for only a few comparisons of that nature. Similarly, each section of the book introduces a different aspect of *'Light Gardens'*, as once again there is not space in this book to fully discuss every aspect of the *'Light Garden'* model for each continent.

Cultural movements for self reliant communities living in harmony with nature, light and beauty are also referred to as examples of implementation of the *'Light Garden'* theme of the book. These movements are quite diverse and include indigenous peoples; organic farming; traditional cultures that have survived and groups using state of the art innovative technology to foster effective action on climate change, biodiversity loss, decision making and so on.

Holding a belief that Beauty is not restricted to the eye of the beholder but that there is high degree of consensus about natural beauty and the life-sustaining principles that it embodies, I also believe it is time to re-examine old notions, such as *beauty is in the eye of the beholder.* Beauty is actually what happens when the Life force is allowed to unfold. Many of us in the modern world have been trained *not* to expect beauty to be part of the attainable, essential and cooperative mosaic of social, economic and environmental justice that is needed for Life as we move through the 21st century. However human perception of beauty both *transcends* culture, and is a common language *between* cultures.

Encompassing beauty, harmony, order and balance is the essence of the Navaho philosophy. That essence is included within the philosophies of other cultures, such as some contemporary African cultures and those of the ancient Greeks and Chinese. It is within our capacity as modern men and women, born to travel on our endless journeys through space as planet Earth rotates, to embody that essence too. It is my hope that this book may help humanity to work collectively towards that goal and be part of the rejuvenation of the living ecosystems of the Earth.

# 10 Factors for the Light Garden

Ten parameters to apply for management of the Earth as a quantum light garden in the 21st century are illustrated below. These apply at both the broad scale and at the local scale. A mnemonic to help remember these in order of 1 - 10 is **Every Summer We Love Matilda Eating Perfect, Crimson, Heavenly Strawberries.** *(E) for energy, (S) for space and time, (W) for waves and particles, (L) for lines and so on.*

*Below* image credit 1.7

Image copyright Anne Whittingham 2019

As the second decade of the 21st century draws to a close, more and more people are calling for transformative change in the way decisions are made about resource management at the global and local scales. For example, as noted by the United Nations "Intergovernmental Science-Policy Platform on Biodiversity and Ecosystem Services (IPBES):

> *"**By transformative change, we mean a fundamental, system-wide reorganization across technological, economic and social factors, including paradigms, goals and values.**"* (2)

In this context, the *'Light Garden'* model proposed in this book gains significance because it points to a future in which the growth of living organisms - and Life processes themselves - are at the centre of the next wave of our local and international cooperative efforts.

> This new wave, (whilst encompassing current work in industry, information technology, science, medicine, food production and a host of other areas), goes beyond current models and puts support for healthy life systems as the central motiving force for collective human activity.

**This wave is an alternative to retaining current, more limited motives** associated with most national government economic programs in the early 21st century. These tend to be primarily motived by factors such as support for profit generating companies and banks, ethnic or national security, growth in gross domestic product, and maintaining social order.

In 2016 Biologist Edward O. Wilson proposed that half the planet's land and water areas be set aside as nature reserves. Supporting this proposal he set out the scientific basis for calculations that 80% of existing living species could be preserved by such action. (3)

Complementing such concepts, the word ***disentanglement*** has come into parlance during the 21st century. It describes the multi-faceted, conscious process of stepping away from what is not needed, whilst rejuvenating local communities and the natural living systems of the planet.

Public awareness is growing about the powerful role of sunlight as one of the driving forces behind these processes. **Sunlight is a resource to be managed equitably,** whether it is valued primarily for the heat it transmits, the light it transmits, the energy it transmits, or for its vital role in maintaining global climate patterns and ecosystems, (including the health and welfare of human beings). As I write in 2019, record droughts, floods, increasing temperatures, loss of biodiversity and human immune system diseases are making headlines around the globe.

> *As part of this new wave of awareness, recognition is growing about the role of sunlight as a global natural resource not to be taken for granted, or corralled into the grip of the rich and powerful.*

In 2014 Sir David Attenborough described high-tech "geo-engineering" solutions to climate change as "fascist" because they put too much power into the hands of advanced nations. (4) Such studies have investigated the effects of spraying particles into clouds, the atmosphere, or onto the surface of oceans. Findings to date indicate that particular projects could each lead to approximately 4 billion people being adversely affected in direct ways, such failure of life-giving rains. (5)

# Scope of the book

*This book begins in Chapter 1 with an overview of the nature of Light and the relevance of Quantum Biophysics to equitable management of global natural resources, (including light), in the 21st Century. Chapters 2 – 9 each focus on a different continent and give examples of how particular concepts of light have been incorporated into the cultures found on those continents.*

Drawing upon the diversity of cultures described in Chapters 2 - 9, the book **concludes in Chapter 10 with testing of *Light Garden* principles for their relevance to decision making that will support rejuvenation of the living systems of Earth**, rather than further depletion of them.

These principles are relevant at the global scale and at the micro scale. They are proposed on the basis that in order to avoid collapse of cities and ecosystems around the globe, humanity needs to collectively take an immediate, quantum leap forward in how the natural resources of the Earth are managed. Working at the global scale but applying a different rationale to resource management during the past decade, many nations have invested billions of dollars in **geo-engineering**. This has attempted to slow global warming by changing the transmission, reflection and absorption of sunlight and heat on Earth.

Studies to date have invariably indicated billions of people will be disadvantaged by geo-engineering. **This book proposes a more equitable approach: applying the principles of quantum biophysics to manage the Earth as a Light Garden.**

1. **Below** Image credit 1.9 **Map location for each chapter.** *For example, Chapter 5 Africa.*

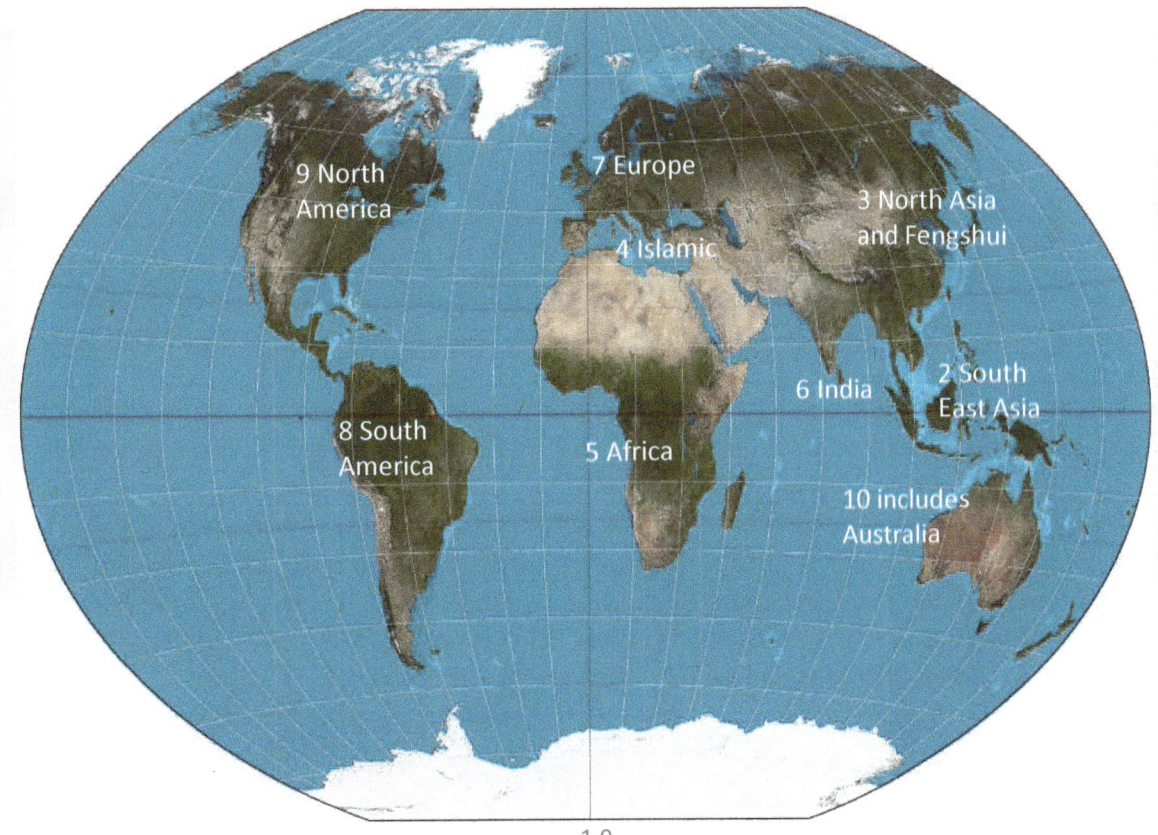

# Replicating ripples: a metaphor for quantum biophysics

As a metaphor for the quantum principles that light and energy travel in discrete parcels, the energy of ocean currents brings sand and water to the beaches in discrete waves.

The particles of sand are deposited as the sea's waves retreat . . . and in their wake new wave patterns form on the shore. As in quantum physics, the probability that one particular grain of sand will come to rest in a particular place is low. However when many grains of sand combine, as illustrated above, they make the familiar rippled pattern of small sand ridges that is found on tidal flats the world over.

Image credit 11.1

# A quantum field is like an inner spring mattress:

touch one part and the vibration moves through the whole. Reminding us of the quantum theory that *matter is forever moving as a resonant, responsive, multifaceted whole*, the pattern of sunlight in the waves is forever changing but forever following the principles of quantum biophysics.

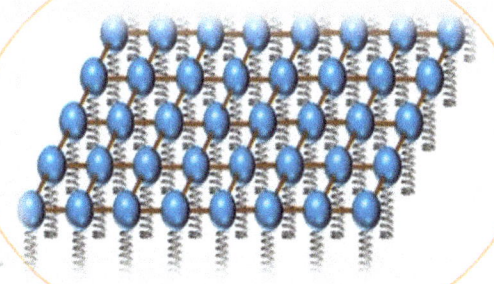

Image 11.1 copyright Anne Whittingham 2019

# The Laws of Nature

*In the 21st century, humanity's whole approach to management of ecology, landscape, urban areas and oceans is predicated by the widely recognised need to simultaneously address multiple global scale environmental, humanitarian and economic crises.*

**The** crises are not isolated but stem from a web of related causes. One of the prime causes is not making decisions based on the laws of nature.

Ironically during the last century humanity and scientists gained a far greater capacity to understand these laws at the galactic, global and sub-atomic scales. However at the global scale, we were, (and continue to be), sadly remiss in applying the laws of nature to maintain ecosystem and human health.

Economist Kate Raworth has effectively summarised the need to address the crises in her 2017 book, *"Doughnut Economics: Seven Ways to Think like a 21st Century Economist".* (6)

As illustrated in her image below, Kate refers to a *"regenerative and distributive economy"* as a necessary part of the doughnut. The *"Light Garden'* model of this book is advocated in that context. It proposes one more step towards working within the laws of nature, through an expanded consciousness of light and quantum biophysics.

**Below left** Image credit 1.12 **The Doughnut Economics** *image of the world in the 21st century. This image was designed for Kate Raworth in 2017. Sourced from https://en.wikipedia.org/wiki/File: Doughnut-classic.jpg . This file is licensed under the Creative Commons Attribution-Share Alike 4.0 International license.*

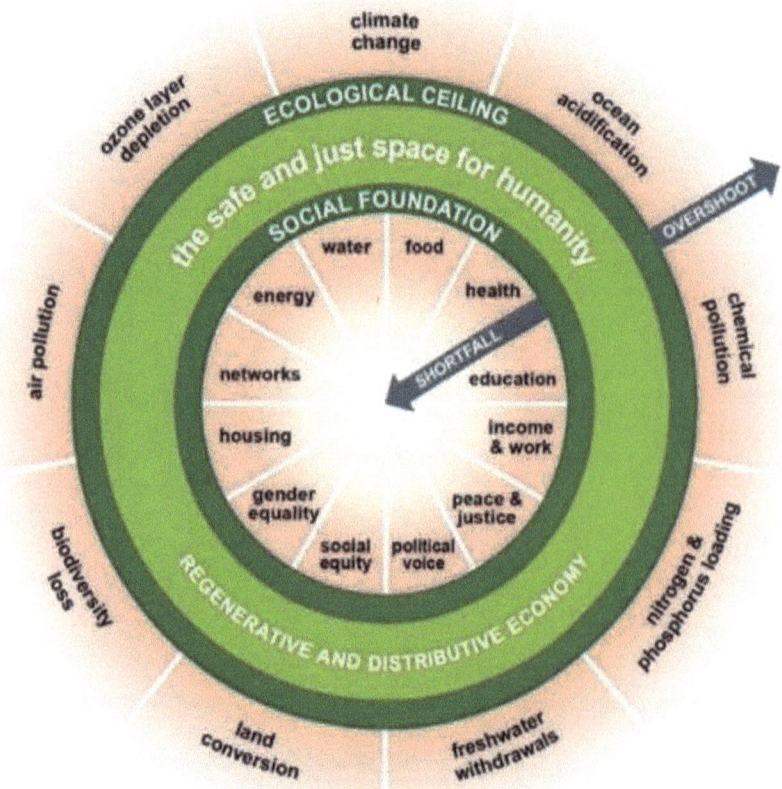

**As this chapter progresses**, I will give a sequential description of some biological processes starting with movement, light and life, then progressing to trees, photons, biophotons, quantum biophysics and biofields.

Both *Light* and *Trees* are common symbols in the traditions and religions of many cultures, perhaps reflecting an intuitive knowledge that both plants and people obtain life-giving energy from the sun.

# Light gardens

It's the light that is indispensable. With it, we co-create places and gardens. We might adapt from tilling the soil on planet Earth to making gardens in space capsules that orbit the Earth, but we still need energy.

**Food energy ultimately comes from light. It is the propellant for growth.** Although there are other processes, photosynthesis in plants is the primary way in which light energy, oxygen and water are converted into the food that underpins plant and animal life on Earth.

Image credit 1.13

# Consciousness of light

*As Galileo said about planet Earth: "It moves". We live on a continually spinning, orbiting, moving globe and as it moves, light also moves. This is not a simple game plan. There's much more involved than hopping between squares on a flat hopscotch board.*

**Each** day is defined by the movement of light from dawn to dusk as the Earth spins on its axis. Our eyes move, absorbing electrons (8) and following the light. Plants move. People move. The moon, sun, stars and galaxies all spin, rotate and spiral.

Our eyes are in continual motion, from perception of what is close to us, to what is far away, or vice versa. We have specialized cells for detecting fast moving patterns of light at the periphery of our vision. We have different retinal cells in our eyes for detecting light and colour in more detail at close range. Over seventy percent of the human brain is involved in receiving and processing light messages received from our eyes.

Utilising these dual capacities to see light with the vision system and realize meaning with the brain, humans often find delight when there is a happy combination of what is near and what is distant. Things that are near may offer refuge or safety. Those that are distant may offer prospect, adventure or inspiration.

People in many cultures have worked to enhance the meaning and purpose of their Earth stewardship and everyday gardening activities with these dual human capacities.

For example, in Bali delightful thatched shrines are found throughout the farms, gardens and villages of the land. They are aligned to face towards Mt Agung. This mountain has great spiritual significance for the people and from a practical perspective, it is the source of the rich volcanic soils and rainfall upon which the food supply and ecology depends. As illustrated at the lower left, the visual link is apparent between what is near, (the thatched shrines) and what is far (the similarly shaped from of Mount Agung).

Moon gates in Chinese gardens also are used in to highlight the psychological transition between what is near and what is further away, on the other side of a gate. A moon gate is not usually a solid gate, but rather a patch of light. As illustrated in Chapter 3, it is a circular opening in a wall through which one steps, as if stepping into the light through a large round window at ground level. Let us now pair that concept with the well known adage: "cause leads to effect".

The intention of doing that is to create the space and light for generating new thinking and new *causes* that will have the *effect* of supporting regeneration of the natural living systems of the Earth. An expanded consciousness of the role of light will be part of that story that this book presents.

Image credit 1.14 **Mt Agung**

1.14

# Cause leads to effect

*"Quantization of energy and its influence on how energy and matter interact . . . is part of the fundamental framework for understanding and describing nature."* (7)

**Trees** are wonderful powerhouses on planet Earth. In addition to their dozens of attributes, such as production of oxygen and control of soil erosion, we know that through the process we call photosynthesis, light energy from our Sun is absorbed by plants and converted into forms of stored energy, such as starches and the like. Once captured in this way, the energy can form food for other creatures as well.

**Have you ever thought of a garden as a food factory, or an energy factory, taking in light and producing packages of food and energy? I am using the word "packages" quite deliberately here, because light, (like all other forms of electromagnetic energy), comes in discrete packages. This is a simple concept. Butter comes in packages when we buy it and so does light.**

There is a need to re-examine the whole subject of the transition between energy, light and matter, if we are to address the challenge of creating new *causes* that will create new *effects* of regenerating of the natural living systems of the Earth - rather than continuing to deplete them.

So let's begin with light: a *quanta* of light is the smallest discrete package of light that exists. A photon is also called a *quanta* of light. Our basic genetic code is stored in DNA. It doesn't engage in photosynthesis but it does absorb and emit biophotons.

Biophotons are photons emitted by living creatures. What are photons? A photon can be produced by acceleration of an electron, which is a negatively charged particle such as visible light. Or it can be produced by a proton, which is positively charged particle, such as a gamma ray. After acceleration, these charged particles retain their electric charge and the neutral photon carries away some of the energy released in the acceleration event. (8)

High energy charged particles rain in on the Earth from all directions. Most of them are produced by the Sun. In the early years of the 20th century, a number of physicians and physicists, including Max Plank and Albert Einstein, were referring to quanta of light, of energy, of matter, of heat and of radiation.

Highly charged particles are emitted as solar wind from the plasma of Suns in our galaxy. So while light is being emitted and absorbed

*Below Image credit: 1.15 **Vegetation helps stabilise soil and many other things but the scale of problems in the 21st century demands a quantum leap forward in our thinking about how to work with nature and address large problems.***

# Plans, movement and spirals

*The world of nature is not full of rectangles and plans on paper. It is a big step from concepts of light and movement, or plan diagrams, to ecologically sound and beautiful creations that fit into the moving, multidimensional dimensional world of nature.*

**(continued** from previous page) from the spiral of our DNA, (and the DNA of all living creatures), it is also emitted and absorbed from the spiral of our galaxy. That light is what we are designing with – and what we are seeking to intelligently manage at all scales of living ecosystems.

Whether planning particular gardens or managing an ecosystem, drawing a plan or diagram is often the first human impulse as a means of communicating what it is intended to construct or change. For example, the Australian Aboriginals are known for their bark paintings depicting pathways, waterholes and other landmarks in the land where they travel.

However, for many people living today with computers, as soon as we enter that *plan* mindset, it's easy to overlook that we are interacting with living creatures and living systems that have evolved in response to moving globes and electromagnetic radiation, which are *not* limited to, or shaped by the mere two dimensions of a stationery plan.

Our conscious design thoughts need to expand to encompass those dimensions. Our unconscious thought patterns have already evolved to do that long ago. For example, many artists utilise their unconscious thought patterns, programed by DNA, to intuitively make artefacts that exhibit the same proportions as found in the shapes created by nature. For example, refer to the sea shell depicted at lower left. Just we admire the natural beauty of a spiral-shaped shell, we also consider some human - made shapes as "*beautiful.*"

IN addition to sea shells, any other spirals are found in nature. For example, our DNA is a double helix spiral axis in three dimensional space. The physical arrangement of genes in the DNA double helix is finely tuned. It provides codes to guide our growth and functions in conjunction with our electromagnetic body. The electromagnetic body underlies our physical, mechanical and chemical structure, just as it underlies the physical, mechanical and chemical structures of all life forms and our galaxy.

So it is apparent that in addition to how plants act with light in photosynthesis, there are other processes at work that we need to understand in order to rejuvenate the life systems of our plants and planet. We need to talk about light in terms that reach beyond trees, photosynthesis and renewable solar energy to encompass a broader view of the laws of natural systems.

**Below** *Image* credit 1.16 ***A sea shell***: *one of the beautiful shapes of nature which humans are intuitively drawn to.*

# What are these energy flows?

*On a previous page, in order to set the scene for understanding how to create gardens and places that embody the energy flows of nature, I outlined my model of ten components involved in Living with the Earth as a Light Garden. I also call this the "Life Force Mandala".*

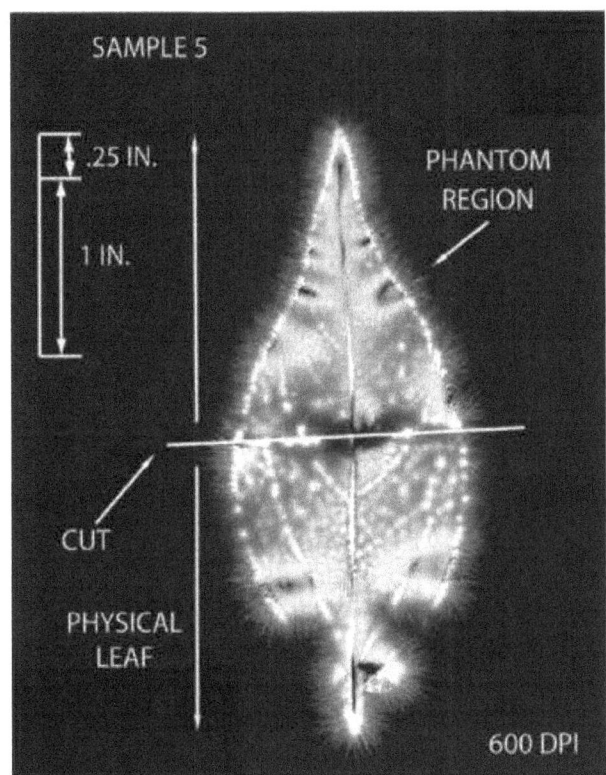

*Above:* Image credit: 1.17 ***Electron flux photograph of a severed leaf.***

**As** Step One in the Life Force Mandala there are the energy flows of nature that direct movement and determine the optimal relative placement of particles and waves. The obvious next questions to me are: What are these energy flows? How are they created and how are particles created?

To answer these questions, I will begin by referring to plasma.

> *"Plasma consists of a gas heated to sufficiently high temperatures . . . that the atoms ionize. The properties of the gas are controlled by electromagnetic force among consistent ions and electrons, which results in a different type of behaviour . . . Plasma is often considered the fourth state of matter (besides solid, liquid, and gas) . . . Most of the matter in the universe is in the plasma state.* (9)

Plasma carries sound and electrical currents through interstellar space and through the bodies of all biological organisms.

> *"From the smallest particle to the largest galactic formation, a web of electrical circuitry connects and unifies all of nature, organizing galaxies, energizing stars, giving birth to planets and, on our own world, controlling weather and animating biological organisms.* **There are no isolated islands in an electric universe."** (10)

The work of Hubacher and other researchers gives us photographic clues about how biological organisms are animated.* As shown above left, the electron flux of a leaf continues unabated above the horizontal line where the leaf was cut away. No physical leaf tissue remained above the cut line but the photon emission and electrical circuitry remained in place after the cut. (11) While our attention if focused on energy, I shall now describe the ten parameters of the *'Light Garden'* model in a little more detail.

---

* This is a broad subject. For example, earlier work by the British mathematician biologist D'Arcy Thompson in his 1917 book *"On Growth and Form,"* covers a different topic. He relates mathematical formula to the gradual evolution of form in organisms, through examples comparing the shape of different skulls. He does not focus on energy.

# Ten components of the Light Garden

*The light garden is a metaphor for how the principles of quantum biophysics can be applied to designing and managing living systems, at the global and local scales. This includes human settlements, nature reserves, agriculture and so on. The ten components of the metaphor are:*

*Image credit 1.18*

1. **ENERGY**. Enhance and work with the energy flows of nature that direct movement and determine the optimal relative placement of particles and waves.

2. **SPACE and TIME.** There is the space through which particles and wave move.

3. **WAVES and PARTICLES**. There are tiny waves and particles that move in energy fields

4. **LINES, PATTERNS and PROBABILITIES.** There are the lines of motion that we perceive and patterns of motion that form. In addition there are uncertainties and probabilities.

5. **MULTIPLICATION.** Multiplication effects arise due to clustering of similar entities into materials that we can feel and feel. For example, one group of carbon atoms might cluster together to form graphite, while another might form a brilliant pink diamond.

6. **ENTANGLEMENT and FOCAL POINTS.** There are points where energy paths intersect and where we perceive focal points to arise. In addition there is the related concept of Quantum entanglement, where particles cannot be perceived or described independently of each other.

7. **PERCEPTION and MEASURE.** There is humanity's measurement and perception.

8. **CONTECT and ENVIRONMENT.** There is the wider environment in which particular patterns form. For example, a labyrinth garden follows a repeatable basic plan but also is influenced by its wider setting and the intention of the people who plan and build it.

9. **HUMAN USE**. There may be restrained human intervention for particular purposes, such as food production, education, control of a parcel of land, water or space and so on.

10. **STORAGE and SHARING**. There is the storage of information, so that the patterns of nature and human use can replicate and evolve.

*Similar patterns at larger and smaller scales.*
*Below left* Image credit 1.20.1, **Curving patterns on a Leaf**
*Below centre* Image 1.20.2, **Labyrinth garden plan & trees**
*Far right* Image 1.20.3,
**Ancient stone engraving of Labyrinth pattern.**

# Biofields and Biophysics

*The term "biofields" was coined by a panel convened in the United States of America at the National Institute of Health (NIH). The panel was convened in 1994 to discuss complementary and alternative medicine (CAM).* (12)

**Biofields** may be defined as an organising principle or information flow that regulates the biological functions and homeostasis of organisms. Biofields operate across a hierarchy of levels from the subatomic scale to the molecular, cellular, organismic, interpersonal and cosmic scale. They are recognised in a number of professional disciplines, including medicine, biology and physics. (13)

Many of the founders of quantum physics, including Max Plank, understood and advocated for "wholeness" in both physics and biology. (14) However biochemists traditionally did not accept the relevance of biophysics to the study of molecular biology and living organisms. (15) (16)

Niels Bohr, The Danish physicist who received the Nobel Prize in 1922, understood how the principle of *complementarity* in quantum physics, (which holds that objects have certain pairs of characteristics which cannot be measured simultaneously), is an important part of understanding biophysics and the complex organisation and synchronisation of activity that occurs in living organisms. These factors cannot be explained by biochemistry alone. (17)

Although biofields exhibit electromagnetic properties, (such as with the phantom leaf effect), they do so within the context of bio-information and quantum field theories. These theories help explain additional properties of living organisms, such as biophotons, interaction with the quantum vacuum, coherence, nonlocality and entanglement. Some of these properties are discussed in examples of 'Light Gardens' which are included in later chapters of this book.

> *"Without the biofield life would not exist and there would be only an inner biochemical mix."(18)*

Since Nicholas Tesla and Albert Einstein released their documentation of Scalar Waves from 1899 onwards, (19) scientific work has continued. Awareness of all forms of electro-magnetic radiation and electromagnetic frequencies (EMF) has grown. EMF naturally occur throughout nature and the human body. However,

> *Electricity and Wi-Fi etc. signals are stronger and foreign EMF, overriding the inherent Human, Nature and essential Human-Nature connection. Undesirable EMF alters the body's electrical system which directs the chemical messaging system in the brain. (20)*

The need for protection against harmful EMF has now been documented by many studies. (21) The insurance underwriters *Lloyd's of London* and *Swiss Re* refuse to include health cover against EMF in their polices, due to the high risk to life forms.

***Below*** Image credit: **1.19 *Albert Einstein***

1.19

# Biophotons

*Biological organisms continuously emit weak light. This light has been referred to as biophotons and is now currently referred to as ultraweak photon emission (UPE). This phenomenon is different from bioluminescence. (22)*

**Biophotons,** or ultra-weak photon emission (UPE), are the discretely sized packages in which electromagnetic radiation occurs within living organisms.

Biophotons are emitted and absorbed by DNA and other living material. Photons are emitted within the light spectrum at a range of 350 to 1270 nanometers. A billionth of a meter is called a nanometer, or nm. (23)

The human eye is able to detect light within the range of 400 to 700 nm. The mechanism by which UPE regulates the activity of living organisms is the subject of much research. One theory states that

> "... neurons contain various light-sensitive neurotransmitters (tryptophan, phenylalanine, tyrosine, and other molecules), and it is difficult to imagine that the nervous system is not affected by the phenomenon of UPE and that such conduction of photons does not transport encoded information." (24)

Other theories refer to biochemical interaction with biophotons at the cellular level. Blood also carries biophotons.

UPE is detected, photographed, recorded and measured with low-noise photomultiplier tubes and imaging using highly sensitive charge-coupled device cameras. (25) The optical coherence tomography (OCT) imaging technique commonly used by Ophthalmologists to obtain cross section images of the layers in the retina of the eye is one example of the use of this technology in the field of medicine.

The general term given to the technology of generating, manipulating and detecting photons is Photonics. Photons and photonics also play important roles in information technologies such as fibre optics. Photons are to fibre optics what electrons are to electronics. (26)

In order to place these concepts within the context of the historical development of relevant aspects of Western philosophy from the ancient Greeks, (Democritus and Aristotle), to the 21st century, a very brief summary is given on page 24 of this chapter. But first, let us recall the words of philosopher Bertrand Russell. (1872 – 1970). They are relevant as we build our understanding of the importance of *'Light Garden Principle Number 9:* Restraint in Human Use."

> " Democritus is the last of the Greek philosophers to be free from a certain fault which vitiated all later ancient and medieval thought ... What is amiss, even in the best philosophy after Democritus, is an undue emphasis on man as compared with the universe." (27)

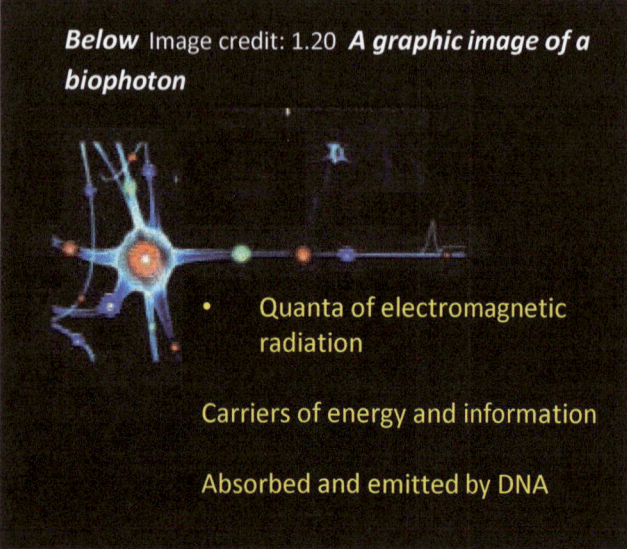

**Below** Image credit: 1.20 *A graphic image of a biophoton*

- Quanta of electromagnetic radiation
- Carriers of energy and information
- Absorbed and emitted by DNA

# Physics and biology in western culture

*A simple summary of concepts of physics and biology that are particularly relevant to the theme of this chapter is presented below under the four consecutive historical categories of Classical, 20th century, Quantum and 21st Century.*

## 1. Classical

**Photosynthesis**: Light is the powerhouse for life on Earth, via the process of photosynthesis, which creates food for plants and other organisms.

**Waves** may be in the form of energy, light or sound. They are measured in terms of their amplitude, velocity and power.

**Particles** found in matter are called protons, electrons and neutrons (plus other smaller particles that are less well known outside specialist scientific circles).

## 2. 20th century

**Plasma** is a fourth state of matter, in addition to solids, liquids and gases. It is composed of ionised gas. It is emitted by the sun and by lighting bolts. The solar wind carries ionised plasma through space, past planet Earth and beyond.

**Plasma** and its associated electromagnetic energy interacts with the biochemistry of living organisms on Earth in various ways. For example, the human body interacts with the Schumann Resonance. This is a wave of a constant frequency, (7.83 Hz), which surrounds the planet in the atmosphere.

## 3. Quantum

**Light** behaves as both a particle, which has mass and as a wave, which does not.

**Light** travels in discrete packages, called photons. Quantum physics helps describe the behaviour of light and energy better than classical physics can. Classical physics can explain the motion of objects that have mass and move in smooth trajectories, such as a ball rolling down a slope.

## 4. 21st century

**Quantum biophysics adds to knowledge of how living** organisms organise their growth and reproduction through their own biofields and light-emitting biophotons. This is in addition to their biochemistry and DNA. **Living matter** is formed by standing waves of energy and quantum entanglement beyond space and time.

# Light, atoms and growth

**This book is about designing with light and the natural living systems of the Earth.** So let us consider how light and living entities are created – and how we can synchronize with that.

By understanding the energy that makes these tiny mandalas that underlie all natural living beauty, we can then apply that knowledge to designing and living in harmony with the Life force -- rather than designing an inherently non-living, non-sustainable system.

*Above: One visualisation of an atom with electrons emitting light as they move around a central nucleus.* Image credit 1.22

## Background to the need for the Life force mandala

**At least as far back as the Greek philosophers, in Western culture there have been two schools of thought about how matter is formed.** One school, attributed to Democritus, is based around the concept that participles are the building blocks of Life - and that Life and can be scientifically understood by examining the component parts, plus the sum that they make. The second school of thought is attributed to Aristotle. He stated that the Life process is wholistic, autonomous, self regulating and evolving in a way that cannot be broken down, understood and reassembled in the manner of building blocks. (28) This school of thought is more closely aligned with tribal cultures, Eastern cultures and the concepts of Hinduism, Buddhism and Taoism.

**Since the early 20th century and the work of Albert Einstein, Max Plank** and their contemporaries, quantum physics has come to be the accepted springboard upon which further scientific study in the realms of physics is based. Quantum physics does not focus on either of the schools of thought associated with Democritus or Aristotle: it provides a third one.

It incorporates principles such as uncertainty, probability, quantum entanglement, non-locality and the so-called vacuum in space. In doing so, it has been found to be better than either of the earlier schools of thought in explaining the behaviour of light, energy fields, waves, electromagnetism and the way in which living organisms regulate their growth, repair, reproduction and collaborative existence on planet Earth. **It is in this context that the need for this book arises and the 'Light Garden' model which is explained and tested herein is proposed.**

**This book addresses fields that deal with living organisms on Earth.** These fields, such as biology, ecology, landscape design, landscape management, human settlement and medicine, have lagged some one hundred years behind the work of the physicists in applying the principles of quantum mechanics to everyday best practice.

# Light, atoms and growth, continued

**Entanglement** is one of the basic concepts of quantum biophysics. In quantum theory, entanglement refers to the phenomenon that particles cannot be perceived or described independently of each other. In an interesting comparison, **"disentanglement" is similar to the centuries-old Japanese Zen aesthetic principles,** which are described in more detail in Chapter 3. These principles include:

- *Kanso*, meaning *"simplicity or elimination of clutter"*
- *Shizen*, meaning *"naturalness"* and
- *Yugen* meaning *"subtlety"*. (28)

> **The goals of the Localisation and disentanglement movements include but are not limited to:**

- Building meaningful, inclusive, place- based communities that have a reasonable level of self government, within a network of larger scale government (29)

- Supporting healthy food and lifestyles of happy restraint

- Prioritising carbon sequestration and avoiding the use of fossil fuels

- Rejuvenating the natural environment and biodiversity , (including reafforestation and biodiversity conservation)

- Restructuring of social support systems through a much greater emphasis on well paid, meaningful careers based around labour-intensive stewardship of land, light, air and water resources. This includes supporting and spreading the knowledge and practices of traditional indigenous people, whilst acknowledging that local businesses and small, biodiverse farms have been shown in a number of studies to provide more local employment and produce more food than is obtained through large companies and large, industrial scale farms.

- Supporting public banking and small to medium scale business economies rather than multinational companies that seek to maximise their profits whilst avoiding paying tax and being accountable for the welfare of local communities.

> In this chapter I have given some introductory information and illustrations about the quantum nature of light and started to outline a framework for how to design and plan for light gardens at all scales from the global to the local.

**Study of the role of living systems and sunlight is not only a recent phenomenon**. It has continued for centuries. For example as described in Chapter 8, the Incas of the 15th century believed that the sun powered not only the growth of the plants they depended upon for their food supply but also that the warmth of sunlight powered the production of life giving rains. Inti, the Sun God, was an important part of their culture.

**Many other cultures have worshipped sun gods and modelled their calendars around seasonal changes in sunlight.** At the more close up scale of the human body, we know, for example, that our bodies work in a circadian rhythm that follows night and day and that energy associated with light is necessary in many biochemical processes. We also know that the cells in the human retina recognize certain colours of light and that blue light, (for example), affects us in different ways from the glow of firelight.

# From the small to the large

*In writing about forests, light gardens and biophysics, I have chosen the broad sense of the word "gardens" that encompasses traditional agricultural practices, temples, sacred sites, management of biodiversity and urban environments and leading to the concept of Earth as a Light Garden.*

**Consciousness** is growing that we are all part of the global community. So too, awareness is growing that natural beauty and natural light are essential natural resources to be shared equitably: they are not peripheral or ancillary facets of modern Life. Humans replace the energy and electrons in their body in three ways: from food; from sunlight and from walking barefoot on the ground. (30)

Natural beauty arises when the processes of nature are understood and allowed to flow, rather than being negated by human activities. Landscape design is a process where gradually -- layer by layer -- detail, diversity and resilience are built into the design. Traditional cultures did this with their gardens and Nature still does this.

This book aims to build that capacity, firstly by giving practical examples from each continent and secondly by developing a model to address the resource management issues of the 21st century. The model is based on quantum biophysics principles such as coherence, inclusiveness, information sharing and teamwork. Swedish schoolgirl Greta Thunberg's words are a clarion call for the immediate need to do this in the first quarter of the 21st century:

> *"I want you to act as you would in a crisis. I want you to act as if our house is on fire. Because it is."* (31)

**Top Left:** Image credit 1.24.1 ***The detailed scale.***
**Centre Left:** Image credit 1.24.2 ***Medium scale.***
**Bottom Left:** Image credit 1.24.3 ***Broader scale:***

# I am the light

**Below:** *Young men seek space and new frontiers. Here they have found some - and pause to soak up the sunlight.*

Image credit 1.25.1

**Why** would you read a book about Light Gardens? Perhaps you have a feeling that light underpins our survival needs. Or perhaps you are drawn to the inspiration it provides, seeking to create a life and a community full of wonder and healthy growth, as we live in harmony with the natural world.

Light is so closely aligned with beauty in the natural world and in the configuration of our minds. It is the light, the space and the pattern arrangements of matter, that create the beauty of an autumn glade. As the shafts of light pass through the spaces between the leaves, our minds recognize beauty. Those same leaves only weeks before were reflecting green light and turning light energy into food energy, as they trapped electrons and ordered protons into the mandalas of matter.

Image credit 1.25.2

# Where to from here?

I shall now move to describe how managing the forests of South East Asia in accordance with *'Light Garden'* principles could make a huge and immediate difference to humanity's capacity to manage climate change at the global scale. This is followed by consideration of the North Asian cultures and Feng Shui, where traditionally there has been a strong emphasis on the *'Energy'* component of *'Light Gardens'*, as well as contemporary efforts to maintain this.

Turning then to consider how quantum biophysics principles are reflected in the way Islamic paradise gardens have manifested over the centuries provides an interesting comparison. Taking the example of what is being done in 21$^{st}$ century Dubai to create sustainable settlements in the desert and arid environments, we also see the potential for this type of *'Light Garden'* to be established as viable new homes for the millions of refugees and global citizens seeking shelter, long term sustainable settlements, meaningful employment and happy communities.

Africa too has millions of people forcibly displaced from their traditional homes as governments and corporations engage in grabs for land, resources, sunlight and water. These conditions create a challenging environment in which to consider the viability of the *'Light Garden'* concept but once again, by comparing some traditional villages to 21$^{st}$ century alternatives, the validity of the basic underlying principles of the *'Light Garden'* model can be seen to unfold as a means to support human rights and equitable management of climate and other natural resources.

Moving from Africa to India, the radiance of light that has underpinned Indian culture for millennia is gradually revealed through a series of vignettes on biodiversity civilization, ancient groves, traditional villages, temple gardens and contemporary developments. In contrast, I shall then describe how the biodiversity and use of light in Europe has been more restrained. However with Europe being the birthplace of the 20$^{th}$ century scientists who developed the principles of quantum physics, that in turn blossomed into 21$^{st}$ century biophysics, there is much to be gleaned from life in that continent.

European culture started impacting on South American cultures in the 15$^{th}$ century, with Machu Pichu being one of the most famous sites that eluded capture by the conquistadors. Like many cultures, the Incas worshipped a Sun God, so we know that sunlight was significant to them. However, after detailed examination of the Machu Pichu site, one can see that it does not rate highly in all the ten "*Light Garden'* criteria. Not surprisingly in that context, the Incas abandoned the site after only one hundred years of use.

North American culture has included many frontiers and milestones in the ongoing development of farming practices, settlements, technology and the use of light. After describing these, they are then considered in terms of how well they rate as *'Light Gardens'*. Some, such as the farming communities of the Amish, rate well as *'Light Gardens'*. Others, such as the famous Butchart Gardens in Canada, operate in a more constrained context. Moving on to consider practical examples of *'Light Garden'* innovations and trends in the 21$^{st}$ century, the book then concludes with testing the *'Light Garden'* model for its usefulness in establishing a new and more effective framework for managing climate change.

# Chapter 2 South East Asia

Previous page Image credit 2.1

# Table of Contents Chapter 2

| | |
|---|---|
| Map of South East Asia | 4 |
| South East Asia: global context | 5 |
| South East Asia: tropical forests | 6 |
| Shared Socio-economic pathway | 7 |
| Modelling for Light Gardens | 8 |
| Forest Cover for Light Gardens | 9 |
| Examples: Malaysia and The Philippines | 10 |
| Introduction: Bali as a Light Garden | 11 |
| *Subak,* light and temples | 12 |
| Forests are part of the *Subak* | 13 |
| The light of God | 14 |
| Mountains, shrines, gardens and thatch | 15 |
| Temples facing the light | 16 |
| Illustrating a traditional Balinese shrine *'Light Garden'* | 17 |
| Water, light and pond life | 18 |
| Light garden: living in harmony | 19 |

# Map of South East Asia

*The countries of the South East Asian region are shown in dark green colour on the map that follows. Examples of work from five South East Asian countries are referred to in this chapter: Malaysia, Bali, Papua, The Philippines and Vietnam.* **Below** Image credit 2.4.1 **Map**

**Below** Image credit 2.4.2 *Batik: a distinctive South East Asian art form.*

**Chapter** two focuses on South East Asia as a broad 21st century example of how it is possible to achieve three of the Light Garden concepts introduced in Chapter One:

- Apply the principles of Light Gardens at the regional, national and local scales.

- Achieve the goal of managing half the planet's land and water areas as nature reserves and

- Rapidly and effectively address climate change at the global and regional scales that are necessary to achieve effective results.

# South East Asia: global context

*in Malaysia, during the period 2015 – 2050, there could plausibly be either be a net gain of 14% forest cover, or an equivalent net loss of forest cover. (1) This may come as a surprise to many people who have developed an attitude that there is nothing that realistically can be done to reverse the trend of recent decades, where the worldwide loss of tropical forests has occurred at unprecedented rates. (2)*

**However** there is much than can and is being done for reforestation of the planet and South East Asia provides examples of this. In 2016 Biologist Edward O. Wilson proposed that half the planet's land and water areas be set aside as nature reserves. In support of this proposal he set out the scientific basis for calculations that 80% of existing living species could be preserved by such action. (4)

In that *Planet Earth* context, the 'Light Garden' theme of this book gains significance because it points to **a future in which the healthy growth of living organisms - and the Life processes themselves - are at the centre of the next wave of our local and international cooperative and scientific efforts, rather than diverting funds away from living systems and into non-living technology, such as ever faster spacecraft, mobile phones or geoengineering.**

This next wave of cooperative efforts includes the sphere of nature conservation, in conjunction with work towards local socio-economic stability. In this chapter, a look at some of the successful cooperative cultures and forest management practices of South East Asia provides an insight into how some aspects of the *"Light Garden"* concept are already being put into practice in some South East Asian countries. The transferability of these practices to other locations will also be considered.

Although it may at first seem an unattainable goal to set aside half the planet's land and water areas as nature reserves, vast areas of the planet's land masses are already covered by forests. Map image 2.9 in this chapter illustrates this. For example, in Russia and North America, 30 – 47 % of the land is forested, whilst in the Amazon, Central Africa and South East Asia, forest cover extends over 47 – 54% of the land area. (5)

This does not mean all of this land has no human habitation, or is not used for commercial purposes, food production or other purposes. It does not mean all of this land is of high biodiversity conversation value. It does not mean that other biomes in the oceans, swamps, peat lands, tundras and grass lands of the Earth do not also contribute to nature conservation, ecosystem functioning or carbon sequestration.

However it does mean that about half the Earth's surface is already covered by forest. This provides a living fabric of natural resources that can be managed to support nature conservation as well as other purposes. It also provides a living baseplate for restoration of forests at a scale that will help with carbon drawdown, in the race to develop effective global practices for climate management.

Image credit 2.5

# South East Asia tropical forests

*While they were once considered a moderate sink for atmospheric carbon-a recent study has indicated that the carbon balance of tropical forests has tilted towards being a net source of carbon emissions, due to extensive deforestation and a reduction in carbon density.* (6)

As an edited collection of scientific research published in 2019 states, there is still a chance for humanity to act collectively to avoid decimation of the human population through climate change. A new climate model published by Springer Nature in early 2019, "Achieving the Paris Climate Agreement Goals", shows that we can only meet the target of remaining below 1.5 degrees C in average global temperature rise by:

> "... ending the conversion of forest and other natural lands by 2030, effectively placing half of the Earth's lands under protection.
> "This major conservation effort would need to be coupled with a forest restoration effort and other natural climate solutions to draw down carbon from the atmosphere (providing 'negative emissions') alongside a rapid transition to carbon free energy, like wind and solar power, by 2050." (7)

By the end of the second decade in the 21st century, tropical deforestation was responsible for around one-tenth of total anthropogenic carbon emissions.(8) For example, replacement of tropical rainforest with palm oil plantations

> " may still show on satellite surveys as forest cover, but the plantations lack the biomass, biodiversity and carbon sequestration capacity of the rainforests." (9)

A palm oil plantation will thus have a lower carbon density than rainforest that was knocked down to make space and light to establish the plantation.

By the year 2019, despite being known for high rates of deforestation in recent decades,
South East Asia contained about 15% of the planet's tropical forests and forests covered 33% of South East Asian land. In addition, 56.68% of land in South East Asia was used for agricultural purposes in 2015, according to the World Bank collection of development indicators. The area of land used for urban purposes in South East Asia increased by 22% between 2000 and 2010 to approximately 10% of the land mass. (10)

Meanwhile, by the year 2019, forests covered about 31 percent of total land area of the globe, or just over 4 billion hectares (ha). (11) South East Asia lost about 80 million ha of total forest cover between 2005 and 2015. A state of the art study published in 2019 examined five scenarios for future forest management in South East Asia. Of these five scenarios, or "*shared socioeconomic pathways*", the best-case outcome indicated that one quarter of this 80 million ha loss of forest could be regained by intelligent resource management during the next thirty years to the year 2050. (12)

The "*shared socioeconomic pathways*" (SSP) scenario study generated useful outcomes, showing plausible ways to achieve a net increase in forest carbon stores, given associated socioeconomic considerations. Under the worst case SSP scenario to the year 2050, a further loss of another 5.2 million ha of forest in South East Asia would occur. (13)

# Shared socioeconomic pathway

As described in the SSP study: *"Considering the multiple interacting **uncertainties and the dynamics** of socioeconomic systems, charting the path of the region's forest future [through the SSP approach] is a challenge, and requires exploratory scenario-based analyses. . . . . Scenario analysis is a structured process of **exploring and evaluating alternatives** aimed at providing insights regarding plausible rather than probable futures.* (14)

**Although** the further loss of 5 million ha in the decades from 2015 to 2050 might at first glance appear comparatively insignificant compared to the loss of 80 million ha during the ten years between 2005 and 2015, further loss of forest in South East Asia is particularly significant at the global scale.

This is because tropical forests cover only 7% of the Earth's land surface but account for 68% of the global carbon stock. Thus any further loss of tropical forests, (in South East Asia or elsewhere), leads to a relatively significant loss in the global carbon stock. (15)

This is a significant issue in the global challenge to manage climate change and natural resources because carbon stocks must be increased, not reduced, as part of a multi-factorial approach to climate and natural resource management. Tropical forests also generate rainfall in countries all around the world, through the water that is transpired into the atmosphere through the forests.

The "shared socioeconomic pathways" approach adopted in the 2019 study is acknowledged as being a significant advance over previous resource scenario frameworks, particularly the *Intergovernmental Panel on Climate Change (IPCC) Special Report on Emissions Scenarios (SRES).* As noted by independent research published in *Nature Geoscience* by Zeng et al:

*" the actual area of forest loss in South East Asia represents 57 percent more loss than current estimations of deforestation made by the IPCC."* (16)

The SSP study is considered an example of significant advances over previous resource scenario frameworks because it was able to prepare rigorously documented alternative scenarios for addressing the numerous uncertainties and socioeconomic realities that natural resource management has to correlate and coexist with.

**The need for a capacity to prepare alternative scenarios given these uncertainties also correlates with the need for adoption of quantum biophysics principles. Such principles underpin practical ways to work with uncertainty and multiplication effects, as described in Chapter One. The "*Earth as a Light Garden*" model in this book is proposed in that context to meet the resource management challenges of the 21st century.**

The need to work with quantum biophysics principles such as "uncertainties" is also apparent once one moves from consideration of forests at the regional and global scale to forests in a particular landscape or place.

For example, as described in a well balanced review of the implementation and management of the UNESCO World Heritage listed Cultural Landscape of the Bali Province, adequate consideration of uncertainties and socioeconomic factors for the local residents was identified as sorely lacking. This report was published by the Stockholm Environment Institute in 2015. (17) Discussion of this Cultural Landscape is included later in this chapter.

# Modelling for light gardens

*The maps below are based on satellite data collection and scientific modelling from 2015 - 2019. They illustrate how forest cover can be lost or gained under different management strategies. They highlight how the continued loss of forest cover is not an inevitable process*

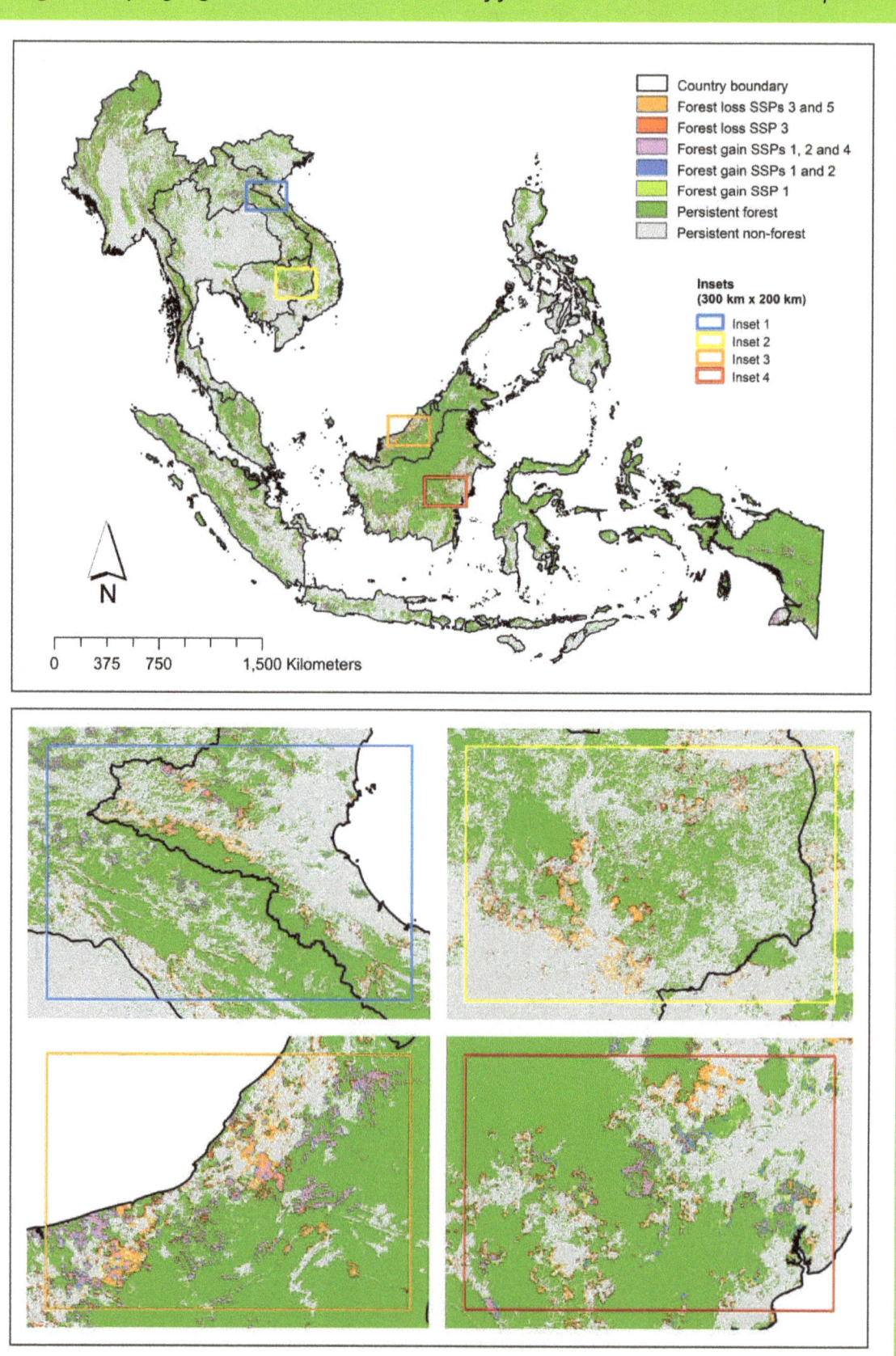

# Forest cover for light gardens

*As illustrated below, South East Asia is one of the three main areas of the world where the sum of the forest cover reaches 47 – 54 % of the land area.*

*The world's three largest areas of tropical rainforest also may be found in these same three regions.*

**Whilst** some people may be sceptical of the dollar value of planting forests despite all the evidence, look at this subject from the other side of the coin: no-one disputes the adverse effects of knocking down trees. Already there are calls for legislation to retain and manage forests so that rain will fall in other parts of the globe.

For example, Egypt and Ethiopia have been negotiating for many years on how to equitably manage water from the Nile. (19) However efforts to equitably share water will be to no avail if deforestation in the Congo basin of Central Africa means rains do not fall in the Ethiopian highlands. Rain in needed for native plants to grow the forests which generate the rain and stabilise ecosystems. There are voices saying:

"Processes such as moisture recycling . . . can, and ought, to be governed." (20)

Similarly - and moving on from access to *water* to consider access to *sunlight* - this is another frontier. Processes such as access to sunlight can, and ought, to be governed..

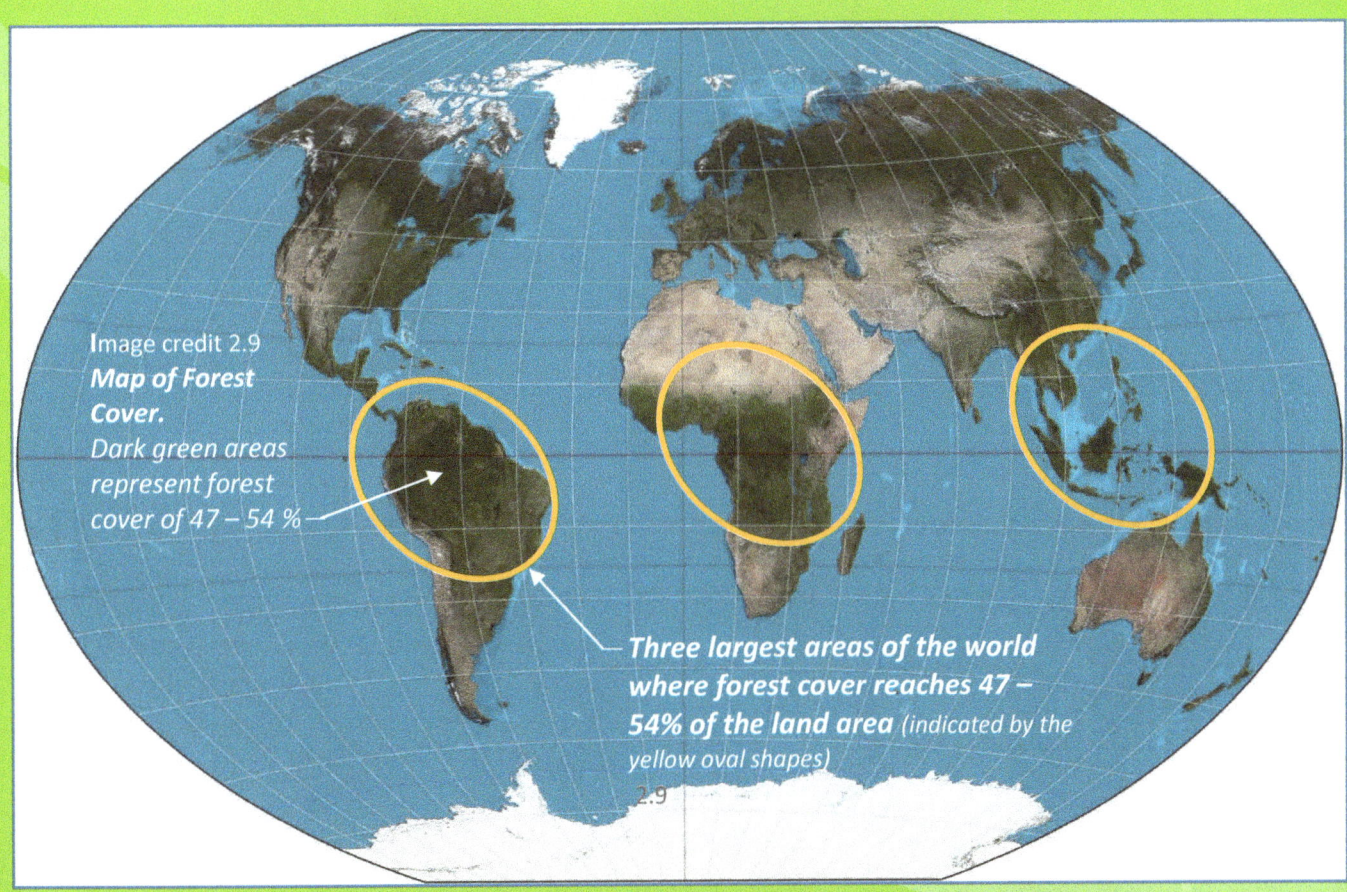

Image credit 2.9 *Map of Forest Cover.* Dark green areas represent forest cover of 47 – 54 %

**Three largest areas of the world where forest cover reaches 47 – 54% of the land area** (indicated by the yellow oval shapes)

# Examples: Malaysia & Philippines

*As illustrated earlier in the mapping of South East Asian forests, Malaysia was one of several South East Asian countries that participated in a study published in 2019. It presented detailed data and modelling to create alternative scenarios for future management of forests. In each country, five different socioeconomic scenarios were used for modelling. The model developed was designed to also inform climate management decisions at the global scale.*

The detailed maps showing areas of projected changes to forest cover highlighted the important contribution that every patch of forest makes as part of the dynamic balance between loss and gain of forests. Sometimes the attitude is voiced that what happens in one patch of forest does not matter, given the huge scale of issues involved, such as soil carbon conservation, biodiversity and climate management.

However by careful management, Malaysia alone could make a difference of 25% between the best and worst case scenarios likely to be achieved within only a few years, using their existing forest resources.

**The difference for Indonesia is even greater. There the difference in outcomes is 88%. There could be a projected net gain of 41% forest cover, or a net loss of 47% forest cover. Appling multiplier effects to those figures for all countries at the global scale, it is immediately apparent that there are huge and achievable net gains to be made in forest cover and associated climate management factors such as moisture recycling, carbon sequestration and temperature control, if appropriate management is adopted.**

**In The Philippines,** the *National Greening Program* was commenced in 2011. It was recently expanded to cover the period 2016 – 2028. Within that twelve year period, the aim is reforest all the nation's degraded, unproductive and denuded forestlands. This comprises an area of 7.1 million hectares. The original program that began in 2011 aimed to plant 1.5 billion trees by 2016 on 1.5 million hectares. Building on that experience, the prospect of planting 7.1 million hectares in a twelve year period to 2028 appears quite feasible.

From its inception the program was designed to

> " *reduce poverty, promote food security, environmental stability and biodiversity conservation, and enhance climate change mitigation and adaptation.*" (21)

*Left* Image credit 2.10 ***In Bali,* the multi-purpose Subak system** was developed during at least 2,000 years of cultural exchange between India and Bali. The forests that protect the water supply and the villages through which the water flows are recognised as part of the Subak. The illustration at left depicts the way of life of the people.

2.10

# Introduction: Bali as a Light Garden

*When initially contemplating South East Asia, such a kaleidoscope of colour and culture presented itself that it was hard to know where to begin in this story of Light Gardens.*

**However** shortly after becoming immersed in this kaleidoscope, I was reading Dr John Tyman's account of living with local people in a Balinese village. (22) I realised he had captured a moment in time that in many ways provided the perfect entry point to describing both traditional and contemporary Light Gardens in South East Asia.

It wasn't an abstract, unattainable idea that people would have difficulty relating to. The concept of Light Gardens wasn't something that only existed with reference to 21$^{st}$ century concepts of quantum biophysics. Once I looked more closely at the account of life in a Balinese village, I felt I had found a real living "Light Garden" culture which had been and to a large extent still was alive and well.

What I was proposing with the Light Garden principles had to be feasible to enact in a variety of cultures and locations all around the world, regardless of whether they existed in the lush tropical environment of Bali, or in more arid areas. **However I knew I needed to find what features existed in the Balinese culture that made Light Garden concepts successful there**.

I then needed to consider whether those principles were transferable to other locations to support the viability of the Light Garden concept for management of natural resources elsewhere. The reasons documented by UNESCO when listing the rice terraces of central Bali as a World Heritage site provide a good starting point to consider that question about transferability. UNESCO did not list just one or two rice paddies. They named the listing as the **"Cultural Landscape of Bali Province: the Subak System as a Manifestation of the Tri Hita Karana Philosophy."** (23)

> Inherent in this naming is recognition of the need for management of natural resources, (including the land, water and light that are needed to grow rice), based around three interdependent factors:
>
> - A philosophy to underpin management of natural resources (*The Tri Hita Karana Philosophy*).
>
> - An effective system of governance and organisation that is derived from the philosophy. *(The Subak System)*
>
> - A landscape scale approach to natural resource management. The listing covers an area of 19,500 hectares. It refers to the *cultural landscape of Bali Province.* Five rice terrace sites with their associated water temples are specifically mentioned within this area. The full area is shown on the map on the following page.

Water temples are a key way in which the philosophy of *Tri Hita Karana* is literally transplanted to the grass roots level of daily farming practice. Water from springs and canals flows through a multitude of temples into terraced rice paddies. Offerings are made at the temples and a collective respect for the divine symbolic connection between the three *Tri Hita Karana* realms of the spirit, human and natural worlds is maintained. (24)

# Subak, light and temples

*Water temples in Bali have drawn inspiration from several ancient religious traditions, including Saivasiddhanta and Samkhyā Hinduism, Vajrayana Buddhism and Austronesian cosmology.* (25)

**As** illustrated below, temples are located throughout Bali. These include the "Light of God", *Lempuyang Luhar* temple, which is located at the eastern tip of the island, where the morning rays of the sun first reach the island as the Earth rotates. (26) Thus we begin to see how the three elements of the Tri Hiti Karan philosophy create the "Light Gardens" of Bali.

Individual farmers are not at liberty to use water as they wish. Decisions about access to water and distribution of water are made through the *Subak* system. Unlike the caste system of India, the Balinese Subak system is based on an egalitarian and democratic decision making process that extends up from the level of individual farmers. The value of this approach has been reiterated during the 21$^{st}$ century as Bali seeks to control the adverse impacts of tourism in the rural areas. These impacts have included water being diverted for tourist use and tempting offers for farmers to sell their traditional farming land for tourist redevelopment, thus taking labour and agricultural land out of production. The Subak decision makers have countered this by requesting fees for tourists to visit farming areas. However much progress remains to be made before such funds can be diverted away from multiple layers of bureaucracy, in order to reach the generations of farmers who built the World Heritage site and upon whom its ongoing maintenance relies. (27)

**Below** Image credit 2.12 *Some temple sites in Bali*

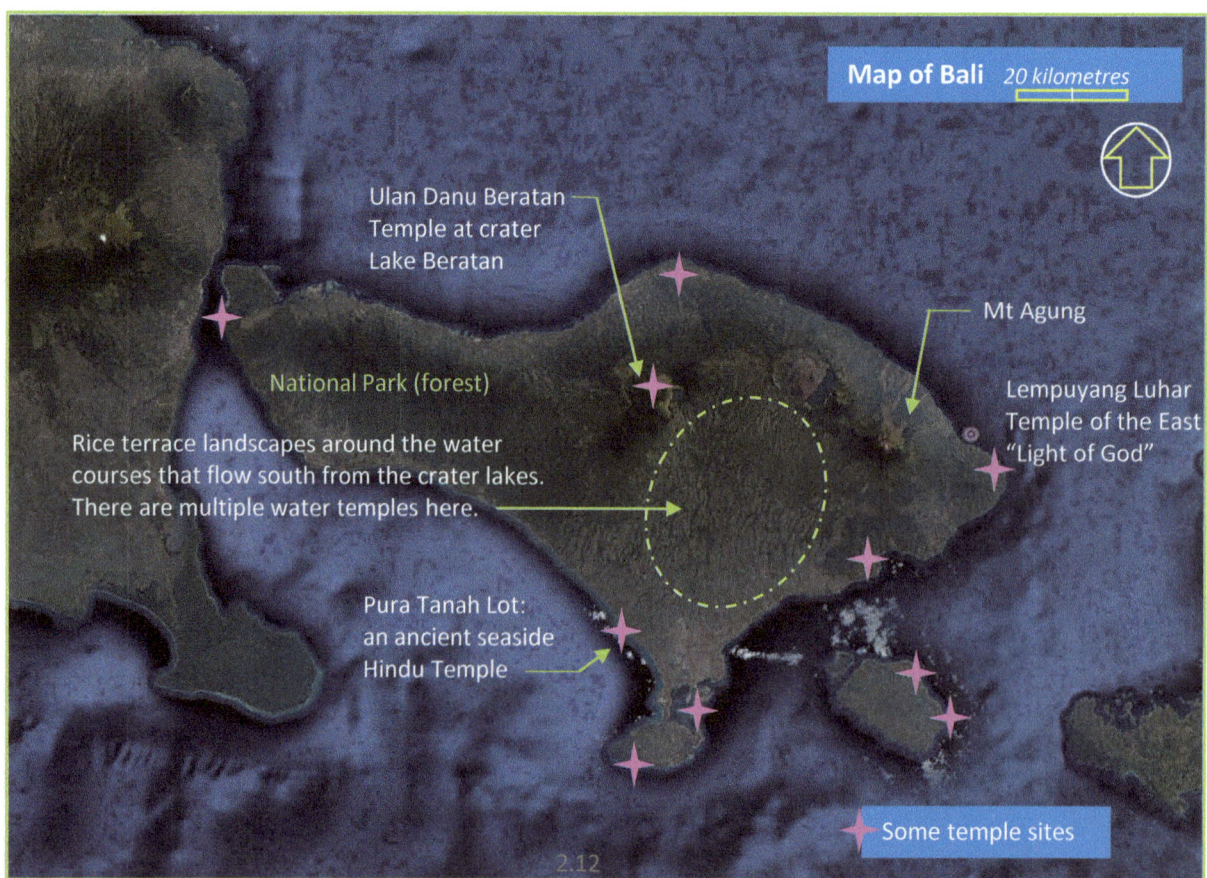

# Forests are part of the Subak

*Below* Image credit 2.13 *Images of Bali*

# The light of God

*As the rays of dawn strike the high volcanic peaks of Bali they are reflected in the waters of the sacred crater lakes. As outlined below, light is a conscious part of Balinese culture.*

**Right**: Image credit 2.14.1 **Lake Beratan.** Set at a cool tropical altitude of just over 1,200 metres, Lake Beratan is one of the main crater lakes from which water flows some forty kilometers to the south across the rice terraces of Bali. The whole island is about seventy kilometers wide from north to south.

**Below** Image credit 2.14.2 **Looking through Lempuyang Temple gates towards Mt Agung.**

**Lempuyang** is one of the six major Hindu Temples in Bali and is relatively small in size. The other five main temples are Andakasa Temple, Uluwatu Temple, Watukaru Temple, Ulun Danu Batur Temple and Besakih Temple. Lempuyang has shrines to padmasana or the shrine of God, plus two shrines which are similar to padmasana and share a single foundation dedicated to Hyang Gnijaya.

In Balinese cosmogony, Lempuyang Luhur is considered the sacred temple of the East, the abode of god Iswara, keeper of the peace. The meaning of the word *Lempuyang* has long been debated but is said to be derived from the words "lampu" (light) and "hyang" (God). Thus the word "lempuyang" means the "Light of God."[28] Another meaning of the word "lempuyang" is derived from the word "emong or empu" that means "guardian." [29]

Part of the Ulan Datu Baratan Temple at Lake Beratan is depicted above. The taller shrine with eleven roofs is for Shiva and the one with three roofs is for the Rice Goddess. Such temples have become popular international tourist destinations during the 21st century, allowing wider appreciation of their sacred religious significance.

# Mountains, shrines, gardens and thatch

**Below** Image credit 2.15.1

Religion is not something that is talked about. It is practiced every day. It binds people together in harmony . . . .

**Above** Image credit 2.15.2

**Over** 80% of the population of Bali identify as Hindus. Hinduism was brought to Bali around the 8th century AD. Since then a unique blend of religions has developed, including Hinduism, Buddhism and the animistic religions that had been practiced on the island for thousands of years prior to the arrival of the Hindus. The Balinese respect mountains as the dwelling of the gods. Mount Agung is believed to be home to Mahadewa, the supreme manifestation of Lord Shiva, considered by many as the supreme god.

*" Some people believe that the mountain [Mt Agung] was first a part of Mount Meru brought to Bali by the first Hindus. Mount Meru is a sacred cosmological mountain that bears heaven on its summit and is considered to be the centre of all universes; physical, metaphysical, and spiritual."* (30)

# Temples facing the light

*There is no understanding Bali without the trees. It is as though the people have never forgotten how pleasant and sensible it is to live in villages where trees provide shelter of every form.*

**A** Shrine in Temple Courtyard

**B** Above: Social and Sleeping pavilions

**C** Below: view towards front gate

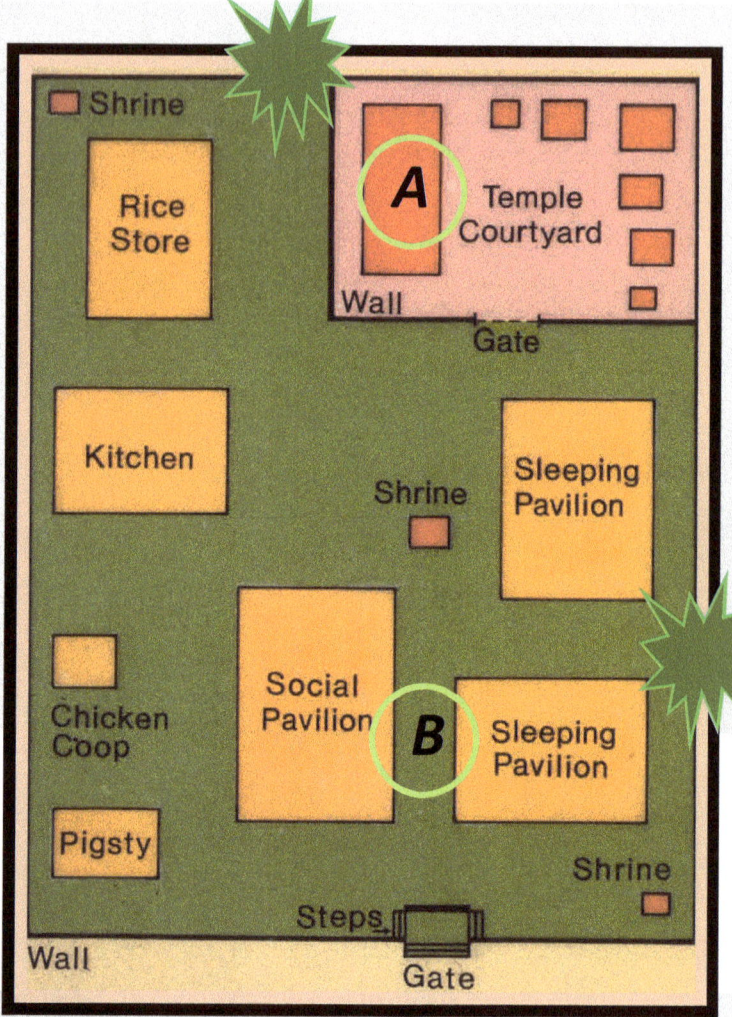

**Above:** Image credit 2.16.1 **Plan of a typical Balinese family compound.**
Carefully located within the walled compound, shrines are part of daily life. Photo locations A, B and C are shown on the plan. Photos are typical images. They are not all from the one site.

*At left photos A, B and C.*
Image credits 2.16.2 – 2.16.4

# Illustrating a traditional Balinese shrine 'Light garden'

*Notes 1 – 10 in the example below illustrate the extent to which the ten Light Garden parameters identified in Chapter 1 are present in the traditional Balinese village shrine depicted below.*

 **Energy.** The sun is the energy source in this village.

**2. Space.** The shrine courtyard has a central *'light garden'* space for activities.

**3. Waves and particles.** Waves of devotees come and go through the shine.

**4. Patterns and probabilities.** The thatched roofs of the shrine buildings follow traditional patterns and the design is highly probable to be the same as other buildings in the village.

**5. Multiplication effects.** This courtyard is framed by a series of thatched roofs which together create a multiplication effect.

**6. Focal Points and entanglement.** The shrine is a focal point. It also relies for its significance upon the courtyard in which it is located. This is an example of entanglement.

**7. Measurement and perception.** Careful measurements and human mindsets appreciative of the cultural significance of what was being built were used to construct this devotional shrine.

**8. Context.** The materials in this village come from the forest and trees that enclose it. The scale of the construction fits within the spaces between the coconut palms and other the trees. These factors help to provide a comfortable and ecologically sound framework for life.

*9. **Human use.** Visitors from the "developed world" sometimes write off Balinese beliefs as "superstition": but if the purpose of religion is to help people live in harmony . . . with one another and with their environment . . . it certainly works in Bali, and works well*

**10. Storage of information.** The design of this village and the lives of the people are based on information stored in the minds of the people and Hindu traditions.

***Below*** Image credit 2.17 ***A shrine within a Balinese village***

# Water, light and pond life

*Although the terraced Balinese rice paddies catch the attention of visitors, in reality there is a complex land use relationship between forests, rice paddies and gardens around dwellings. For example Dr John Tyman described one property as: "a tropical garden of 2,000 square metres .. a rice growing area of 3,000 square metres - and not least of all, a lily pond where they raised fish, frogs and lily roots to add to the diet."* (31)

**Top below** Image credit 2.18.1 *Balinese landscape*
**Centre below** Image credit 2.18.2 *Balinese fish pond*

**Bottom left** Image credit 2.18.3 *Balinese ducks*
**Below** Image credit 2.18.4 *Non-balinese fish farm*

**Dr** Tyman's description above is a good illustration of the light garden concept where, (in an intensive agricultural system that is acknowledged as likely to be the most productive in South East Asia), light is harvested for a complex series of interdependent uses. The area of land actually devoted to rice paddies in full sunlight is roughly equivalent to the land area managed with more tree cover. Land with tree cover incudes forest water catchments, plus trees and gardens around and within the rice paddies and dwellings.

Comparison between the non-Balinese trout farm depicted immediately above and the Balinese fish pond at centre left, tells the tale of a culture where religion is reflected in the way daily activities are carried out. The lotus is a symbolic, sacred flower that grows unsullied out of the mud as it reaches for the light. It's leaves shelter aquatic life and its roots are also edible, making the harvesting of light in this fish pond much more diversified and ecologically stable than in the modern trout farm. Chickens roam the gardens around the pond, while geese chase frogs in the rice paddies and cattle assist with the ploughing.

# Light garden: living in harmony

*" Visitors from the "developed world" sometimes write off Balinese beliefs as "superstition": but if the purpose of religion is to help people live in harmony . . . with one another and with their environment . . . it certainly works in Bali, and works well. Christian missionaries were sent here long ago but were unable to make any converts."* (32)

*"In Bali people don't just talk about religion, they live it."* (33)

As depicted at right, this Balinese woman is drawing water in contemplative mode from the mountain stream that sustains her village with its modestly scaled, carefully tended gardens. The background foliage in this view of the garden contains the venerated Tulsi plant, which is worshipped by Hindus in the morning and in the evening. (34)

The older village residents depicted playing in a local gamelan are likely to also be seen ploughing the local rice paddies, as illustrated below. The music and the farm work has artistic and religious significance, so not surprisingly , the artwork depicted below right includes a shrine amidst the rice paddies. This is a common sight in Bali.

**Above:** Image credit 2.19.1 **Ploughing**
**Top right** Image credit 2.19.2 **Balinese woman**
**Centre right** Image credit 2.19.3 **Gamalan**
**Bottom right** Image credit 2.19.4 **Balinese shrine** *(on the far left of this view of a rice paddy).*

# Chapter 3 North Asia & Feng Shui

Previous page Image credit 3.1

# Table of Contents Chapter 3

| | |
|---|---|
| Introduction | 4 |
| Mapping the locations | 5 |
| Hangzhou and West Lake in China | 6 |
| The Light of inspiration | 7 |
| From the distant to the near | 8 |
| Korean Feng Shui | 9 |
| Huwon and walking in Nature | 10 |
| Austerity and military imperatives | 11 |
| Up to the light: A Sky Garden | 12 |
| Restoration of Qi | 13 |
| Feng Shui and Light | 14 |
| Brining in the Light and energy | 15 |
| Before and after garden with Feng Shui | 16 |
| Light in a Japanese Garden | 17 |
| Japanese Garden Pools of Light | 18 |
| Lanterns and Pools of Light | 19 |
| Supplementing and Suppressing | 20 |
| Buddhism: beyond the dualism of light and dark | 21 |

# Introduction

***Light*** *and **Feng Shui** – what an ideal match.*
*For light is a form of energy and Feng Shui works with balancing the energies of the earth, air, fire, water and wood. It also works with yang and yin, the masculine and feminine energies identified in the Feng Shui system.*

*Go Puo, Chinese:* 郭璞; (AD 276 – 324), was an eminent writer and commentator on ancient texts. He was the author of *The Zangshu*, otherwise known as *The Book of Burial*. He is considered the first and most authoritative writer on the ancient doctrine of Feng Shui. (1) Shephen L. Field, PhD, translated *The Zangshu* to English in 2001. (2) Within that translation he defines the meaning of the term Feng Shui as "Wind Water." (3)

經曰，
氣乘風散，
界水則止。
古人
聚之使不散，
行之使有止，
故謂風水。

The Classic Says:

*" when qi rides the wind it is dispersed,*
*when it meets a boundary of water it is retained.*
*The Ancients were able to gather it to prevent dispersion,*
*to guide it and retain it,*
*hence it was called Wind Water "* [ *Feng Shui*]. (4)

This translation of the meaning of Feng Shui refers to *"qi"*. *"Qi"* or *"chi"* may be described as:

> *" Natural Laws are regarded as the highest guidance of all aspects of human endeavours and Chi is the very essence of the universe . . .*
>
> *"We all want to reside in a living environment that nourishes us with good health, harmonious relationships, career success, and overall happiness." (5)*

Describing the difference between Chinese traditional landscape design and Western landscape design, Junying Pang, a 21st century landscape planning student said:

> *" Chinese traditional landscape design emphasized the understanding and development of the natural beauty, whereas Western landscape focused on the refining of the natural elements as an abstract sense of order and formal beauty." (6)*

Whilst this subject is infinity debatable and relevant to the concept of 'Light Gardens', I will defer considering it in more detail until later in this chapter and subsequent chapters of this book.

Firstly I will describe concepts of Feng Shui in a little more detail then give particular examples of places and 'Light Gardens' in the countries of China, Korea and Japan.

# Mapping the locations

*As an indication of how universally admired is the beauty of Feng Shui gardens, a number of them are included on UNESCO's register of World Heritage sites. Two of these gardens, (within their landscape settings), are considered in this chapter: West Lake in the city of Hangzhou in China and Huwon in Korea*

**The** symbolism of light in North Asian Buddhist gardens is quite different from that in Hindu, Islamic or Christian gardens.

Not surprisingly, there is a greater emphasis on being in an environment that emulates nature, with the enlightenment experience arising from meditation and the realization of the "oneness" of all beings. This concept aligns well with the 'Light Garden' concept. This is because there are ten principles that need to act in unison to create the overall quantum biophysics synchronicity of the 'Light Garden." This synchronicity aligns well with the Buddhist concept of "oneness" of all beings, where the needs of all become synchronised in diverse, interactive ecosystems and societies.

Highlighting the alignment of the 'Light Garden' concept to Buddhist symbolism is not to imply that other cultures have less affinity with the 'Light Garden" model. This will become apparent by progressing through the examples given in each chapter of this book.

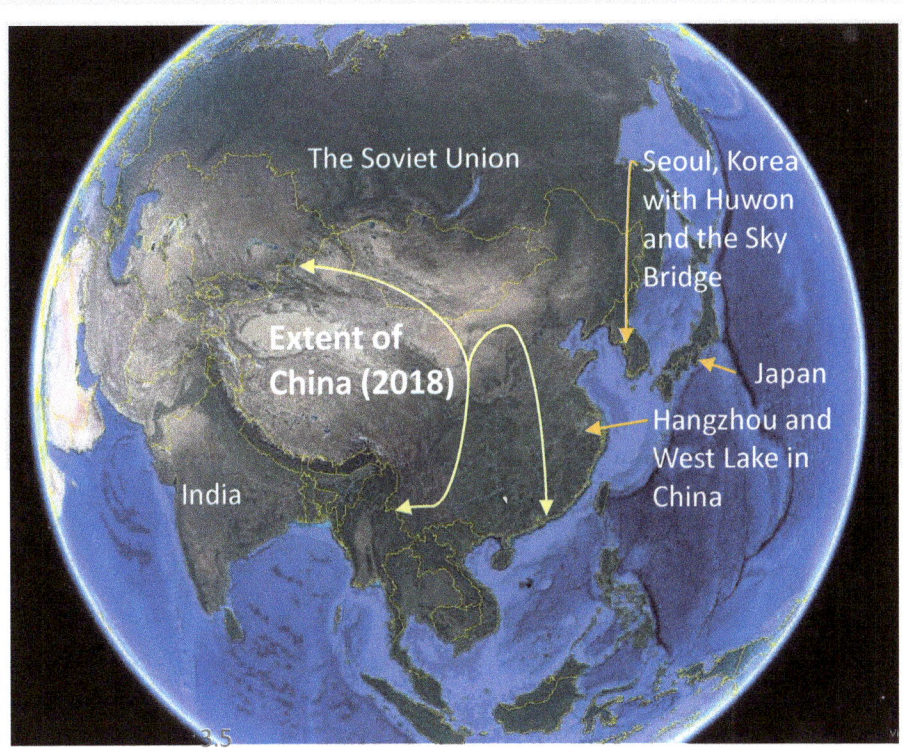

**Right** Map Image credit 3.5
***Map of North Asia (2018)***

# Feng Shui and light

*I am proposing in this chapter that consideration of Feng Shui is combined with consideration of Light. For what is light but electromagnetic energy from the sun and what is Feng Shui but aligning with Earth's electromagnetic energy?*

## Feng Shui

*The Eight Life Aspirations style of Feng Shui is referred to here. Feng Shui has many variations, that have developed over thousands of years. A Feng Shui Bagua to guide design for gardens, places and landscapes in the southern hemisphere is given below.*

**Traditional** Feng Shui was developed in the northern hemisphere. The same principles apply in the southern hemisphere, except that North and South are reversed, while East and West remain the same.

**Whilst there is controversy over how to interpret this**, in the Northern Hemisphere the *Fire* Element is located in the South. I use the chart below for reference in the southern hemisphere. This chart includes the feature of *Love and Marriage* in the North West, between the *Fire* Element in the North, and the feature of *Children and Creativity*, which manifests in the West.

| North West<br>Earth Element<br>Love and Marriage | North<br>Fire Element<br>Fame | North East<br>Wood Element<br>Wealth |
|---|---|---|
| West<br>Metal Element<br>Creativity/ children | Centre<br>Heart Yin/ Yang point | East<br>Wood Element<br>Health |
| South West<br>Metal Element<br>Helpful people/ Blessings | South<br>Water Element<br>Career/ Path in Life | South East<br>Earth Element<br>Spiritual Growth/ Cultivation |

*At left* Image 3.6 *A Feng Shui Bagua for the Southern Hemisphere*

*Feng Shui encourages a mindful abundance of natural light. For example, in interior design, there are rules for the placement of mirrors, so they either reflect light into areas needing more energy, or alternatively, they are placed to avoid directing light away from areas where it is needed.*

**In landscape design, instead of a mirror reflecting light indoors, a pond of water** might reflect light and bring energy into an area, as illustrated later in this chapter at the West Lake site in China. This can be considered in conjunction with the description of *wind water* given in the Introduction to this chapter:

" *when qi rides the wind it is dispersed, when it meets a boundary of water it is retained. The Ancients were able to gather it to prevent dispersion, to guide it and retain it, hence it was called Wind Water."* (8)

# Bringing in the light & energy

*The Vedic system of Vastu has similarities with Feng Shui. So too does the Japanese system of Kanso. This chapter provides a brief overview of the how light is used in each of these systems. As briefly introduced in the remainder of this chapter, Buddhist gardens often display a sensitivity to space, light and natural materials that is more in accordance with Light Garden principles and more subtle than the none the less very useful, tried and true basic Feng Shui principles outlined in the table below.*

| Fengshui Direction | Fengshui Element | Fengshui unction | Fengshui Feature |
|---|---|---|---|
| South | Water | Career/Life Path | Water feature |
| North East | Wood | Wealth | Gold bells in water feature |
| East | Wood | Family & Health | Greenery & wood dragon |
| South East | Earth | Spiritual Growth | Spiritual symbol |
| North | Fire | Fame & recognition | Lights, BBQ |
| South West | Metal | Helpful People | Business seating area |
| West | Metal | Children & inner child | Playground & yoga area |
| North West | Earth | Love and Marriage | Flowers, Outdoor furniture |

## Feng Shui

The five elements (Fire, Water, Earth, Wood and Metal), are listed in the table at left. These differ a little from the five elements of Vastu.

## Vastu

The five elements of this Vedic system are Fire, Water, Earth, Air and Space. There are other significant similarities between Vastu & Feng Shui.

## similarities

Both are concerned with the universal flow of energy and with reverence for the sacred and spirit worlds, especially with regard to temple design and the passing of the dead.

Image 3.7 copyright Anne Whittingham

# Before and after Feng Shui

*Feng Shui principles can be applied to the design of a place, garden or landscape. Here is an example of landscape design to reestablish native vegetation and make a recreation area around a lake that remained after quarry operations had finished.*  **Below** *plan image credit 3.8.1*

**The proposed earthworks around the lake are shown on the inset plan at right and additional works are shown below.**  *At right* Plan Image credit 3.8.1

*Below* Image credit 3.8.2

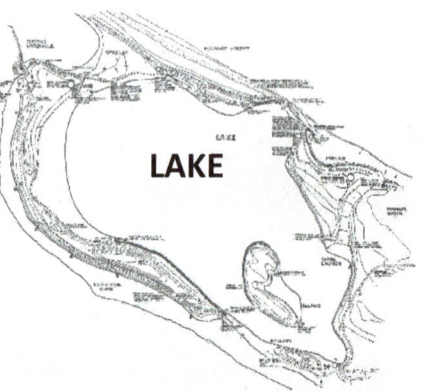

**Red is in the North with the Element of Fire** and the function of fame and recognition. Place lights or fire pits here. Image credit 3.8.3

**Purple and gold in the North East** is the Element of wood, with the Function of Wealth and Prosperity. Add features such as gold and purple flowers. Image credit 3.8.4

**In the East is Green and the Wood** Element, with the function of Health and Family. A wooden dragon may be placed here. Image credit 3.8.5

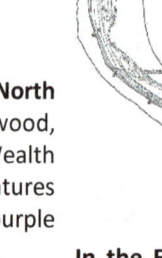

**Pink in the North West** with the Element of Earth and the Function of Marriage and happy personal relationships. Image credit 3.8.10

**In the South East, beige, pink and earthy colours** are associated with the Earth element and the function of Spiritual Growth and Knowledge. Image credit 3.8.6

**White in the West** is the Element of Metal, with the Function of Children and Play. Image credit 3.8.9

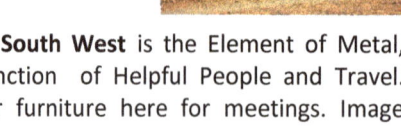

**Grey in the South West** is the Element of Metal, with the Function of Helpful People and Travel. Add outdoor furniture here for meetings. Image credit 3.8.8

**Blue in the South** with the Water element and the function of Career and Life Path. Image credit 3.8.7

# Hangzhou & West Lake in China

***West Lake*** *(Chinese)* 西湖*, pinyin Xī Hú; Wu Si-wu) is a freshwater lake in Hangzhou, China. After centuries of dredging, three main causeways divide the lake into five sections. There are numerous man-made temples, islands, pleasure craft, walkways and gardens in and around the lake.* (9)

Below Image credit 3.9 **Map of West Lake**

**By** the 21st century, Hangzhou had grown to be a city with a population of 9.2 million. It may be reached by a one hour train journey to the south west of Shanghai.

The history of West Lake includes many themes from Feng Shui and Buddhism, as well as practical water storage and distribution schemes for agricultural, recreational and urban use. West Lake was once a lagoon adjoining the nearby Qiantang River. In AD 610, the Qiantang River was effectively linked to the other four major rivers of China, (the Yellow, Hai, Yangtze and Huai), via the construction of the Jiangnan Canal. (10)

This waterway linkage boosted the regional economy of Hangzhou, which in turn supported the development of a class of poets, painters and travelers who celebrated the West Lake landscape. The name "West Lake" is recorded as first appearing in the poems of Baui Juvi. One of these is known as "*Bestowed on guests as returning from West Lake in the evening and looking Back to Gushan Temple*" (西湖晚歸回望孤山寺贈諸客). (11)

The significance and beauty of the light of the setting sun in Chinese culture, (as seen to the west across the waters of the lake), is underlined by the naming of the lake as *West Lake*. This name has remained in use ever since the days of Baui Juvi. Millions of visitors continue to come to the site each year. In 2011 it was listed on the United Nations Educational, Scientific and Cultural Organisation's (UNESCO's) World Heritage List. (12)

# The Light of inspiration

*The West Lake Cultural Landscape of Hangzhou illustrates the profound metaphysical importance of natural beauty in Chinese culture. In the view illustrated below, we see an example of how this could be considered as an example of principle number nine in a 'Light Garden' landscape, where human use is retrained within the capacity of the natural resources.*

**Hangzhou** and the West Lake Cultural Landscape in China is one of the inspirational landscapes which underpin the art of Chinese landscape design and planning. Its beauty has been celebrated by writers and artists since the Tang Dynasty (AD 618-907). The factors contributing to the beauty of West Lake and other inspirational landscapes were analysed long ago and gradually documented into the system of Feng Shui that we know today.

The idyllic lake scene depicted above appears as though the pavilion has been placed in the natural setting of a lake, forested hills and sky. However, the West Lake landscape has been gradually created over a period of at least 1500 years. For example, the main artificial elements of the lake, (two causeways and three islands), were created from repeated dredgings between the 9th and 12th centuries. (13)

The locations of particular structures in and around the lake, such as the viewing platform depicted above and pagodas on the edge of the lake are selected with Fengshui in mind.

**Below** Image credit 3.10 **West Lake** (**Chinese** 西湖; **pinyin:** *Xī Hú*; **Wu:** *Si-wu*)

# From the near to the distant

*In the three photographs below, we see the progression from a a close up view of a lakeside pavilion to a more distant view across the lake. This series illustrates the need for timeless underlying Feng Shui. principles that are applicable at all scales when designing landscapes.*

**Since** the Southern Song Dynasty (thirteenth century), ten poetically named Feng Shui scenic places, (such as illustrated on this page), have been identified at West Lake. They embody idealised, classical Chinese landscapes that are regarded as examples of the perfect fusion between man and nature.

As noted in the UNESCO World Heritage listing information for site, in order to make them 'more beautiful' the islands, causeways and the lower slopes of the hills around West Lake have been 'improved' by the addition of numerous temples, pagodas, pavilions, gardens and ornamental trees which merge with farmed landscape. (14)

Although you don't see the crowds in these photographs, during peak holiday times the 3,322 hectare West Lake site caters to over 1 million visitors per day. (15) In comparison, the highest average daily attendance at the hectare 341 hectare (16) Central Park site in New York is 220,000 people. (17)

**Top right** Image credit 3.11.1 *a close up view of a West Lake* **Pavilion**

**Centre right** Image credit 3.11.2 *a more distant view of the West Lake pavilion with mountains behind it*

**Below right** Image credit 3.11.3 *a yet more distant view to mountains across the foreground of West Lake*

# Korea, Huwon and walking in nature

*Korean gardens place a greater emphasis on creating a naturalistic setting and the experience of walking through the actual landscape in which the garden is located.*

**Huwon** is an example of the unique Korean form of Feng Shui, which is known as Psungsu – jiri – seol.  This form was developed by Doseon Guksa, a Korean Buddhist monk, AD (826 – 898).

He is honoured in Korea because of his genius in studying, then adapting existing Chinese Feng Shui theories for use in the different conditions of Korean culture.

**Below**   Image credit 3.12 *Changdeokgungi Palace within the Huwon garden.*

**Doseon Guksa** emphasized the effects of these theories on communities and the nation as a whole, rather than on more individual endeavours, such as the creation of personal fortunes or the placement of furniture.

**Korean Feng Shui** and the cultural connection to Nature can be traced to the Korean religious spectrum known as Seondo, which includes prehistoric traditions of animism, shamanism and the belief in mountain and forest spirits, as well as Feng Shui.

In comparison to Chinese and Japanese gardens, Korean gardens place a greater emphasis on creating a naturalistic setting and the experience of walking through the actual landscape in which the garden is located.

**At Huwon,** the small pavilions were built along the stream flowing through the site.  There were also areas provided for archery, banquets, military drills, entertaining and withdrawal from the royal court. Kings and Queens used their time in the gardens to perform court rituals, experimental farming and silk cultivation in ceremonies to show leadership to the people of Korea. (18)

Although the Kings and Queens are no longer in residence at Huwon, the enthusiasm of the people of Korea to develop their connection with Nature and rural enterprises continues to grow. For example Bukhansan National Park near Seoul  is reported to have the highest number of visitors per square meter of any

# Austerity and military imperatives

(continued) National Park in the world. It has an average of five million **visitors per year, exemplifying the national enthusiasm for hiking in the countryside and celebrating the changing seasons.** (19) The modern approach to gardens in the city of Seoul also reflects this ethos, as trees and gardens are planted in all available public spaces along roads, as well as on private balconies and rooftops. Seoul's *Sky Garden* is a 21st century example of this, as discussed later in this chapter.

*Korean landscape architecture and garden design hinges on reverence for nature. The theory is that structures and garden features are used sparingly - and they are carefully located to complement natural settings.*

**Right** Image credit 3.13.1 ***Ongnyucheon stream (Hangeul: 옥류천; Hanja: 玉流川),*** in the rear garden of Changdeokgung palace, Seoul, South Korea.

**Below Right** Image credit 3.13.3 ***A Temple in Korea***

**Below left** Image credit 3.13.2 ***The Korean Gyeong Palace,*** which was originally built in 1395..

Today the relatively austere garden at Gyeong Palace may be a reflection of the military imperatives behind the reconstruction after it was destroyed during the Japanese invasion of 1592 – 98. In a similar manner the South Korean capital city of Seoul was rebuilt after devastation during the 20th century Japanese occupation and the Korean War of the 1950's. (20)

# Korean Feng Shui

*Below* Image credit 3.14 ***An historic painting of Changdeokgungl****, showing the landscape setting. This site is located within the city of Seoul and dates from the 14th Century to present times.* The garden includes

> "a small rice field, where the king would farm rice to aid his understanding of the hard work of farmers and show his solidarity with the farmers. The dried rice plants would be used to thatch Cheonguijeong". (21)

*Below* Image credit 3.14 ***A painting of Changdeokgungi***

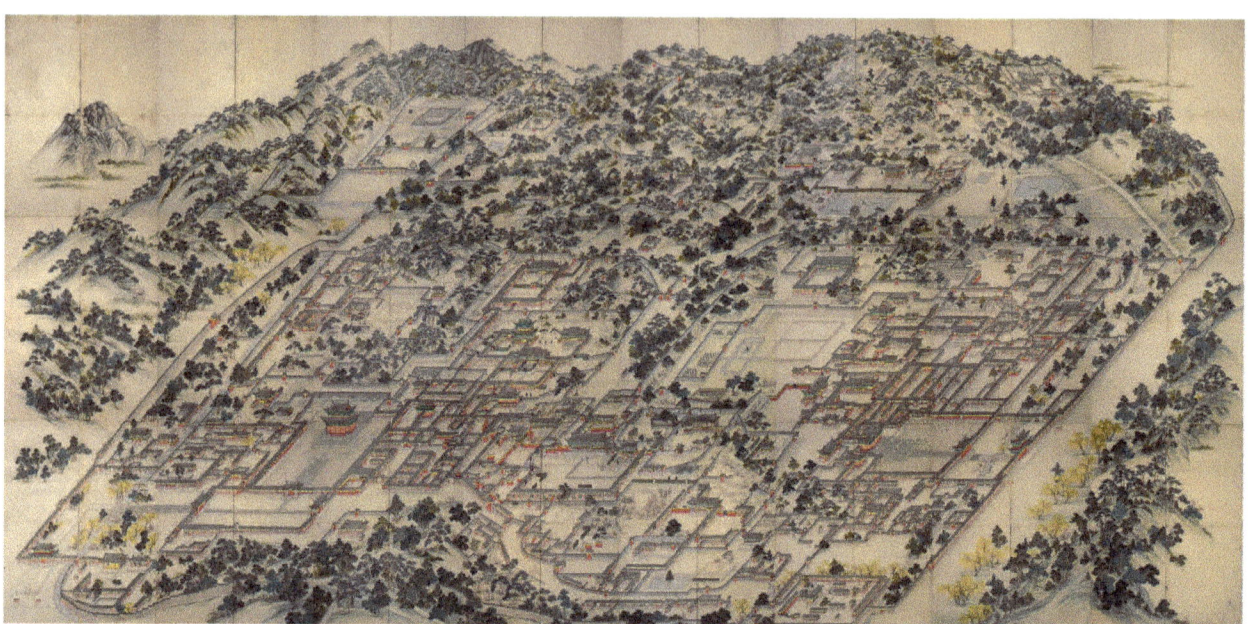

**Huwon** garden was designed to embrace the topography in accordance with *pungsu,* (or Feng Shui), principles on the site of the Changdeokgungi Palace in Seoul. This site dates from the fourteenth century to the present times. There is a hill behind the buildings on the site and a small stream to the front, which is regarded as good *pungsu*. The entry and palace buildings were located on the southern side of the site, which is associated with the Sun element. Huwon, the 32 hectare rear garden, was constructed on the northern side of the site, which is associated with the Water element. (22)

Huwon is also known as Biwon, or the Secret Garden. It was originally constructed for the use of the royal family. However, it is not an extravagant garden. A signboard at the front of the garden was inscribed by King Jeongjo, with words that translate as 'Gather the Universe'. Joseon kings chose to relax, study and write poems in this tranquil garden setting. Pavilions were built on the edge of a square lily pond that was set in a forest glade. Other halls and a library were located nearby. (23)

Korean culture still values a strong connection with Nature. In contrast to the millions of daily visitors to the gardens of the West Lake Cultural Landscape District of Hangzhou, visitor numbers to Huwon are limited to fifty per tour. Visitors must book one of the two or three popular daily guided tours to enter this garden, which today is located within a city of ten million people. (24)

# Up to the light: a Sky Garden

*Opened to the public in 2017, Seoul's new 'Sky Garden' literally illustrates how opening up to the sunlight and its rejuvenating, life-enhancing properties has caught the imagination of the public and of contemporary designers.*

**Top right** Image credit 3.15.1 **The Sky Garden site in the city of Seoul**
This projects demonstrates creative re-use of an existing 1970's motorway flyover that was no longer deemed safe for its original purpose.

It aims to regenerate and connect places in Seoul near the main railway station. These public spaces had been fragmented by roads and railway tracks. The Sky Garden is open 24 hours per day and is part of a larger plan to transform Seoul into a more pedestrian friendly city.

**Centre left:** Image credit 3.15.2
**The safe pedestrian access** provided by the Sky Garden to link with public open space, sunlight and trees was immediately taken up by the citizens of the city, as illustrated here.

**Bottom left** Image credit 3.15.3
*Map derived from Figure 6, Seoul Green Network Plan* **for major green-spaces and its potential network in Seoul.** (Seoul Metropolitan Government, 1997.)

**Legend:**
    ━ ━  Main network of green space
    ━ ━  Main network of water space

This plan illustrates the influence of Feng Shui principles, where the city planning aimed to incorporate the symbolism, character and guidance of the Feng Shui elements of mountains (earth), water, forests (wood) and open space (fire and air).

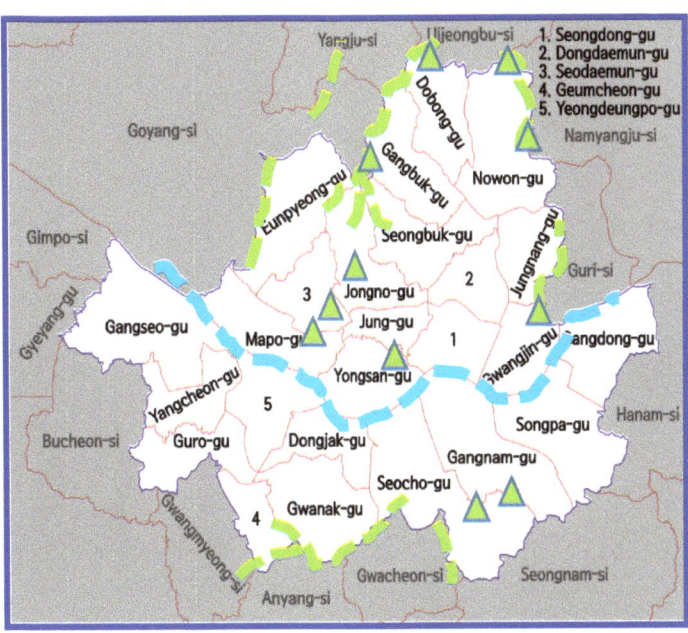

# Light in a Japanese garden

*Although there are many principles followed in the design of Japanese gardens, they do not include specific reference to light.*

**Lanterns** of stone are a characteristic feature of Japanese gardens but the seven principles of Zen aesthetics as set out below, do not include specific reference to light:

*Simplicity or elimination of clutter – Kanso (簡素)*
*Asymmetry or Irregularity – Fukinsei (不均整)*
*Naturalness – Shizen (自然)*
*Subtlety – Yugen (幽玄)*
*Break from routine – Datsuzoku (脱俗)*
*Stillness, tranquillity – Seijaku (静寂)*
*Austerity – Shibui/ Shibumi (渋味)* (25)

In that context, it is interesting to see in the photograph above below that there is a quite deliberate use of the contrast between light and dark elements. The light coloured walls and paving contrast with the dark timber frame of the entry and the dark trunks of the nearby black bamboo and Syzygium trees. Perhaps it is the combination of the seven principles of Zen aesthetics in this garden that leads to a pleasant sense of natural light, without it being obvious how it is achieved.

**Below** Image credit 3.16 ***Japanese garden***. Design by the late Kenzo Ogata, Landscape Architect. Location: Mt Coot tha Botanic Gardens, Brisbane, Australia

# Japanese & Korean gardens

***Below*** Image credit 3.17.1 ***the Japanese Garden at Mount Coot-tha Botanic Gardens, Brisbane.*** This garden, designed by Master Landscape Architect Kenzo Ogata, was originally built in 1988 as a gift from the Japanese people to the people of Australia at the time of Expo 88. The garden falls within the *stroll garden* category of Japanese gardens.

The rounded forms of the clipped, light green shrubbery and lawn in the centre of this view correspond well with the pool of light that falls upon them. The purpose of neatly clipping so many shrubs in this garden is evident, as the form of each is subsumed within the pattern of the whole.

The right hand half of this view of the garden is illuminated by a large light well in the surrounding tree cover. The light well occurs over the pond, the surface of which also serves as a source of reflected light in the centre of the garden.

**Above right** Image credit 3.17.1 Upon passing through the entry gate of the garden, this view unfolds. It includes a grey stone lantern beside the path in the centre foreground. In keeping with the relative subtlety, (*Yugen*) of the design, this lantern is much smaller than the one depicted in the garden on the following page.

**Right** Image credit 3.17.2 **Seoul** The yellow colouring and intricate patterns on the end of the seats bring extra light, character and interest to the welcome shelter of trees in the inner city of Seoul.

# Lanterns and pools of light

*The stone lantern is a key focal point in this garden, by day and by night. The bright red handrails are another focal point, enhanced by their colour, contrast and form.*

***Oriental garden*** Image credit 3.18

**Space** and light in this part of the garden are used subtlety in combination with the focal points o create *legibility*. The bridge is not only a means of passing through the garden, it also adds to the legibility of the garden in another way.

The bridge allows us to pause and stand upon it, suspended there in space and time. Safely above the water, yet in close proximity to the plants and aquatic organisms, our minds can relax and derive meaning from the experience of being in contact with Nature.

As the pool of light reflected from the surface of the pond in this garden is much smaller than the one in the Japanese garden depicted on the previous page, it serves to illustrate how a combination of symbolic garden elements, (the lantern, bridge and small pond), can be used to evoke the experience of being in contact with nature.

Buddhists in other parts of the world are more likely than the Japanese to include a statue of Buddha in a garden. In the subtle Japanese way, the analogy of Buddhist enlightenment is provided through lighting, lanterns and the opportunity to stop and reflect upon nature in the stillness, simplicity and tranquillity of the garden. After all, it was while sitting outdoors under a tree that Buddha gained enlightenment.

# Restoration of Qi

*The Cheonggyecheon (Stream) restoration project in urban Seoul is an example of the application of Feng Shui principles to city planning and design. In particular, this project represents restoration of Qi, which is described as the life force, as living energy or the energy flux. ( 26)*

**Top right** Image credit 3.19.1
**The site of Cheonggyecheon in 2004, before the restoration** project began.

The raised motorway was above the stream, which is not visible beneath the cars in this photograph. By the end of the second decade of the 21$^{st}$ century, Seoul had a population of approximately 12 million people.

**Centre right:** Image credit 3.19.2
**The same view as the photograph above, overlaid with the design illustration for** restoration of an eleven kilometre long section of the stream through Seoul.

Note that the design included a wide river corridor with sloping grass riverbanks and plenty of pedestrian access to sunny lawns and public open space, amidst the dense urban environment.

**Bottom right** Image credit 3.19.3
**An 'as constructed' view** of the Cheonggyecheon Stream project.

This project is an example of how Qi has been at least partially restored in this part of the city by provision of public open space with access to trees, water, sunlight and air, (representing a balanced energy mix of the five Feng Shui elements of Earth, Air, Fire, Water and Wood. This project was also planned as part of the broader Seoul Green Network Plan illustrated on a previous page.

# Supplementing & suppressing

*Fengshui theory is also concerned with creating and managing Fengshui elements, resembling modern ecological restoration technology in some ways.*

**Ecological** restoration (and the explanation of such projects to the general public in North Asia), engages two main streams of Fengshui concepts. Firstly there is the concept of addition or supplementing *elements in the landscape. This is called "Bibo"* in Korean. For example, forest restoration projects can support ecological restoration through improvements to the local climate, biodiversity and water systems.

Secondly, there is the concept of removing or suppressing improper and unnecessary open spaces and structures in the landscape. This is called *"Apseung"* in Korean. For example, removal of nuclear power plants in geologically unstable areas can support long term ecological restoration. (27)

**Top left** Image credit 3.20.1 **Roan-ji in Kyoto, Japan.** This is an example of suppression or removal of elements in a garden, leaving a space that is none the less conducive to meditation.

**Centre left** Image credit 3.20.2 *Japanese garden at the Mount Coot-tha Botanic Gardens in Brisbane.*

**Bottom left** Image credit 3.20.3 **West Lake at Hangzhou in China.** This is an example of supplementation by the addition of a moon gate in the foreground of a view across the lake.

# Buddhism: enlightenment beyond dualism of light & dark

*"Beyond dualism, every object – by whomever or in whatever manner it is made – finds salvation."* (28)

**The** concept of dependent origination is one which distinguishes Buddhism from Christianity and other monotheist religions. It is descried in the following text which is attributed to Buddha Shakyamuni (Siddhartha Gautama), who lived during the 6th century BCE:

> *" He who experiences the unity of life sees his own self in all beings and all beings in his own Self and looks on everything with an impartial eye."* (29)

For those Buddhists who seek liberation from impure dual perception, a garden and landscape may be seen as an expression of the unity of life and an opportunity to immerse oneself in it, in order to more fully develop *an impartial eye*. A 20th century Japanese text by Seotsu Yanagi also notes:

> *" . . . from the Buddhists' point of view, the 'beauty' that simply stands opposed to ugliness is not true beauty . . . In the Muryoju-kyo ('Sutra of Eternal Life'), the following statement is attributed to the Buddha:*
> *" . . . If in the land of the Buddha there remains the distinction between the beautiful and the ugly, I do not desire to be a Buddha of such a land . . ."* (30)

As an example of the Buddhist way of life, the former Korean royal families chose to immerse themselves in gardens within natural settings. Their chosen activities, dedicated to the benefit of the nation, were ritual, study and contemplation around the natural streams that flowed through the palace grounds.

Thus the symbolism of light in Buddhist gardens is quite different from that in Hindu, Islamic or Christian gardens.

Not surprisingly, there is a greater emphasis on Naturalness (*Shizen*) in Buddhist gardens, with the enlightenment experience arising from meditation

This is a different concept of light from when it is valued for its symbolic role in religious cultures. For example it may be a source of divine inspiration, a way of approaching an understanding of God, or a symbol of the triumph of good over evil, as described in various scriptures.

**Below** Photo credit 3.21 a ***Buddha statue: an aid to meditation***

# Chapter 4
# Islamic gardens

Image credit 4.1    www.nefertitigarden.com

Previous page Image credit 4.1

# Table of Contents Chapter 4

| | |
|---|---|
| Introduction to Islamic gardens | 4 |
| Examples of Islamic Gardens | 5 |
| The Light of Paradise | 6 |
| Nur Jahan | 7 |
| Versailles comparison of plan with an Islamic Garden | 8 |
| Arches and Inscriptions | 9 |
| Reflections on the Taj Mahal | 10 |
| Comparison of an Italian Garden with a Moorish Garden | 11 |
| The Alhambra | 12 |
| Phi in the Sky | 13 |
| Islamic Plans: the finite and the infinite | 14 |
| Living with the Earth as a Light Garden | 15 |
| Light Gardens linking to Islamic concepts | 16 |
| Ten components example | 17 |
| Evolution in One Generation | 18 |
| 21st century Dubai Is Changing | 19 |
| Sustainability City Light Garden | 20 |
| Burj Al Arab and tradition | 21 |

*God guides whoever He will to his light (1)*

# Introduction

*Islamic gardens are often described as paradise gardens, based on the principle that there are four rivers in paradise. The rivers are represented in a garden by four channels of water. These channels or rivers divide the land into four quadrants, each of which is filled with flowers, plants and birds. (2)*

> " *God is the Light of the heavens and earth. His Light is like this: there is a niche, and in it a lamp, the lamp inside a glass, a glass like a glittering star, fuelled from a blessed olive tree from neither east nor west, whose oil almost gives light even when no fire touches it - light upon light - God guides whoever He will to his Light; God draws such comparisons for people; God has full knowledge of everything - shining out in houses of worship. God has ordained that they be raised high and that His name be remembered in them, with men in them celebrating His glory morning and evening." (3)*

In Islam, as in Judaism, God is not depicted. However an understanding of the God may be developed through reference to light. This practice is described by the Qur'an, which Muslims believe to be the actual word of God sent down to the Prophet Muhammad. (4)

From this mind stream the Islamic garden emerges. As I will try to describe in this chapter with reference to examples, it is almost as though the role of light, like that of God, cannot be described through reference to the physical world, or to the four quadrant principle of paradise gardens. However, through the experience of being in such a garden, one can approach an experiential understanding of these concepts. This may occur in a similar way to the description from the Qu'ran that is quoted above, where the Light of God shines *"out in houses of worship"*.

Although Islamic gardens were not designed for use by non-believers, several of them, such as The Alhambra and the Taj Mahal, are often included in lists of the world's most popular pilgrimage and tourist destinations. (5) These sites are also listed as being of World Heritage significance by the United Nations Educational, Scientific and Cultural Organisation (UNESCO). (6) As described later in this chapter, although these gardens were built with high ambitions, their patrons probably never imaged the world wide influence that they would have upon the consciousness of people from all nations in the 21st century, as the internet has facilitated the spread of images across the globe.

This illustrates the underlying ability of these Islamic gardens to appeal to the human soul, regardless of culture. The fact that many visitors to Islamic sites cannot read the inscriptions they contain but are none the less inspired by the experience of being in the gardens, is testimony to the validity of the goal for peaceful, spiritual coexistence between human souls that is upheld and promoted by many Islamic and other religious leaders of the 21st Century. One of the goals of this book is to support evolution in that direction through greater conscious use and sharing of the resource of light on Earth.

# Examples of Islamic gardens

*The map below (date 2019) focuses on that part of the globe where Muslim majority countries are located. There are significant Islamic populations in all the countries in the band between points A and B on the map. For example, the county of India falls within this band. Although India is not regarded as an Islamic culture in the same way as say Saudi Arabia is, there is a significant Islamic population in India. Places referred to in this chapter are labelled on the map*

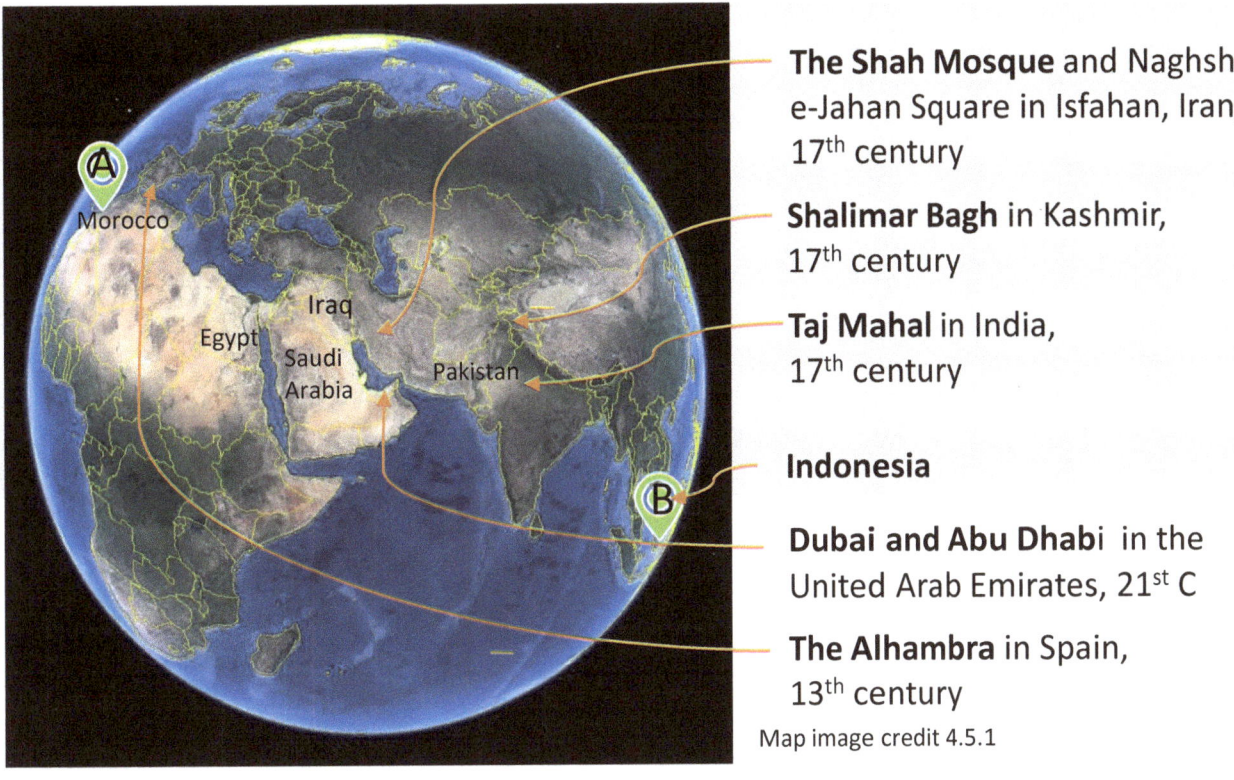

**The Shah Mosque** and Naghsh-e-Jahan Square in Isfahan, Iran, 17th century

**Shalimar Bagh** in Kashmir, 17th century

**Taj Mahal** in India, 17th century

**Indonesia**

**Dubai and Abu Dhabi** in the United Arab Emirates, 21st C

**The Alhambra** in Spain, 13th century

Map image credit 4.5.1

**In Islamic countries, the call to prayer** that rings out from the mosques five times per day sets the rhythm for the whole community. Illustrating the importance of sunlight in this ritual, it is the passage of the sun through the sky that defines these five times:

"*Salat al-fajr*: dawn, before sunrise.
*Salat al-zuhr*: midday, after the sun passes its highest.
*Salat al-'asr*: the late part of the afternoon.
*Salat al-maghrib*: just after sunset and
*Salat al-'isha*: between sunset and midnight." (7)

Image credit 4.5.2

# The light of Paradise

*"Agar Firdaus bar rōy-e zamin ast, hamin ast-o hamin ast-o hamin ast.* (8)

**As** depicted below, the dazzling play of light in the centuries old fountains of the central water channel at Shalimar Bagh are likely to induce us to pause and enter a reflective moment of the 'paradise' experience.

*Shalimar* was an ancient sacred site long before *Shalimar Bagh* was created by the Moghul Emperor Jahangir in 1619. Foreshadowing the words of the Persian poet Amir Khusrau, the Sanskrit word *Shalimar* translates to English as "abode of love." (10)

The Vale of Kashmir has been immortalised through ancient myths and plays that are set in this area. One of the earliest preserved historical records tells us that amidst the natural springs that flow from the foothills into Dal Lake, the Hindu ruler Pravarassena II built a garden there in the 1st century CE. (11)

**Above** Image credit 4.6. ***The Moghul Gardens at Shalimar Bagh in Kashmir.*** *This 12.5 hectare garden is now owned and operated by the Jammu and Kashmir Tourism Department as a public park.* (9)

Around the shallow edge of the lake, below the formal gardens of Shalimar Bagh, is a band of swamp meadow about 1.6 kilometers wide. Groves of willow trees, rice paddies and vegetable gardens were established there centuries ago. (12) As is still the case today, plenty of food was needed in this paradise garden!

Among the formal gardens of Shalimar Bagh as depicted below left, we see a design that illustrates an understanding of the interplay of light and dark, as it invites us to walk and pray in the colonnades of paradise.

Creating such experiences was regarded as an activity fit for Moghul rulers to spend their lives engaged with. Inscriptions on the walls of the buildings in this garden include the words of the Persian poet Amir Khusrau:

> *"Agar Firdaus bar rōy-e zamin ast,*
> *hamin ast-o hamin ast-o hamin ast".*

> In English, this translates as:

> *"If there is a paradise on earth, it is here, it is here, it is here."* (13)

Despite the early good intentions, in the 21st century, Lake Dal has floating islands and weed choked waterways. Approximately fifty thousand residents and visitors now dwell around the lake. They live in the town of Srinagar and on the many tourist houseboats that anchor around the edges of the lake.

Government programmes with the aim of rejuvenating *paradise* have been commenced. Problems include lack of law enforcement to stop pollutants such as untreated raw sewerage, excess sediments, rubbish and other materials that flow into the lake. (14)

# Nur Jahan 'light of the world'

*Below: As the setting sun shines over Lake Dal and the terraced gardens of Shalimar Bagh, it is not difficult to see how successful Emperor Jahangir was in celebrating the inspirational light of the Islamic scriptures. It is also recorded that he built this garden to celebrate his Queen Nur Jahan. The Queen's name translates to English as "light of the world".*

**So many of the famous Islamic Gardens are built to take full advantage of light from sunsets over water**. Shalimar Bagh is no exception. High in the Himalayas, It's central watercourse steps down through a series of four terraces across a length of 539 metres to the swamp meadows that line the shores of Lake Dal. Built during the period 1569 – 1627 as a retreat from the scorching summer heat of the Indian plains, (15) such visions of paradise have on-going appeal to earthly, as well as heavenly sensibilities.

In Islam, rather than providing an analogy for God, light is recognised as a quality that can be perceived and understood by humans, whilst also being a quality that most closely resembles God. (16) For more detailed discussion of this subject in relation to Islamic thought, refer to reference (16), for example.

Recognising the universally appealing qualities of the Islamic paradise gardens, it has been said, for example, that the design of Versailles in France was influenced by them. Versailles was commissioned by the French king Louis XIV in the 1660's, about one century after the main gardens of Shalimar Bagh were constructed. As illustrated on the following page, the plan of Versailles includes a prominent, central intersection of water channels. Some have interpreted this plan view as reminiscent of the plans of Islamic gardens.

However, contrary to the analogies of God's light in Islamic gardens, Louis XIV considered himself king by divine right. He chose the sun as his own personal symbol, naming himself the **Sun King** (*Roi Soleil*). The 800 hectare site of Versailles was built to impress others with his power, not as a place to help others invoke an understanding of God. (17)

The garden of the *Roi Soleil* is depicted on the following page. The aesthetic impact of views at Versailles is entirely different from that at Shalimar Bagh. Applying the *"Light Garden"* parameters identified in Chapter 1 of this book to identify why this is so, I would say that human use of the landscape is more restrained at Shalimar Bagh, (Principle Number 9,) and views to natural landscape features of mountains and water are more integrated into the garden experience at Shalimar than at Versailles, thus illustrating successful application of Principle Number 8: *"Context and Environment"*.

*Below* Image credit 4.7. ***Landscape Design for the paradise garden at Shalimar Bagh** included channelling of a natural stream. It flows through terraced ponds down to Lake Dal, as the light of the sun is reflected in the waters.*

# Versailles plan comparison

*The long geometric axis of the Versailles site terminates at point A, as illustrated in the aerial photograph plan view of the site below. On this plan, the Palace entrance at point B is approximately 3.5 kilometers away. Point A is also identified in the photograph at the bottom left of the page.*

**Below** Image credit 4.8.1 ***Versailles,*** *Google Earth image 2019*

**By** comparing the photographs below of Shalimar Bagh and Versailles, we can see the similarity between the main structures of the gardens. Versailles was constructed approximately one hundred years after Shalimar Bagh.

**Below left** Image credit 4.8.2 **the main axis at Versailles**

**Below right** Image credit 4.8.3 **the main axis at Shalimar Bagh, looking towards Lake Dahl**

# Arches and inscriptions

*Another interesting comparison between Islamic gardens and Versailles is found in the type of detailing and inscriptions. For example, as illustrated below in the Moghul Garden of the Taj Mahal we see inscriptions from the Qu'ran but at Versailles, we see Louis XIV's own self appointed symbol: the Roi Soleil, (the Sun King). (18)*

**Above** Image credit 4.9.1 **symbols at Versailles**

**As** documented in the 21$^{st}$ century during a comprehensive study headed by the Spanish Government, fewer than ten percent of the inscriptions on the walls at another famous Islamic garden, The Alhambra, are actually quotes or verses from the Qu'ran. (20)

Although the name of Allah was frequently inscribed by the masons, this study identified that many of the other inscriptions extol the virtues of the architecture itself, or of the rulers who commissioned the work. (21)

Other textural inscriptions at The Alhambra, such as those in the Hall of the Two Sisters, give us an insight into the imagery of light that pervades the poetic stream of Moorish thought and infuses its gardens:

> " The portico is so beautiful that the palace
> competes in beauty with the sky . . .
> How many arches are high on its summit,
> on the columns that are adorned by the light,
> like spheres that turn above the glowing pillar of the dawn! " (22)

Archways *"adorned by the light"* and covered with inscriptions are often an important part of Islamic paradise gardens. They gain significance as symbols of the passage between light and dark, life and death, paradise and hell. (23)

**Below** Image credit 4.9.2. **The Taj Mahal**

# Reflections on the Taj Mahal

*If anyone doubts the importance of light in the Islamic Mogul Gardens of India, let them remember that were it not for Shah Jahan's vision that the Taj Mahal should be fully reflected in the waters of a wide river, it is likely that it would have been built some 800 kilometers to the south of its current site. (24)*

**Above** Image credit 4.10 ***The Taj Mahal and the Yamuna River***

**Shah** Jahan originally chose a site for the Taj Mahal in Burhanpur, by the banks of the Tapti River in central India. Burhanpur was the headquarters from which Shah Jahan spearheaded his military campaigns into central India and it was there that Mumtaz Mahal died in childbirth with her fourteenth child, whilst accompanying her husband on his military exploits.

To honour Mumtaz Mahal, the Shah wanted the Taj to be built of white marble, which could only be sourced from Makrana in Rajasthan. That site was a long way from Burhanpur. He also found that the River Tapti was not wide enough at Burhanpur to fully reflect his intended vision for the Taj Mahal. In addition, the rock foundations may not have been strong enough for the huge weight of the intended structures. (25)

So upon finding a site with firm foundations, with reasonable access to the white marble supplies of Rajasthan and on the banks of the wide Yamuna River at Agra, the decision was made to build there.

Such tombs were disapproved of by some Islamic leaders because of the Muslim tradition forbidding elaborate decorations on graves. There is also debate about whether the Taj was primarily a symbol of love, or of power. Others point to the inscriptions from the Qur'an on the walls of the building and say the Taj Mahal is more than a grave.

Regardless of these concepts, the bodies of Mumtaz and Shah Jahan were placed in a relatively plain crypt beneath the inner chamber of the Taj Mahal tomb, with their faces turned to the right and towards Mecca.!26)

In a twist of fate, legend has it that after construction of the Taj Mahal, when Shah Jahan was overthrown and locked up by his son, Aurangzeb, the only thing he could see from his prison cell was the Taj Mahal. From that distance he would not have seen the marble inscriptions of the Qur'an on the walls but he would no doubt have cited them as he gazed upon the reflections in the river. (27)

**Comparison of an Italian Garden (top left) with the Moorish gardens at the Alhambra in Spain.**

**Top Left I**mage credit 4.11.1. **Unlike Islamic gardens, the rectangular** form of this Italian Renaissance style garden at Pisa in Italy does not include water courses that divide the lawn into four quadrants.

**Top right and lower left and right:** In comparison, at **The Alhambra,** the Moorish gardens do have water courses that divide them into quadrants. This is in accordance with descriptions of paradise contained in Islamic texts.

**Top right** Image credit 4.11.2.**Lower left** Image credit 4.11.3.
**Lower right** Image credit 4.11.3.

# The Alhambra

*Built during the 13th to 15th centuries CE, the hilltop fortress gardens of The Alhambra are quite different in their impact from the gardens of Shalimar Bagh or the Taj Mahal in India. However these three places were all built to reflect the same principles of Islamic paradise.*

**Above** Image credit 4.12. *The Alhambra*

**Challenging** both the notion that appreciation of beauty is constrained by culture *and* the old saying that *Beauty is in the eye of the beholder*, there is a high degree of consensus about the beauty of the The Alhambra.

The site has World Heritage status under the United Nations Educational and Scientific Organisation, (UNESCO) accreditation programme. (28) It also is the second most visited site in Europe, according to information published by tripadvisor.com. (29) The Alhambra was originally established in the mid thirteenth century as a Moorish palace on the site of earlier Roman fortifications that date back at least as far as the 8th Century CE. The Alhambra now exhibits a blend of Medieval Islamic, Renaissance Christian and Modern styles. (30)

Its popularity demonstrates the cross-cultural nature of the principles that are considered in this book - and which underlie all beautiful gardens and the natural world.

Set high in the southern mountains of Spain, The Alhambra takes advantage of its hilltop location and glorious views to distant mountains, masterfully juxtaposing these with the more intimate surrounds of walled Islamic paradise gardens on the site itself. As described earlier in this chapter with reference to Shamiar Bagh, "*paradise*" is not just *here*, ("*Agar Firdaus bar rōy-e zamin ast, hamin ast-o hamin ast-o hamin ast*"). (31) "*Paradise*" also lies in the juxtaposition between what is *here* with what is *far away* in the sky and hills.

# Phi in the sky

*The view below of The Garden of the Partal (Jardines del Partal) is an example of the type of image that is featured in travel brochures for the site. Such views tend to repeatedly attract people to admire and photograph them. The design of this Islamic garden demonstrates an awareness of how to apply principles that humans of all cultures respond favorably to and which enhance human perception of their connection with the divine cosmos.*

**One** of these principles is the presence of the phi ratio (1:1618). In this case, we also see the presence of *'Light Garden'* principle number five, *"focal points"* and principle number six, the *"multiplication factor."* Multiplies of the phi ratio frame the focal point in the central arch.

**To test for the presence of the phi** ratio in this view, I superimposed two golden mean rectangles with sides in the ratio of 1:1.618. As illustrated below, we can see that both the pink and the red rectangles frame the central distant arch.

In this view, the pink golden mean rectangle is formed when the **arched facade of the building is framed by the roof and hedge.**
I think this would have been consciously designed because, for example, the dark green foreground hedge is trimmed so that it is just the right height to form the base of the pink rectangle.

The sense of perspective in this view is heightened by the second red golden mean rectangle that frames the whole view. It runs from the edge of the foreground pool and out to the countryside beyond with a pleasant sense of transparency. The upright date palm and conifer trees add foreground presence and balance as they frame the view.

**Above** Image credit 4.13. *The Alhambra*

# Plans: the finite & the infinite

*In the case of The Alhambra, the Phi ratio is used to frame our perception of movement from discrete units in the garden foreground, out to the apparently limitless expanse of the distance. How does this relate to the "Light Garden" theme of this book ?*

**Consider** the concept of moving our perception from a discrete unit in the garden foreground out to the apparently limitless expanse of the distance. This can be seen as analogous to the concept of a discrete unit taken from a larger field, which is part of 20th century Quantum Theory. That theory was developed by scientists such as Albert Einstein. It includes, for example, the concept that light travels in discrete parcels called photons.

When we draw, we need light to see what we are doing. We tend to start drawing at a particular point. This is the case whether we are drawing in the sand to make a symbol of something we want to build on the ground, (such as a garden, a farm, or a village), or we are drawing with a pen or a computer.

We then move from a starting point to create lines, areas and spaces to represent something that is in our minds. As a way of describing this process, the Greek Pythagoreans are attributed with developing the Tetractys symbol depicted below. It is thought to have been developed during the 6th to 5th Centuries BC. (33) The Tetractys was used to represent t the musical, arithmetic and geometric ratios which underlie the structure of the universe – and to represent the process by which our which minds tend to move in steps as we develop a plan concept. (34) However this is a simplified model of how the human mind

**Above** Image credit 4.14.1 **The Tetractys**

**Left** Image credit 4.14.2 *Patterns at the Alhambra*

works and Quantum biophysics includes many more concepts to address other factors that come into play, such as multiplier effects, quantum entanglement, wave motion and so on.

On the following page I have illustrated the ten *'Light Garden'* parameters described in Chapter One over a photograph of The Alhambra. This is to give an example of how each of these ten parameters is relevant to nature of the place that has been created - and why it has such universal appeal.

# Living with the Earth as a light garden

*Every culture has its own way of working with light, albeit often unconsciously. For ease of reference and to make the process more tangible, the ten "Light Garden" parameters set out in Chapter One are listed below and linked to features of this view of The Alhambra.*

# 'Light garden' concepts and Islamic concepts

As illustrated below, not only the Phi ratio but also a proliferation of geometric shapes and patterns is found at The Alhambra and at Islamic sites in general.

**During** the 8th and 9th centuries:

*" the expansion and development of geometry through Islamic art and architecture [was related to] significant growth of science and technology in the Middle East, Iran, and Central Asia . . . such progress was prompted by translations of ancient texts from languages such as Greek and Sanskrit (Turner, 1997). By the 10th century, original Muslim contributions to science became significant". (35)*

Bearing this in mind, let us return to discussion of the Tetractys and the Pythagoreans. The point at the top of the Tetractys triangle symbolises zero dimension (or a point). The second row has two points, making a line. The addition of third row represents a two dimensional flat surface, which in this case is a triangle. The fourth row introduces the concept of three dimensional space. In the case of the Tetractys, the space is a tetrahedron. (33) The influence of the Pythagoreans extended to Islamic scholars, to Plato and many others. As Leonora Leet said of Plato's work, it

*" implies that every number presupposes a definite and discrete unit taken from a limitless, homogeneous field. Contemplation of it thus provides access to the contemplation not only of a limit, but also of the limitless. These extremes are the fundamental tension in Pythagorean thought. " (34)*

This concept of discrete units taken from a larger field is analogous to contemporary Quantum Theory. As described earlier with reference to a photograph, the courtyard design depicted at The Alhambra fosters contemplation of what is near and what is far away: of *"a limit but also the limitless."*

As Petruccioli has described in detail, (36) there are three pre-Islamic roots from which the diverse range of Islamic landscapes emerged: Arab, Turkish and Persian.

Although each of these roots had strong agricultural underpinnings and different concepts of nature, space and light, there is some sense of unity within that diversity. It is to that sense of unity which I have tried to refer to in this book, whilst leaving readers to ponder more detailed texts such as Petruccioli's (36), if they need further clarification about the diversity of these cultures.

**Below** Image credit 4.16 **Patterns at The Alhambra**

4.16

# Ten components example

*Further description of the ten Light Garden parameters as assessed at The Alhambra and illustrated on the previous page is provided below.*

**Below** Image credit 4.17

| Component | Description |
|---|---|
| Energy | This garden is fully open to the sky and the energy of the sun by day and by night. By night, the light of the stars and moon is reflected in the water. . |
| Space | The garden design consciously frames a transition through space of what we see in the foreground, through to what we see in the distance. For example, in the foreground the space around the pools is framed by paving and hedges. In the middle ground, the space is framed by the walls and arches of the building, plus the tall trees. |
| Waves and Particles | The motion of light in the form of particles or waves moving through this garden at the macro, visible scale is not an important feature of the design. This more a static garden, where the light is quite static, even though it changes with the motion of the sun and stars through the sky overhead. This is consistent with Islamic gardens being designed for rest, reflection and contemplation. (36) |
| Lines, Patterns and Probabilities | The primary line of perceived motion through this garden is along the central visual axis from the foreground, through the arches of the building and on to the distant hills. The probability of any garden elements falling outside the formal geometric pattern is low. The places where people walk in this garden also fall within the formal geometric pattern. |
| Multiplication effects | Atoms multiply and cluster together to form the different basic materials of this garden: water, space, plants, paving and buildings. The archways of the building and the reflections in the pool are examples of shapes that are multiplied. The reflection from the pool is part of this symbology of paradise. |
| Entanglement and Focal Points | The beauty of this garden is an example of the concept of quantum entanglement, where the beauty of individual parts cannot be perceived or described independently of each other but rather it is the sum of all the parts that leads to the beauty of the proportions and the relationship to the landscape beyond. |
| Perception and Measurement | The striking beauty of The Alhambra is universally admired. The site has been studied and measured in detail by many scholars and it is listed on UNESCO's World Heritage Register. |
| Context | Islamic principles were applied to help people reach an understanding of God not only in this immediate garden settings but also in the wider landscape setting. |
| Human Use | The paradise garden is specifically designed for human use, including providing a contemplative setting in which people may approach an understanding of God. |
| Storage and Sharing of information, skills and so on | The design of this garden is based on information about the paradise garden concept that has been stored and shared for centuries in the Quran. |

# Evolution in one generation

*Islamic gardens have strong agricultural roots, and are usually part of a landscape of settlements, shelters and food cultivation nodes in a broader, more harsh environment or desert. As illustrated below, often the sequence of moving from the old to the new may have changed little in centuries but in Dubai, big changes have occurred rapidly.*

**Top Left** Image credit 4.18.1 **The Taj Mahal** which was constructed in India in the 17th Century.

**Middle Left** Image credit 4.18.2 **Sheikh Zayed Grand Mosque** constructed between 1996 and 2007 in Abu Dhabi.

**Lower Left** Image credit 4.18.3 **Sustainability City** constructed 2013 – 2020 in Dubai, the United Arab Emirates.

"The Sustainable City", is the first "Net Zero Energy" development in Dubai. The concept of "Net Zero Energy" has emerged during the 21st Century to refer to developments that have zero energy requirements from the energy grid because they generate as much of their own electricity as they consume. Solar energy as well as energy from on-site composting is being used. This AED1.25 billion project has received personal support from His Highness Sheikh Mohammed bin Rashid Al Maktoum, the Vice President, Prime Minister and Ruler of Dubai. (37)

A related concept of "Net Positive Development" was proposed by Dr Janis Birkeland in her 2008 book "Positive Development: From Vicious Circles to Virtuous Cycles through Built Environment Design". Net positive development means a project contributes more to, or rejuvenates more for environmental, social and economic well-being than it consumes or takes away. For

# 21ˢᵗ Century Dubai is changing

*As illustrated below, the night time skyline of Dubai could well be called a City of Lights. The people of Dubai in the 21ˢᵗ Century are turning away from this type of high energy consumption urban development and looking to create a more diverse future, in which there is a much greater emphasis on the type of examples discussed in this chapter.*

(continued) **example a net positive energy development** would contribute more electricity to the grid than it consumed. (38)

In 2006 the United Arab Emirates was declared by the World Wildlife Fund as the country with the greatest ecological footprint per capita in the world. (39) Announcing a new vision for the city in 2018, His Highness Sheikh Mohammed bin Rashid Al Maktoum, said that the *Sustainability City* project is:

> " . . . establishing sustainability's pillars as a key component of our development journey, which is part of the national agenda. We are committed to sustainability, which is a top priority that we strive to implement taking into consideration environment conservation, and balance between economic and social development, to provide people the best quality of life and ensure happiness of community." (40)

Upon completion, the *Sustainability City* project will support Dubai's aims to produce 75% of the city's energy from clean sources by 2050. (42) The developers of the *Sustainability City* project cite their mission as:

> " Striving to safeguard the natural world by helping people to live more sustainably". (43)

**At right** Image credit 4.19 ***Dubai CBD*** *(c 2018)*

As Robert Kunzig noted in his 2017 article for National Geographic:

> " A decade ago Dubai had one of the largest ecological footprints of any city in the world. By 2050 it wants to have the smallest." (44)

Sustainability City does not look like a typical town, urban development, educational institution or farming enterprise. Instead, the 46 hectare site has a tree lined, six kilometer long exercise trail; eleven food producing "bio-domes" located in the parkland spine that runs through the centre of the site and solar powered charging stations for electric cars.

There is also a mixed-use zone, which includes a school, an eco-hotel and a hospital and health rehabilitation centre which is open to the public. Although much of the development in this zone looks similar to contemporary international style, some of the features of traditional settlements in the Arabian peninsular area have been included. These include wind funnels to help cool small outdoor squares where people can gather in the evenings and planting of palm trees to foster an oasis-like atmosphere. (45)

# Sustainability City *'light garden'*

*Sustainability City has some notable statistics that illustrate how the Light Garden concept can be applied in 21st Century settlements. For example, with over ten thousand trees on the site, there is a ratio of five trees for every residence. With careful planning it also has been possible to locate a 10,000 Kilowatt/h/p solar installation over buildings and car parks.*

**The** on-site light-harvesting solar installation produces 20 Kilowatts of electricity per residence. This illustrates the efficiencies that can be gained with this type of 21st century *Light Garden* technology when applied at the community scale. Composting of waste material is also carried out. The system provides sufficient electricity to operate the free charging stations provided on site for long range subsidised electrical vehicles and free, on-site buggy transport.

Being located in the dry desert fringe of Dubai, *Sustainability City* also demonstrates that *'Light Garden'* living is achievable to establish in other harsh desert environments and remote locations such as refugee camps and military settlements. As the 21st century proceeds, this type of landscape and community is likely to proliferate. We need to conceive of these camps and settlements as opportunities to create viable, livable places for the millions of people who will call them their long term *'Light Garden'* home on planet Earth.

With an investment of appropriate security, training and technology for waste recycling, food production and the like, living conditions and vocations in these new settlements could be better than what has been left behind in war torn areas.

The innovative *MyHive* project established at *Sustainability City* in 2018 highlights another vital aspect of the worldwide *'Light Garden'* concept. Bees are essential for pollination of food species and for biodiversity, (not to mention when trying to establish plants in harsh environments where bees may be scarce or absent). The *MyHIve* projects sponsors bee hives and appropriate training.

**At left** Image credit 4.20. **The International Center for Biosaline Agriculture,** another project in Dubai which has a broad sustainability agenda and which is transforming formerly arid lands.

# *Buri Al Arab* and tradition

The Buri Al Arab is shaped like a three cornered sail found on traditional fishing dhows in the Persian Gulf. Rising from the sea on it's own island, Buri Al Arab is now a city icon for Dubai. At night, floodlighting of the structure makes it's unique Arabian character all the more apparent.

Dubai has been a fishing village and trading port for many centuries. In the 20th Century, an oil boom and a real estate boom then transformed it into a city with one of the world's most dense collections of skyscrapers, the world's tallest building and as of 2018, the third busiest port in the world.

Modern critics such Salmar Samar Damljui have said of the Buri Al Arab, *"both the hotel and the city, after all, are monuments to the triumph of money over practicality. Both elevate style over substance."* (48)

The same could well be said for the Sydney Opera House, the Taj Mahal and many other iconic structures that none the less reflect vast amounts of white light and perform their function well as cultural icons and landmarks. On the other side of the coin, Damluji has also noted that:

> *" Viewed in the context of the specific environment and cultural fabric of this desert region in Arabia, the coming of modern architecture has been coupled with extensive cultivation projects implemented in an originally barren landscape. Simultaneously, the cities have also remained true to their heritage and recognized the importance of their vernacular architecture and, in a fascinating contrast to the rapid modernization, today there are also many reconstruction and heritage projects underway."* (49)

***Below top*** Image credit 4.21.1 ***The Buri Al Arab in Dubai***
***Below bottom*** Image credit 4.21.2 ***a fishing dhow***

# Chapter 5
# Africa

Image credit 5.1

Image credit previous page, 5.1

# Table of Contents Chapter 5

| | |
|---|---|
| Introduction: Africa and the Nile | 4 |
| 'They make a desert and call it peace' | 5 |
| Map of African locations | 6 |
| The shamba of Jorama Onjimbo | 7 |
| Traditional village garden plan | 8 |
| The shamba of Jimmy Adjani | 9 |
| Plan of Jimmy Adanji's shamba | 10 |
| Violence makes refugees | 11 |
| New ways versus the traditional village | 12 |
| Plant a tree for Peace | 13 |
| That there is light, despite all the darkness | 14 |
| African gardens, old and new | 15 |
| 2.5 million people on 6% of the land | 16 |
| 500 million people targeted for light, water and land | 17 |
| 'Before and after' food gardens | 18 |
| Small holder gardens and farms | 19 |
| Africa: unique and ubiquitous | 20 |

# Africa and the Nile

**Africa** is a wonderfully vibrant and culturally diverse place, despite the sad truth that it has been the battleground of colonial powers for centuries. In a report published in February 2018 the Rights and Resources initiative estimated that 500 million people, who depend on 3.46 billion acres of farmland in sub-Saharan Africa, have been a target for foreign governments and investors looking to produce food for populations outside of Africa.

Examples abound throughout the continent of foreign interests coming in to plant crops like sugarcane, palm oil, and jatropa on huge tracts of land that were already inhabited, or that could be used for growing food to feed local populations. (1)

So when considering the following questions:

- What is unique about African gardens, places and landscapes?
- What is unique about the light that sustains them?

a disturbing theme of exploitation emerges.

In that context, I would then ask: What is the relevance of the *'Light Garden'* model for rejuvenation of African natural resources and cultures? In this chapter I will begin to explore these questions with reference to examples of both traditional African settlements and the urban conditions under which many people live in the 21$^{st}$ century. Although the colonial powers continue to exploit African resources, (such as light, water, land and labour), the economic champions of these colonial cultures are under no illusion about the competency and benefits of their leaders in supplanting traditional African gardening, farming and land management practices.

For example, the following quote comes from the popular 20th century American economist Milton Friedman:

> *"If you put the federal government in charge of the Sahara Desert, in five years there'd be a shortage of sand."*
> (2)

His political philosophy advocated a free market economic system with minimal government intervention. However, his statement about the Sahara indicates that he realized the limited value of America seeking to act as a colonial power managing African resources and lives.

Although "a free market system with minimal government intervention" could not be said to describe the ancient Egyptian culture, the concept does apply at least in part to aspects of the traditional tribal systems of governance that prevailed in Africa prior to the colonial period. Although Friedman's ideas continue to influence the policies of conservative governments in the 21$^{st}$ century, he also had more liberal views, such as his announcement that his proudest achievement was his work towards eliminating military conscription in the United States.

# *They make a desert and call it peace* (3)

**Albert** Einstein, another prominent international citizen, had a similar progressive development of his views during his lifetime. After contributing significantly towards the development of the atomic bombs that America dropped on Japan at the end of the Second World War, Albert Einstein awakened to the destructive power that his ideas had unleased. For the rest of this life, he was a public advocate *against* nuclear proliferation and *for* peace.

Perhaps in a similar way, Milton Friedan realized the destructive power of the economic polices he had advocated when they were imposed by colonial powers in Africa and other places, then chose to turn his mind towards the more humane concept of eliminating military conscription, which so often goes hand in hand with objectives for economic and political power. Against this background, we begin to see the relevance of the 'Light Garden' concept for management of natural resources and maintenance of traditional cultures in Africa. For example, one *Light Garden* concept that was illustrated in Chapter One is that a quantum field is like an inner spring mattress. Touch one part and the vibration moves through the whole. This reminds us of the quantum theory that "matter" is forever moving as a resonant, responsive, multifaceted whole.

Considering "matter," such as economic resources and natural resources in this way is consistent with how the ecosystems of nature operate as diverse, interconnected networks. It is also consistent with those traditional cultures which have sustainably managed natural resources, such as the Balinese culture which was described in Chapter Two and the "Shamba" of Jorama Onjimbo which is described later in this chapter.

*Below*  Image credit: 5.5 *A composite satellite image of Africa (centre) with the other continents.*

**The global extent of arid lands and deserts are is apparent from the images below. Deserts are beige in colour. Snow and ice are white. Forests are green.** The Sahara Desert, the largest on Earth, has steadily expanded in recent centuries. Research published in 2018 shows that during one century alone, (the period 1920 – 2013), the Sahara expanded by ten percent. (4)

The northern climatic extent of sub-Saharan African is indicated by the line ▬▬▬

# Shamba of Jorama Onjimbo

*Having briefly outlined the threats to traditional African gardens and livelihoods on the previous pages, let us now consider what a traditional village garden looks like.*

Traditional garden and pastoral activities in the Shamba of Jorama Onjimba are illustrated at left. The photographs were taken in northern Kenya during the 1980's. A plan view of the nine hectare property is shown on the next page. Various types of pastures and fields for cropping are identified on the plan.

*Upper Left* Image credit: 5.6.1 **One of Jorama's wives, digging sweet potatoes.** One third of the property was used for a diverse range of activities, including dwellings, cassava, taro, beans, vegetables, trees and waterways. Jorama lived with his two wives and eight children. Six other children had died in infancy. (5)

*Centre Left* Image credit: 5.6.2 **Jorama Onjimbo in his pasture.** Approximately one third of Jorama's shamba was devoted to this type of pasture. In the early 1980's, Jorama had two cows in milk, 2 calves, 1 heifer, 4 oxen, 3 sheep, and half a dozen chickens. The animals were a vital part of the diverse range of agricultural activities conducted by this self sufficient family. Another third of the property was used to grow maize for consumption by the family, with some surplus for local sale.

*Lower left* Image credit: 5.6.3 **A thatched, mud walled hut,** similar to the cluster of huts where the family lived. In many ways, this family lived in accordance with *'Light Garden'* principles and by using local materials to build their own dwellings, were more self sufficient than the Amish communities of North America, (as described in Chapter 9).

# Traditional village garden plan

*Below* Image credit: *5.7.1* **A scale drawing of a traditional village garden and pasture in Kenya, Africa.**

**Jorama's garden and farm** was considered to be quite large in comparison to farms in the more southerly regions of Kenya, where the population was higher and the roads more highly developed. Traditional pastures had survived in Jorama's region, where commercial pressures were fewer.

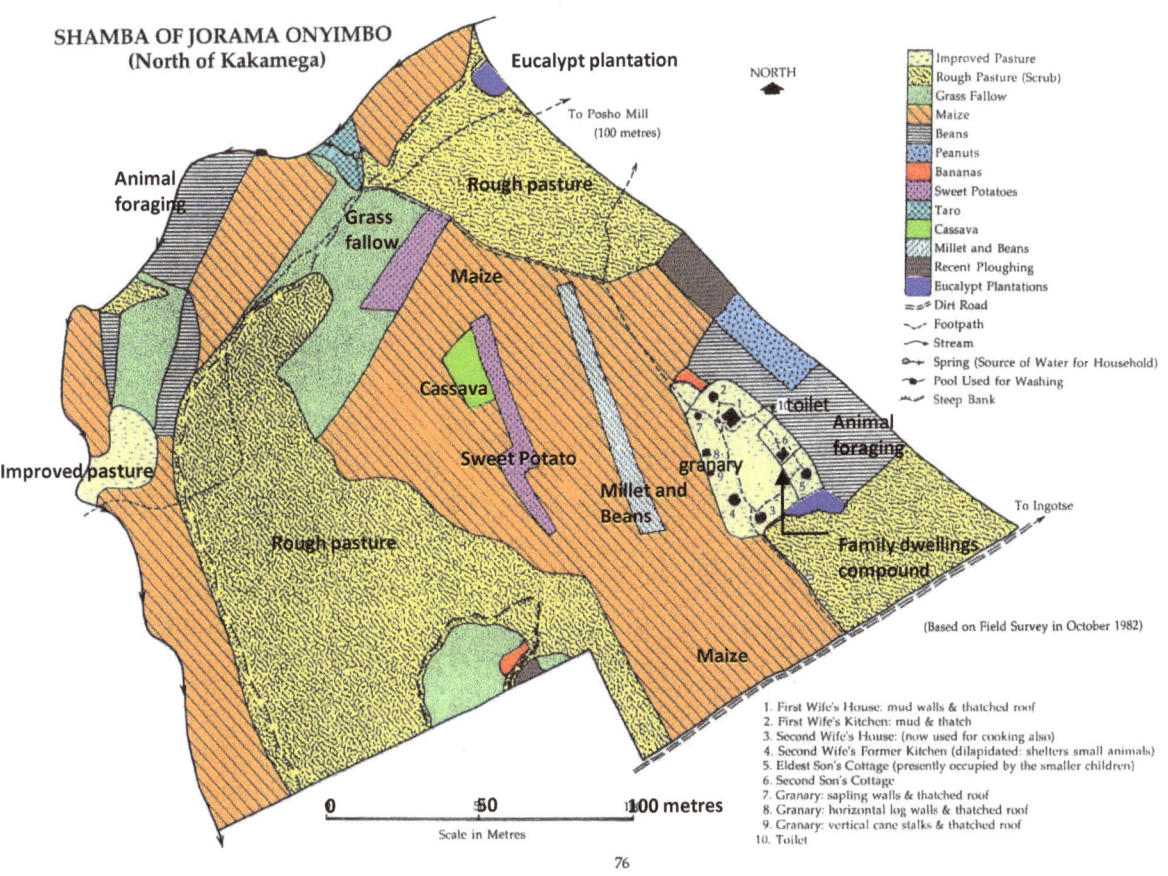

On the following page there is an example of another shamba – that of Jimmy Adanji in Kenya.

On Jimmy's shamba, pasture and land devoted to maize and vegetable growing had been significantly reduced. This was in order to accommodate the export crop of sugar cane. (6)

*At right* Image credit: *5.7.2* **Jorama's wife milking their cow**

# Shamba of Jimmy Adanji

*Although both Jimmy Adanji and Jorama Onjimba began their lives in traditional Shambas in Kenya, Jimmy has not worked in his village all his life. His Shamba is different from Jimmy's too. Photographs on this page were taken in northern Kenya during the early 1980's.*

**Top left** Photo credit 5.8.1
**Jimmy Adanje** served in the (British) Royal Air Force during the Second World War, and was later employed for many years on construction work in Tanzania and other parts of East Africa. The money that he earned helped him develop his *shamba*, financed his marriages, and paid for his children's education. *(the photograph shows Jimmy Adanje, on the left with a friend.)*

**Centre Left** Photo credit 5.8.2
**Jimmy's first wife Marita,** a mother for thirty years, still at work in the vegetable garden. Vegetables were grown for household use. The family also owned ducks, several chickens, three goats, three cows, one calf and four sheep. Groups such as https:/one.org/us are devoted to working with African woman to encourage the artisan economy as an additional source of income. For example in one project in Rwanda, 72 percent of women participants reported in 2016 *that they now never run out of food (versus only 5 percent in 2008).* (7)

**Lower Left** Photo credit 5.8.3
**View of the property.** The dates of planting for sugar cane are determined by the mill owners, and are staggered between districts so as to provide a continuous supply of sugar. The small-holder does the planting and the weeding (7 times!) but the company provides the fertilizer and the cane. (8) A plan view of the property is shown on the next page.

# Plan of Jimmy Adanji's shamba

*A comparison of the plan of Jimmy's shamba with Jorama's shamba, (refer to the previous pages), shows that although he has sugar cane, Jimmy has virtually no land upon which to graze his animals. In addition, the proportion of his garden devoted to vegetable and taro growing is much smaller than in Jorama's garden, despite having two wives and fifteen children to feed.*

Jimmy lived near Ingotse, 10 km north west of Kakamega, and his *shamba* was small for that area -- only half the average size. Despite this, as can be seen on the plan below, over half the good arable land was devoted to production of sugar cane. Sugar provided him with a cash income but he was compelled as a result to buy much of the corn needed to feed his family. His family was no longer self reliant in food production The strip of land around the edge of the cane field reflects the policy of the sugar company: growers are required to maintain a firebreak of evergreen crops. (9)

**Below** Image credit 5.9.1 **A scale drawing prepared in 1982 showing a traditional village garden that had been changed to include sugar cane production in Kenya, Africa**. *It may be compared to the drawing two pages earlier showing a village garden that had not moved into sugar cane production.*

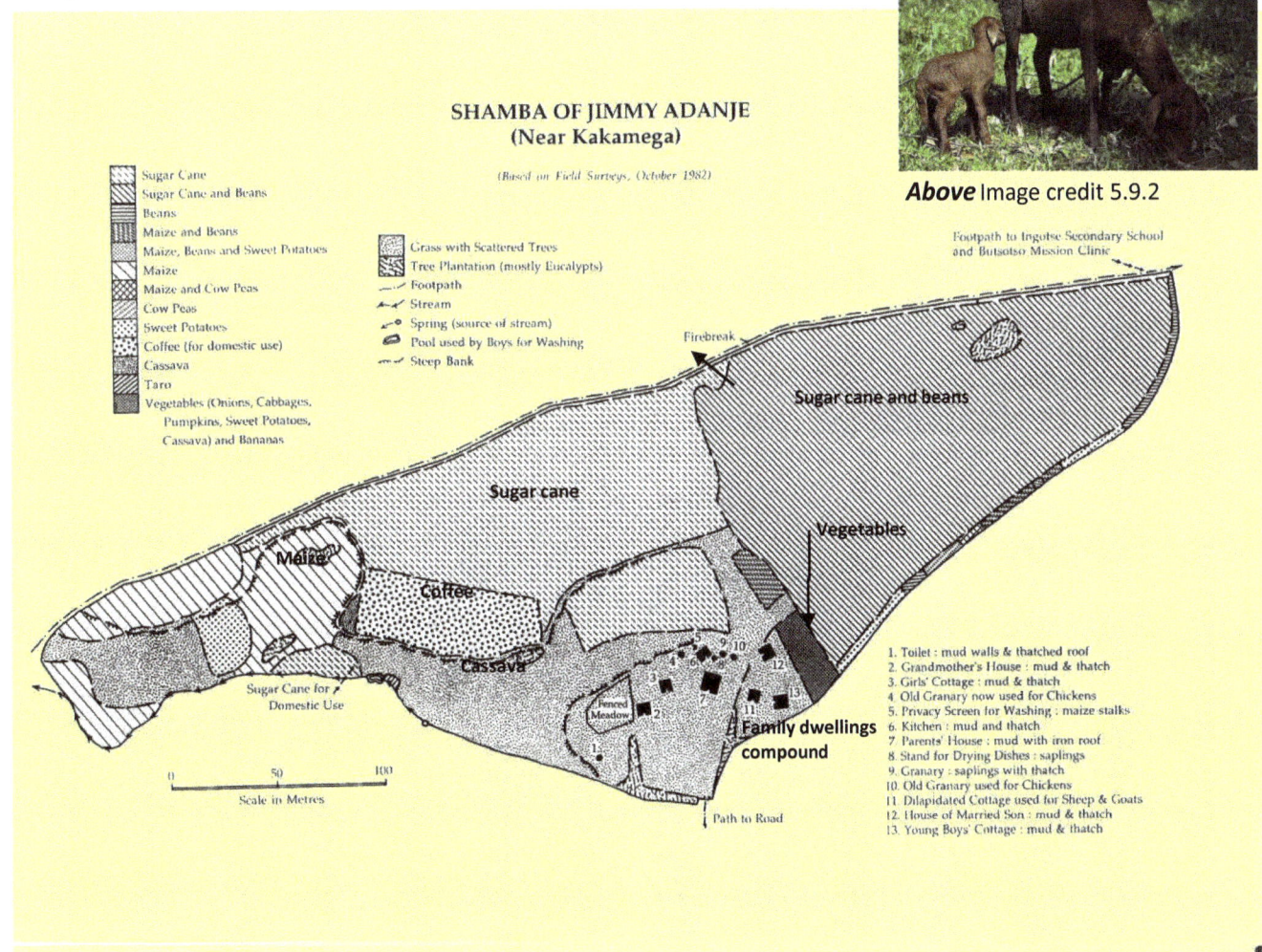

**Above** Image credit 5.9.2

# Violence makes refugees

*Millions of African people have moved during the past century from life in villages to life in cities and refugee camps. The need for greater security from violence and warfare is one of the prime causes for making these moves, which have entailed changes to housing, gardens, livelihoods and social fabric.*

**Left** Image credit 5.10.1 **Homes destroyed gives a clear message to** local people: abandon your property and livelihood. Flee for your life. You are now a refugee.

**Centre Left** Image credit 5.10.2 **Forced to flee to a refugee camp** to escape a killing spree in her home area, this woman was separated from her children, husband, home and livelihood. She became one of the estimated 18 million people in sub-Saharan Africa who were of concern to the United National Humanitarian Commission for Refugees (UNHCR) in 2018. This sub-Saharan population represented about 27 percent of the total global population of refugees and displaced persons. (10)

**Lower Left** Image credit 5.10.3 **What chance for gardens in town when gangs** destroy the water tanks? At least in the countryside villages there were wells and streams for water.

**Below** Image credit 5.10.4 **With no police assistance, men sit under the stars all night**, *defending their families as best they can.*

# New ways vs traditional village

*Having considered how sunlight is harvested as the energy source to grow crops, raise livestock and manage natural resources in the traditional "Shamba" way of life, let us consider other reasons, (in addition to imposed violence and warfare), why people would chose to move from this self-sufficient lifestyle to live in urban areas.*

**Other** reasons cited for making the move include over-population in the villages, droughts and a shortage of productive land for gardens and farms.

Dr John Tyman has described the story of Kibera, one the largest peoples' settlements in Nairobi, where people have moved to an urban lifestyle then demonstrated great determination and resourcefulness to survive:

> " . . . Thousands of families and single men and women struggle to survive in a community with almost no services and few opportunities for remunerative employment. Kibera is situated 7 kilometers from the centre of the city, on the Motoine Ngong, a tributary of the Nairobi River, and overlooks the Nairobi Dam, which is highly polluted with waste from the settlement." (11)

**Top Left** Image credit 5.11.1 **Kiberia is located on marshy ground** but clean water is in short supply. As one mother said, *Water is Life but here it can mean Death.* This woman was speaking of death due to contaminated water and disease. (12)

**Centre Left** Image credit 5.11.2 **Open mud waste disposal drains run among the homes in Kiberia.** This waste management system is so different from the composting toilets and recycling of materials found in traditional thatched hut Kenyan villages. For example, refer to the plan of Jorama Onyimbo's Shamba that is featured earlier in this chapter.

**Lower Left** Image credit 5.11.3 **Thousands of people throng each day to the bus station in Nairobi.**

# Plant a tree for Peace

*"And young men who had previously been perpetrators of violence once more planted trees, working together in the interests of the wider community. The slogan then was 'Plant a tree for Peace'. "* (13)

**Top left** Image credit 5.12.1 **Kiberia today**
As illustrated here, there are no trees and gardens on one side of the railway track at Kiberia. The wealthy citizens of Nairobi have trees around their residences to the left of the track. Once there was a forest of trees and a peaceful settlement at Kiberia. But now, with over 250,000 people forced to relocate from their rural farms and villages to live in the crowded, insecure conditions of Kiberia, no trees remain there.

**Centre Left** Image credit 5.12.2 **The 1980's.**
**During the early 1980's in Nairobi**, rival election candidates represented different tribal groups. These groups enlisted gangs of youths who roamed the streets. Amidst the terror, looting and burning, over a thousand people (1,133) lost their lives in nationwide violence; 3,561 were wounded, and 117,216 properties were either damaged or destroyed. Roads were barricaded. Drivers were dragged from trucks then beaten or killed. The trucks were torched. (13)

**Lower Left** Image credit 5.12.3
**After the violence subsided,** young men planted trees in gestures of peace. They had grown up surviving from day to day, with little prospects for land ownership, traditional male roles in their community, paid work, business opportunities or training. The settlements where they lived were shanty towns and in most cases, they had no legal right to occupy the land, no security of tenure and virtually no police protection.

# . . . that there is light despite all the darkness

Hope is being able to see that there is light despite all of the darkness.

*Left* Image credit 5.13.1 **Archbishop Desmond Tutu**. He and Nelson Mandala are but two of the brave and tireless African leaders who have sought to redress injustice and bring the light of international human rights principles to the structure of societies in contemporary Africa.

*Below* Image credit 5.13.2 **Foreign governments have targeted Africa for a long time. For example, refer to the quote below by Tewodros II, emperor of Ethiopia in the mid 19th century.**

**Article 23 of the Universal Declaration of Human Rights:**

(1) Everyone has the right to work, to free choice of employment, to just and favourable conditions of work and to protection against unemployment.
(2) Everyone, without any discrimination, has the right to equal pay for equal work.
(3) Everyone who works has the right to just and favourable remuneration ensuring for himself and his family an existence worthy of human dignity, and supplemented, if necessary, by other means of social protection.
. . . (14)

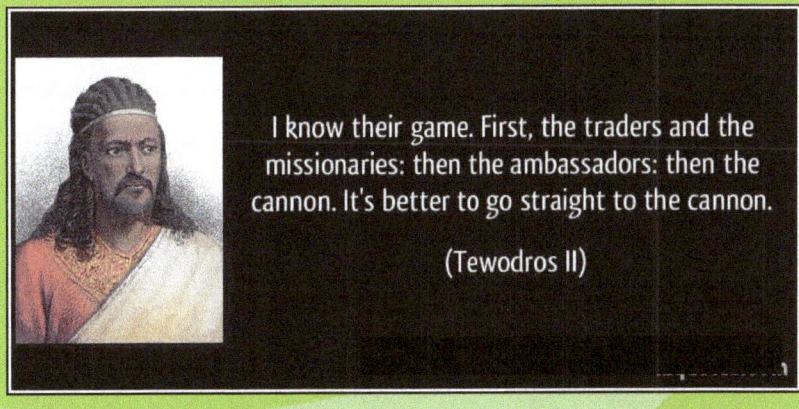

I know their game. First, the traders and the missionaries: then the ambassadors: then the cannon. It's better to go straight to the cannon.

(Tewodros II)

*Right* Image credit 5.13.3 **African women at work, growing food for their families**.

# 2.5 million people: 6% of land

*In 2018, Kibera had a population of 250,000 people. It has been described as the biggest slum in Africa and one of the biggest in the world. Of the 3.5 million people living in Nairobi, 2.5 million live in such settlements, which are located on 6% of the land. The land is often on the fringes of the city.* (15)

**How** did a word from the ancient and revered kingdom of Nubia come to be the namesake of the largest slum in Africa?

**Kibera is a Nubian word for *forest*. The following historic account is worth telling because it reveals how access to land and light has been at the core of the creation of this settlement and others like it. It is also a tale of just how vital for human welfare it is to have access to adequate sunlight, space, land and clean water. Thirdly, it reveals a process that was replicated in similar ways around the globe to disenfranchise traditional communities and gain control of the sunlight, space, land and clean water that they once relied upon for their livelihoods.**

When we speak of sunlight, we are speaking of the energy that drives not just forests, but also human survival. The Nubians came from their home lands of Egypt and the Sudan to live at Kibera following a mutiny in 1897 amongst warriors who had been recruited to fight for the British. At that time, the British military rescinded its earlier decision to repatriate the Nubian warriors and instead dispersed them to Kenya. (16)

When they first came to live in Kenya the Nubians called the forested military base where they were stationed *Kibera*. They continued to be excellent solders. However, by denying them title deeds to land, the British ensured that Nubians could only build temporary structures. Many warriors from Nubian villages in Kenya fought for the British in World War I, (1914 – 1918). However after the war they were demobilised without compensation, unlike the Indians who had fought for the British.

Nubians were not accorded the privilege of British citizenship, despite their long and loyal service to the British Crown. When constructing Kenya's social structure, the British colonial authority consolidated ethnic groups and designated them to native reserves. They deliberately excluded the Nubians from the process because they considered them as a detribalised community rather than as a Kenyan tribe.

This Nubian position was ameliorated to some degree by the passage of a new Constitution in 2010. This recognised the Nubians as the 43rd tribe of Kenya. However earlier in 1963, the Kenyan government had already taken control of the land at Kiberia and made it available for informal occupation by other people moving into the area. (17)

Photo credit 5.14 **Kibera.**

5.14

# African gardens, old and new

*As the story of African culture is vast, let us now return to comparison of the old ways and the new ways, when it comes to managing light and gardens. Although gardens are one of the most ancient of human activities, the open flowing water of the paradisiacal pools in ancient Egypt and Morocco is rarely seen in the daily lives of Africans today.*

**Above** Image credit 5.15.1 **An irrigation system supplies water to a farm.** Drip irrigation reduces water consumption because the water is delivered directly to the soil root zone.

**The** transfer of drip irrigation technology to African village gardens during the past century illustrates Principle number ten of the global 'Light Garden' concepts described in Chapter One: *Storage and Sharing of information.*

**Comparison** of the 21st century food garden shown at left with the diet of the ancient Egyptians highlights how in ancient Egypt the diet consisted of much more than plants and livestock that could be raised in specific gardens or farms. The diet included a variety of fish and wildfowl caught in the reeds along the waterways, plus beef, goat and mutton. They also grew onions, leeks, garlic, beans, lettuce, lentils, cabbages, radishes, turnips, dates, figs and melons. (18)

The two sacred flowers of ancient Egypt were the lotus and the papyrus – both of which are found along the Nile River. The lotus, *Nymphea caerulea,* was regarded as a symbol of the sun..

> *"At Heliopolis, the origin of the world was taught to have been when the sun god Ra emerged from a lotus flower growing in "primordial waters". At night, he was believed to retreat into the flower again".* (19)

**Right** Image credit 5.15.2 **Ducks**
**Below right** Image credit 5.15.3 **Hieroglyphics at Karnak**
**Below** Image credit 5.15.4 **Lotus**

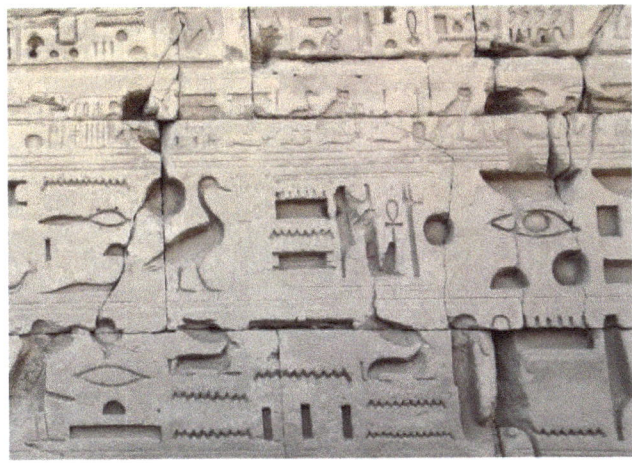

# 500 million people targeted for light, water and land

*Food, gardens, land, people and light are not superficial subjects in Africa. They are hotly contested. The number of people affected is approximately 500 million. In the context of the following examples, perhaps the relative stability of ancient Egyptian dynasties has appeal.*

**The** annotated map on the following page illustrates some examples of African people being displaced from their homes, land and access to natural resources. As we have seen on the preceding pages, this includes being displaced from free access to the energy source of sunlight.

For example, at least 8.8 million acres of Ethiopia's most arable land has been leased to China. China has established export cropping enterprises on this land. As documented by the organisation Human Rights Watch, at least 70,000 people have been displaced from the leased land. *(20)*

In addition, as reported by Friends of the Earth International, numerous elephants have been displaced too. An Ethiopian elephant sanctuary has been cleared, so that more land can be devoted to agrofuel export cropping. (18) However China is not the only nation engaging in such activities. Companies from the United States, Norway, Germany, Israel and other places are involved too, as illustrated overleaf.

> *"In Congo-Brazzaville, President Sassou-Nguesso has ceded 10 million hectares of fertile land to South-African farmers to grow staple food crops for export without any percentage to remain in Congo, alongside 70,000 hectares granted to the Italian oil company ENI to plant oil palm monoculture plantations for agrofuel production, threatening Africa's last precious tropical primary forest."* (21)

As also noted in the Friends of the Earth report which documented the above situation in the Congo, "agrofuel" or "biofuel" crops are often seen by overseas based governments and companies engaged in biotech and agricultural industries as a way to enter the African market. For example, they also are conducting research into genetically modified crop varieties to use in Africa, (thus excluding local farmers from participating in the market with traditional, locally used crop varieties). They also claim that their activities will help the global community tackle climate change. (22)

However, such activities would not pass the *'Light Garden"* model test from the perspective of the human rights of African citizens, as *'Light Garden'* decision making entails reference to criteria such as *'Storage and Sharing of Information'* and *'Consider Context and Environment: work for the greater good'*. More detail on *'Light Garden'* decision making processes is provided in Chapter 10.

**Below** Photo credit 5.16

5.16

# Before and after food gardens

*The map below, based on one in the Rights and Resources Initiative report (2018) shows a number of projects in Africa where local farmers have been displaced by land deals with international corporations wishing to use the land, water and light to grow export crops such as sugarcane, jatropa and oil palm.* (23)

**Sierra Leone** Swiss based Addax Bioenergy obtains 26,000 ha for sugarcane.

**Ghana** Italian based Agrolis obtains 105,000 ha.

UK company Jatropha Africa acquires 120,000 ha.

Scanfuel (Norway) cultivates 10,000 ha and has contracts for around 400,000ha. Galten (Israel) has 100,000 ha.

**Kenya** Japanese, Belgian and Canadian companies plan to acquire up to 500,000 ha.

**Tanzania** 1,000 rice farmers forced off their land to make way for sugarcane.

**Mozambique** investors aim for 4.8 million ha. Over 183,000 ha currently allocated to jatropha. Companies in UK, Italy, Germany, Portugal, Canada and Ukraine.

**Benin** Proposed 300,000 – 400,000 ha of wetland to be converted for oil palm.

**Nigeria** Over 100,000 ha in land acquisitions by the state using foreign capital and expertise.

**Above** Map image credit 5.17.1 **Some examples of projects in Africa**

**Left** image credit 5.17.2 **A young farmer in Africa**

**Below** Image credit 5.17.3 **The Ugandan National Flag**

### A snapshot of Uganda's food production and economy (2018)
**Population** 36.3 million.
**Main Exports:** Tea, cotton, tobacco and sugar.
**Main diet of the local population for food and agricultural commodities:** Plantains, Cassava, Potatoes, Sorghum, Corn and Groundnuts. (24)

# Small holder gardens & farms

Approximately 50% of farm work is done by women in sub-Saharan Africa. Some more data, as provided below, helps to flesh out the picture of the agricultural base of 'Light Gardens' in Africa.

## 75 %

of the world's food is generated from only 12 plant and 5 animal species, making the global food system highly vulnerable to shocks.

Biodiversity is a key strength of many smallholder systems that keep thousands of rustic and climate-resilient plant varieties and animal breeds alive. (28)

Bees are part of this living network.
They are needed for pollination of many food plants.

*Above right* Image credit 5.18.1 *Bee*

*Below* Image credit 5.18.2 *Farmers in Rwanda*

## 80% of food

Smallholders supply 80% of overall food produced in Asia, sub-Saharan Africa and Latin America through farmers, artisan fisher folk, pastoralists, landless and indigenous people. (25)

## 570 million

The majority of the 570 million farms in the world are small. In addition, 70% of the 1.4 billion extremely poor people live in rural areas and 75% of these rural poor are also smallholders. (26)

## < 10 hectare

*Smallholders* are small-scale farmers, pastoralists, forest keepers and fishers who manage areas varying in size from less than one hectare to ten hectares. (27)

# Map of African locations

The map below shows the borders of countries in Africa. There are 54 countries in Africa (2018). In summary, some of those referred to in this chapter are labeled on the map.
**Below** Image credit 5.19.1 Desert in Namibia and **Map of Africa** image credit 5.19.2

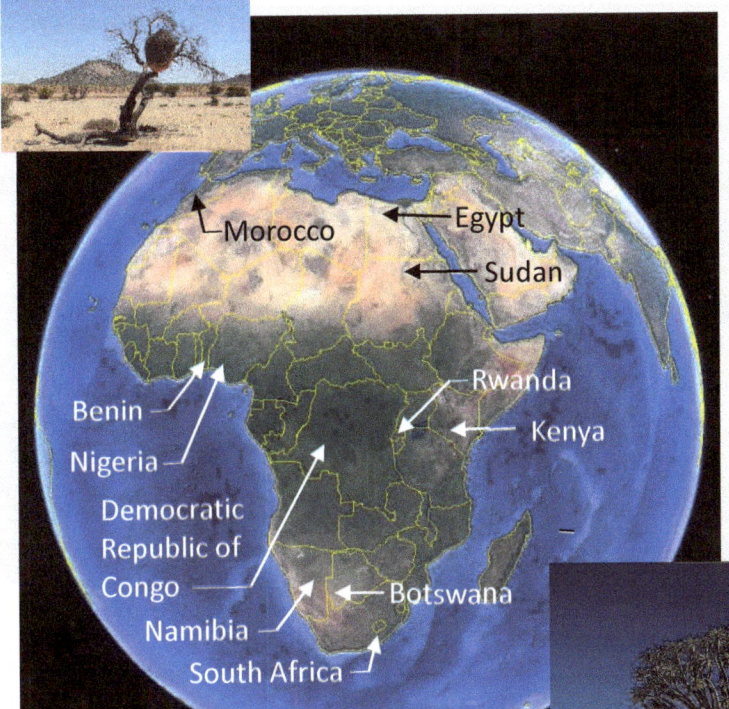

**Below** Image credit 5.19.3 *Women farmers walking in a garden in Sudan.*

**Below** Image credit 5.19.4 *A quiver tree.*

**Above** Image credit 5.19.5 *Children in Botswana*

**At right** Map image credit 5.19.6 **Climatic zones in Africa.**
1. **Sub-Saharan Africa** - the Sahel and the Horn of Africa in the north (**yellow**).
2. **Tropical savannah** (light green)
3. **Tropical rainforests** (dark green)
4. **The Kalahari Basin** (yellow)
5. **The "Mediterranean" coast** (olive)
6. **The Sahara and patch of West Coast** (orange)

**Inset right** Image credit 5.19.7 **Fynbos heathland with white flowers near Capetown**

# Africa: unique and ubiquitous

*The style and lighting of gardens in the three large Southern Hemisphere continents of South America, Africa and Australia can look remarkably similar. So what is unique about Africa?.*

**Each** of the continents of Africa, South America and Australia has a vast array of different landscapes and thousands of native plants. In South America, Burle Marx first came to fame internationally for his innovative use of native plant species from the jungles of Brazil.

Looking on this page at the photographs of the famous Kirstenbosch National Botanic Garden at Capetown in South Africa, it might be difficult to distinguish whether the gardens were located in Brazil, Africa or Australia, were it not for the distinctive form of the background mountains. Although many African native plants are featured in this garden, there may well be plants that originated in other continents, before being planted in Africa.

However, the pink King Protea flower illustrated at right provides an example of how the character of the Kirstenbosch gardens is definitely associated with the distinctive forms of the native plants, as well as with the local people and mountains. This is an example of *'Light Garden'* principle number 5: Multiplication Effects and Scale at work, as well as principle number 8: Context and Environment.

*Above* Image credit: 5.20.1 A ***pink King Protea flower, a native of South Africa***
***Top left*** Image credit 5.20.2 ***Kirstenbosch National Botanic Garden at Capetown in South Africa.***
***Centre left*** Image credit 5.20.3 ***Kirstenbosch***
***Bottom left*** Image credit: 5.20.4 K***irstenbosch***

# Chapter 6
# India & Bangladesh

Previous page Image credit 6.1

# Table of Contents Chapter 6

**Introduction**

**Part 1 Ancient groves**

1. Statistics about tree biodiversity in the ancient groves of India & Bangladesh
2. Mallur Gutta near Hyderabad in central India.
3. Shankaracharya forest grove temple at Srinagar in Kashmir
4. Alappuzha and the Western Ghats in Kerala and southern India

**Part 2 Biodiversity culture**

1. The words of Gandhi, mixed with environmental justice
2. Biodiversity civilisation
3. The biodiverse small farms and gardens of India
4. Civilisations of India
5. Light persists: a lifelong quest for truth and justice
6. Gandhian principles
7. Baskar Save, the Gandhi of natural farming

**Part 3 Traditional villages**

1. Ziro Valley in the north east Himalayas

**Part 4 Famous Gardens**

1. Taj Mahal
2. Vastu Shastra

**Part 5 Temple, festival and pilgrimage gardens**

1. Temples as places of pilgrimage
2. Diwali, the festival of light
3. Trees and gardens in the life of Gautama Buddha
4. Meenakshi Amman temple in Madurai, Tamil Nadu
5. The temple, the light, the city

**Part 6 Gardens of the 21$^{st}$ century**

1. Rivers of Refugees – cultivating and practicing an enlightened tolerance
2. Bangladesh's floating gardens
3. Jaipur's rooftop terraces & organics
4. Chapter Summary

# Types of gardens, farms & landscapes in this book

To help understand both the traditional culture and the 21st century culture, gardens and farms in India today, this chapter is divided into six parts, which are listed in the Map Legend table below. Refer to the map on the following page.

| Part | Map Code | Type of garden and landscape | Examples in this chapter |
|---|---|---|---|
| 1 | (green) | Ancient groves | • Mallur Gutta in Telegana<br>• Shankaracharya in Kashmir<br>• Alupuzza in Kerala |
| 2 | (yellow) | Biodiversity gardens & farms | • Navdanya in Uttar Pradesh<br>• Kaplavruska in Gujarat |
| 3 | (blue) | Traditional village gardens & farms | • Ziro Valley, Aranchal Pradesh |
| 4 | (pink) | Temple gardens | • Varanasi and the Ganges<br>• Meenakshi Amman, Tamil Nadu<br>• Bodh Gaya |
| 5 | (orange) | Famous gardens and festivals | • Taj Mahal<br>• Diwali Festival |
| 6 | (black) | 21st century sites & Vastu Shastra | • Kutupalong microgardens<br>• Roof terraces in Jaipur<br>• Floating gardens in Bangladesh<br>• Ahmedabad - Vastu Shastra |

Legend for map on facing page

*Table Image 6.5 Types of landscapes and gardens  Copyright Anne Whittingham*

In addition to considering the six types of places listed above, I will include reference to the enduring influence of Mahatma Gandhi, who is one of India's and the world's most well respected historical figures. His work drew upon the ancient Indian traditions and developed a way forward for the nation through complex legal, political and philosophical matters during the 20th century, as well as initiating practical assistance with the day to day lives of the people. Details of the principles for living that Gandhi developed and discussion of the

# Map of India and Bangladesh

*Although India's most famous places and gardens tend to be iconic sites such as the Taj Mahal, there are a great many others throughout the land. I have considered examples of this diverse range of places and gardens under six different categories, as shown on the map below, described in the map legend on the previous page and listed in the Table of Contents.*

(cont. from previous page) relevance of them to humanity's way forward in the 21st century is discussed in Part 2 of this chapter. For example, the biodiversity movement is one of many groups that still quote and cite Gandhi's principles for living. One organic farmer, Baskar Save of Gujarat, has been called the 'Gandhi of Natural Farming' because the principles he lived by had much in common with Gandhi's.

***Map*** Image credit 6.6

- Shankaracharya grove, Srinagar in Kashmir
- Ziro Valley traditional village gardens and landscape near Itanagar in Aranchal Pradesh
- Sikkim, India's and the world's first fully organic State
- Navdanya Biodiversity Farm
- Jaipur terrace gardens
- The Taj Mahal at Agra
- Varanasi
- Ahmedabad temple with Vastu Shastra
- Bodhgaya
- Microgardens at Kutupalong Refugee Camps in Bangladesh
- Kalpavruksha, organic garden farm near Dehri in Gujarat.
- Mullar Gutta grove near Hyderabad
- Bangladesh's floating gardens
- Meenakshi Amman Temple at Madurai, Tamil Nadu.
- Alappuza grove in Kerala

# Introduction

*The current borders of India, Pakistan and Bangladesh were established after the partition of India in 1947. Over two thousand years earlier, the land in these countries was part of the Mauryan dynasty of 265 BCE.*

**Below:** Map Image credit 6.4 *India*

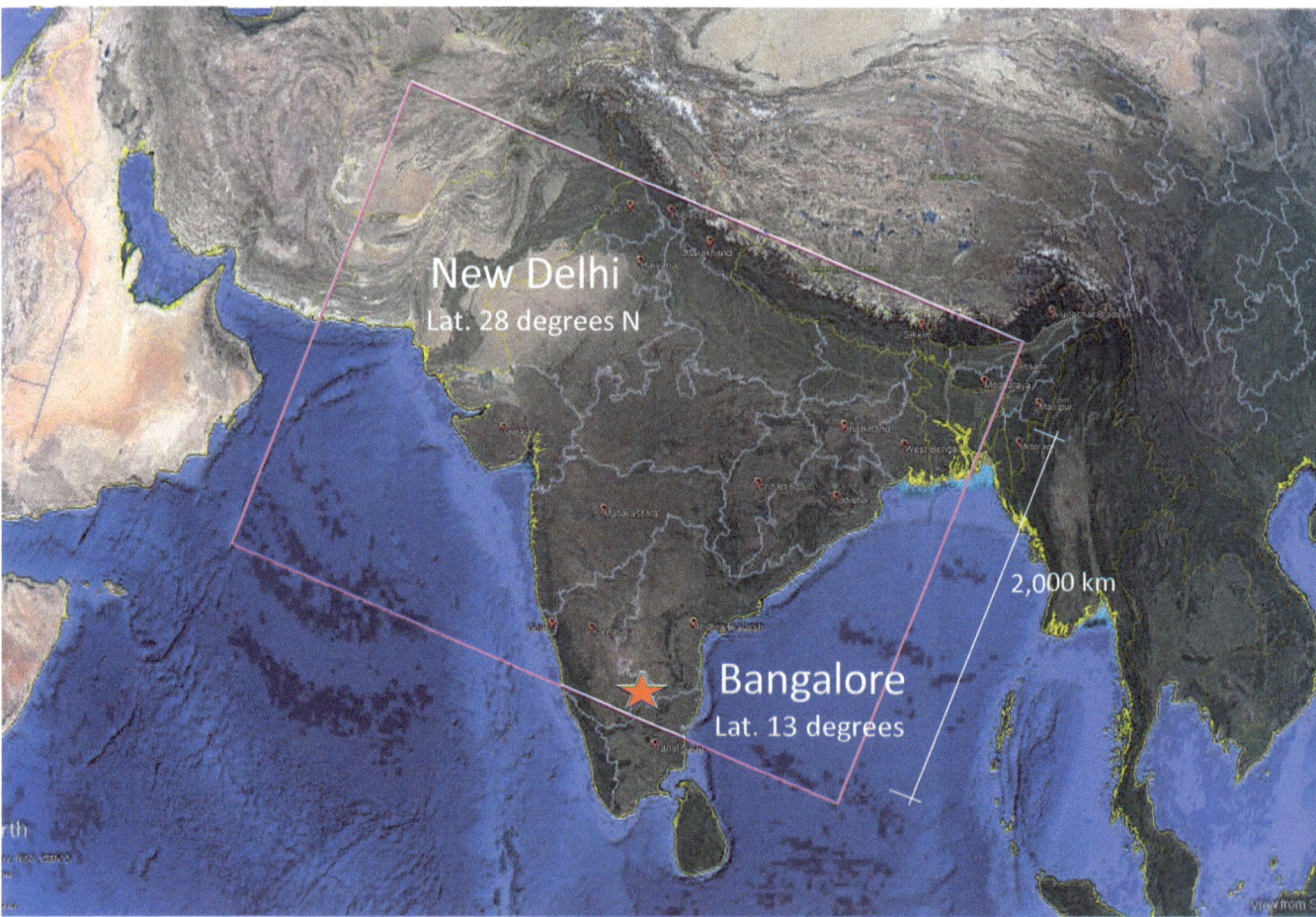

**The** pink rectangle on the map shows the extent of the Mauryan Dynasty, one of many that has existed within the current territories of India, Pakistan, Afghanistan and Bangladesh. The Mauryan Dynasty was the first to control large parts of northern India, as well as extending into more southerly regions. (1

In speaking of Indian culture and the *'Light Garden'* theme of this book, there is not one central connection but a great diversity, which I have categorized under Parts One to Six of this chapter. For example, in Part Two, I draw a parallel between the *'Light Garden'* theme of this book and Gandhi's philosophy of Swaraj, which entailed each person voluntarily adopting a lifestyle of self-restraint, whilst also engaging in community work. People acting both as a group and independently with self restraint, is symbolised by the *'Light Garden'* Principle Number Two: Waves and Particles.

The *Waves* are group activity and the *Particles* are individual activity. Light itself behaves as both a wave and a particle, thus illustrating the quantum biophysical connection between humans and the natural world. Each part of this chapter and each chapter in this book contributes detail to this theme in a diversity of cultural milieu.

# Part 6.1
# Ancient groves

6.1.1 Statistics about tree biodiversity in the ancient groves of India and Bangladesh

6.1.2 Mallur Gutta near Hyderabad in central India.

6.1.3 Shankaracharya forest grove temple at Srinagar in Kashmir

6.1.4 Alappuzha and the Western Ghats in Kerala and southern India

# 6.1.1 Statistics tree biodiversity

*"Experts believe that the total number of sacred groves [ in India] could be as high as 100,000. . . It is estimated that around 1000 km² of unexploited land is inside sacred groves."* (1)

**Throughout** the world cultures have incorporated various ways of worshipping nature. The protection and veneration of scared groves and forests is one of these which has long existed in India.

According to information available in 2018 from the United Nations Food and Agricultural Organsiation, in Bangladesh there were 750 – 800 known tree species. (2)

As reported by the Indian Ministry of Environment, Forest and Climate change there are over 18,000 species of flowering plants in India. This category includes conifers, flowering trees and other forms of flowering plants, such as shrubs and groundcovers. (3)

I have not been able to find any statistics about how many tree species are recorded in India. However the Indian government is currently engaged in work to record the forest cover of the nation and an estimate of the number of tree species may be made at some time in the future.

dolatry. Following from this, although there are many contributing factors, we now find vast areas of Europe and the Middle East devoid of ancient groves of trees. The biodiversity of Europe in the 21st century is less than 1% of that of the tropical forests of the world. (6) )

Thus we see how vital it is that any *'Light Garden'* proposals put forward in this book support the cultural base upon which the protection and veneration of scared groves has rested for thousands of years.

In Europe, there are 250-500 tree species, compared to 40,000 – 53,000 species of trees that grow in the tropical forests of the world. (4) There are 60,000 tree species globally. (5)

In contrast to the protection of sacred groves by Hindus, Buddhists and ethnic cultures in India and Bangladesh, in past centuries the religions of Christianity and Islam have regarded worship of trees as

**Above** Image credit 6.8.1 *Laurebina Yak, in the Nepalese Himalayas near northern India*

**Left** Image credit 6.8.2 ***Shankaracharya forest grove***

# 6.1.2 Mallur Gutta and diversity

*The Mahua (Madhuca longifolia) tree is worshipped by local people in the Mallur Gutta sacred grove. It's seeds may be seen in the photograph below.*

**Mallur** Gutta is a sacred grove in forested hill country near the city of Hyderabad. Although this grove is larger than many, the reasons local people value this grove are typical of the reasons why sacred groves have been valued all over India for millennia. In most places, local people still care for and protect the groves, although in the 21st century accumulated plastic litter left by tourists, lack of legal protection and intrusion by large development corporations have become problems in many groves.

In 2016 a team from Hyderabad University published their studies about Mallur Gatta. (7) During the previous 6 years they had worked in consultation with local people to document 470 species of plants found in this 1500 hectare grove. This diversity of plants highlights why such groves are valued by local communities as sources of medicinal plants.

Also found within the grove are Hindu temples for Lord Sri Laxminarasimha Swamy and Lord Hanuman, as well as prehistoric burial sites, the sacred *"Chintamani"* perennial stream and sites for ethnic worship of the Mahua tree. (8) This tree species is keenly conserved by those dwelling near the grove, as fat from its numerous seeds is used in skincare, as a vegetable butter and as a fuel. Its flowers are used to produce a ceremonial alcoholic drink and several parts of the tree, including the bark, are useful for medicinal purposes. No wonder it is regarded as sacred. (9)

Although we do not have all the details, this description of the use and protection of the Mahua tree starts to build a picture of management of the sacred Mallur Gutta grove in accordance with *'Light Garden'* principles. One of these principles, Number Three, is based around the concept of 'Act as both a Wave and Particle, (as light does).' One could say there is a wave of diversity with many individual particles, each acting as language speakers and protectors of cultural and biological diversity.

As reported by the Indian Ministry of Environment and Forests in 2001, they manage a network of 85 National Parks and 448 Wildlife Sanctuaries covering 4.2% of the land area of India and containing 20% of the world's recorded plant species. Of the 18 biological diversity hotspots in the world, two are found in India: the Eastern Himalayas and the Western Ghats. (11)

Paralleling this diversity of ancient groves, is the multiplicity of languages and human cultures in the India. Census data from 1961

*" identified no fewer than **1,652** mother languages in the Indian subcontinent. Twenty-nine of these, according to a census taken 40 years later in 2001, are spoken by over a million citizens each."* (10)

Image credit 6.9 **The Mahua tree**

# 6.1.3 Shankaracharya at Srinagar

*The locality of Sringagar attracted numerous scholars over the centuries. Some ancient groves such as Shankaracharya are associated with the ongoing religious, historical and strategic importance of the Himalayan region – and may have inspired visions of 'Paradise.' (13) These groves are not unlike a form of the 'Light Garden' concept that is presented in this book.*

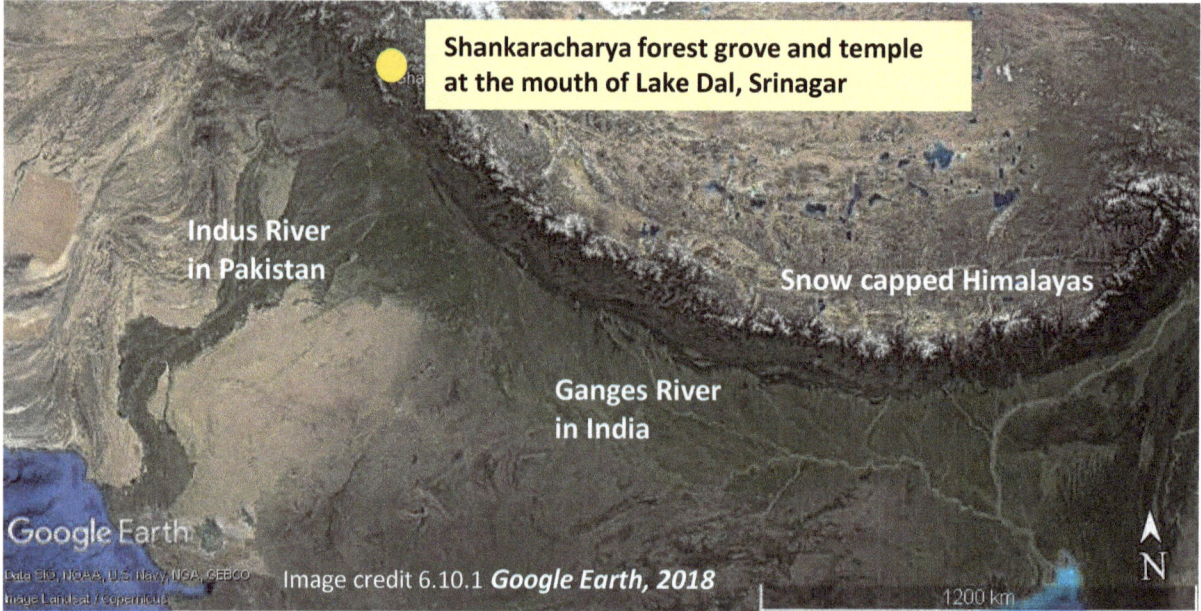

Image credit 6.10.1 *Google Earth, 2018*

**The** Ancient Islamic texts describe 'Paradise' as a garden where four rivers intersect at a central pool, surrounded by lush green trees and beautiful flowers. (14) The natural landscape of Lake Dal may once have mirrored this, with the Shankaracharya hilltop forest grove strategically located at the southern end of the lake.

The oldest of the Hindu scriptures, which some claim are dated back to 7,000 – 4,000 BCE, were probably composed in the north western region of the Indian subcontinent. The Rig Veda, a collection of Vedic Sanskrit hymns to the gods, is likely to have been composed around 1700 – 1100 BCE. (12)

*Below* Google Earth Image credit 6.10.2 ***The town of Srinagar** has grown along the 5 km length of Lake Dal.*

# 6.1.4 Alappuzha, Western Ghats

*Ancient groves are part of the Hindu, ethnic and Buddhist cultures of India but numerous pressures are dampening the flame of faith that keeps these groves alive and well.*

**The** Western Ghats are a chain of mountains which run down the entire west coast of India from north of Mumbai to the southern tip of India. Although there are no comprehensive studies of the area under sacred groves across the Western Ghats,

> " There are hundreds of groves which have not been documented at all . . . "Many tribal communities consider areas within forests to be sacred, but these are not even acknowledged as sacred groves." (15)

In 2014, researchers who set out to update the current status of documented groves in Kodagu, a rural district in the Western Ghats, found that many groves were smaller than previously documented. More than two-thirds of the smaller groves were not forested at all, or could not even be found.

> " . . . many family owned groves have been destroyed by the "lack of faith in old cultural beliefs, lores and myths among the youth, and the migration of outsiders to the neighbourhood who do not understand the cultural significance of groves . . . " (16)

In Maharashtra and Kodagu roads have been made inside groves and elaborate temples constructed. A research associate at the Nature Conservation Foundation has studied attitudes towards groves.

He asked local residents if the change that has occurred in groves was culturally significant to them. He referred to forests changing from dense, biodiverse forests into quite disturbed forest remnants. He found that only 14% of respondents said the change was culturally significant to them.

Parking lots at temples in forest groves are now common. People can be driven right up to the temples, without walking through the forest. In Kerala, the Mannarshala temple parking area accommodates up to 200 vehicles. However many non-resident visitors to India leave without even knowing that sacred groves exist.

> *"The forests seem to be becoming less important than the temple within it,"* says Anand M. Osuri, research associate with the Nature Conservation Foundation . . .
>
> *"It is important to understand what this means for conservation"* he says. (17)

**Below** Image credit 6.11 ***Alappuzha sacred grove in Kerala***

# Part 6.2 Biodiversity culture

6.2.1 The words of Gandhi, mixed with environmental justice

6.2.2 Biodiversity civilisation *

6.2.3 The biodiverse small farm and gardens of India

6.2.4 Civilisations of India

6.2.5 Light persists: a lifelong quest for truth and justice

6.2.6 Gandhian principles

6.2.7 Baskar Save, the Gandhi of natural farming

- The term biodiversity civilization was the major theme for the International Biodiversity Congress 2018 at Dehradun, India.

- "Biodiversity for Ecological Civilization: Vasudhaiva Kutumbakam or 'Vasudhaiva Kutumbakam' which means 'the world is one family', as inscribed in Maha Upanishad, is essentially the Indian philosophy towards living in harmony with every living being in the planet, and an appeal towards undertaking a transformation from industrial civilization to biodiversity civilization, a human civilization strongly rooted in biodiversity consciousness.

# 2.1 The words of Gandhi, mixed with environmental justice

*Mahatma Gandhi is best known for this work towards gaining Indian Independence. He was assassinated in 1948, the year after the British Parliament passed the Indian Independence Act. However his words live on to this day, for he was concerned with a revolution in Indian society that went far beyond gaining independence from British rule.*

*"Recall the face of the poorest and weakest man you have seen, and ask yourself if this step you contemplate is going to be any use to him".* (1)

The manner in which the nation of Bangladesh has accepted nearly a million desperate refugees from neighbouring Myanmar during the past few years provides an exemplary contemporary response to that question.

Whilst Gandhi publicly supported the continuation of the caste system in order to avoid the chaos that dismantling it would entail, he none the less spent huge amounts of energy promoting the welfare of the weakest citizens amongst the power hierarchy of Indian society.

His approach was both philosophical and practical, as described in more detail on the following page. This conjunction between visionary inspiration and practical implementation characterises the guiding light that gardening and farming has become as a way of implementing the principles that Gandhi advocated for the nation as a whole.

*"When you are doing the right things for the earth, she gives you great company."*

**Above** Image credit 8.15.1 and quote by **Dr Vandana Shiva** is a contemporary advocate of Gandhian principles and she has added to them in her work as an internationally renowned advocate for social and environmental justice, sound scientific research, biodiversity conservation and organic farming.

# 6.2.2 Biodiversity civilization

*'Vasudhaiva Kutumbakam', from the Maha Upanishad, means 'the world is one family'.* (2) *It is the Indian philosophy of living in harmony with every living being in the planet. It is an appeal to make a transformation from industrial civilization to one of biodiversity consciousness..*

*Ancient* 'Asudhaiva Kutumbakam', philosophy was applied in the early years of 21st century as the concept of "biodiversity civilisation" arose. Biodiverse, small farms are very much in accordance with Gandhi's philosophy of Swaraj, which he worked tirelessly to implement.

To *Gandhi, Swaraj* entailed the fruits of the tireless work and devotion to the good of the community. Swaraj would be achieved firstly though each person voluntarily adopting a lifestyle of self-restraint and regular self-cleansing, plus secondly through each person also engaging in constructive work. This is a more sophisticated concept than Principle Nine of the *'Light Garden'* model, which is proposed in this book as *restrained human use* of natural resources.

Gandi's concept of the *Seven Social Sins* is also aligned with Swaraj:

> *'Politics without Principles*
> *Wealth without Work*
> *Pleasure without Conscience*
> *Knowledge without Character*
> *Commerce without Morality*
> *Science without Humanity*
> *Worship without Sacrifice'* (3)

Inherent in Swaraj is a philosophy of universal participation and empowerment. This is to be achieved by the elimination of discrimination, oppression, domination and segregation, hand in hand with government policies proactively supporting meaningful work for all in a network of self-reliant local economies at the village scale throughout the land. (3)

This might seem like a difficult goal to achieve but it may well be possible, given the success of recent movements in India such as the Dal Yatra and the major theme for the 2018 International Biodiversity Congress, which was "Biodiversity for Ecological Civilization: Vasudhaiva Kutumbakam." (4)

This theme has inspired hundreds of thousands, if not millions of people to join the movement *towards* organic biodiverse gardens and farms in India and *away* from industrial agricultural monocultures, farmer suicides and debt during the first two decades of the 21st century.

**The northern state of Sikkim** in the Himalayas was recognised in 2017 as India's first, (and the world's first), entirely organic farming state. The use of commercial pesticides and fertilisers is now illegal in Sikkim.

As part of an integrated approach to environmental management, tourism, employment and food production, the Government of Sikkim has recognised the need for financial planning and support for the State's farmers. They face competition from suppliers of non-organic produce who are trucking it in from neighbouring states. This produce is sold at lower prices, undercutting the sale of local organic items. (5)

In 2018, at the International Biodiversity Congress held at Dehradun in India, the goal was announced that all the eight Himalayan states in India would become devoted to organic, biodiverse farming and environmental management. (6)

# 6.2.3 Farmers & gardeners

*"For fifteen years we have been analyzing the small farms of India - in the wet areas of Kerala, in the high Himalayas, in the deserts of Rajasthan - and our research has shown, again and again and again, that biodiverse small farms using ecological inputs, produce three to five times more food than industrial monocultures." (7)*

***Top right*** Image credit 6.15.1 ***Vandana Shiva of Navdanya Biodiversity Farm***

Image credit: The film "Economics of Happiness", was released in 2011 by Helena Norberg-Hodge, Stephen Gorlick and John Page. It gives an international perspective to work being done in India and includes numerous interviews with people from all around the globe. All illustrations and quotes on this page are from the film and are used with written permission.

***Centre right*** Image credit 6.15.2 ***A biodiverse small farm and garden in India.***

***Lower right*** Image credit 6.15.3 ***A gardener and farmer*** in his light-filled Indian garden who said:

"All I need is a complete integrated farm of one acre and I can feed twenty people. We don't need agricultural scientists, we don't need hybrid seeds, we don't need GM. We don't need anything. We just need to be left along to do our farming . .

"This is our vegetable garden. It's 100 per cent organic. You can see the yield of these. Basically we get very good yields because we don't use fertilisers. The soil if it is managed well . . . the productivity is unbelievable . . .

"There is only one economics that will make sense. Local Economics. Everywhere." (8)

# 6.2.4 Civilisations of India

*The origin of the word Hindu is derived from the word Indus, as in the Indus Valley civilisation. As indicated in the time line below, the civilisation is dated from 3,500 BCE. (9) The word "Biodiversity civilisation" arose in India in the second decade of the 21st century and in many ways is a natural extension of India's cultural heritage.*

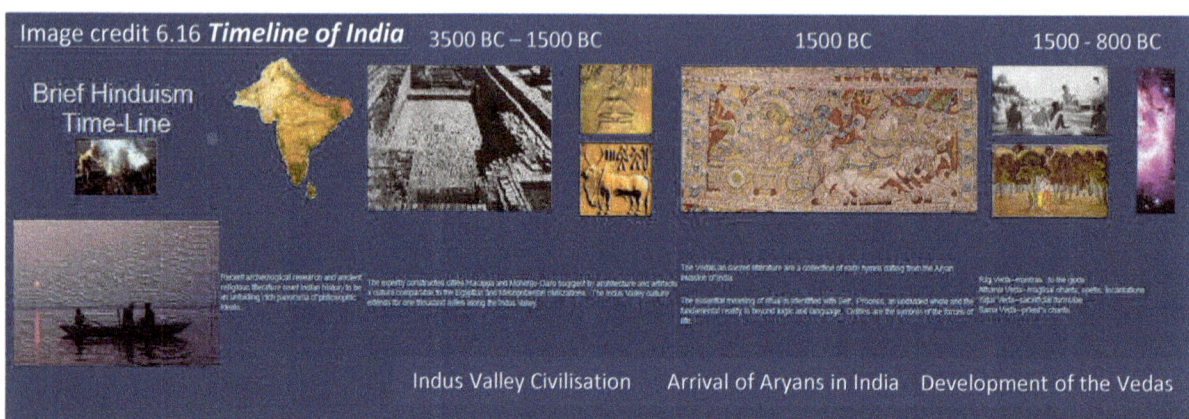

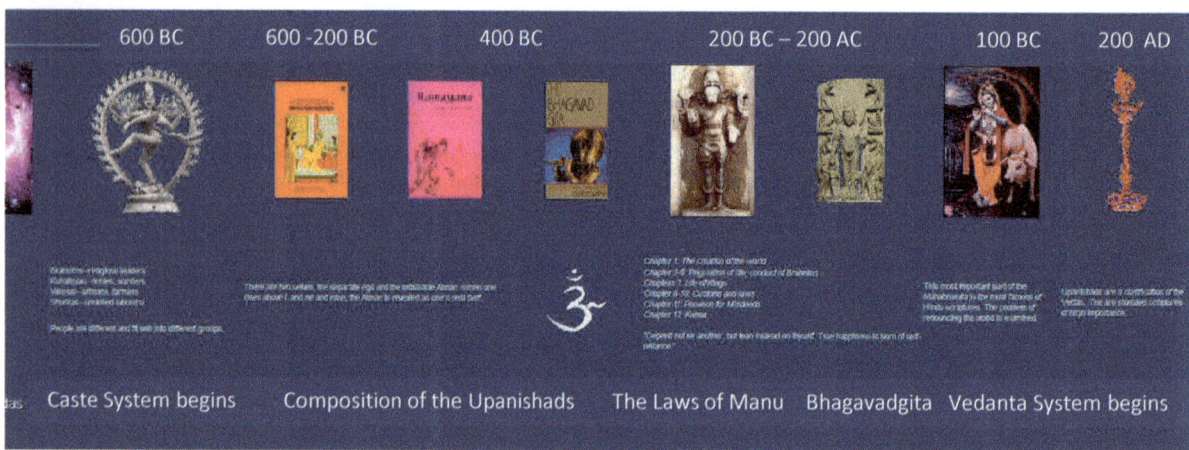

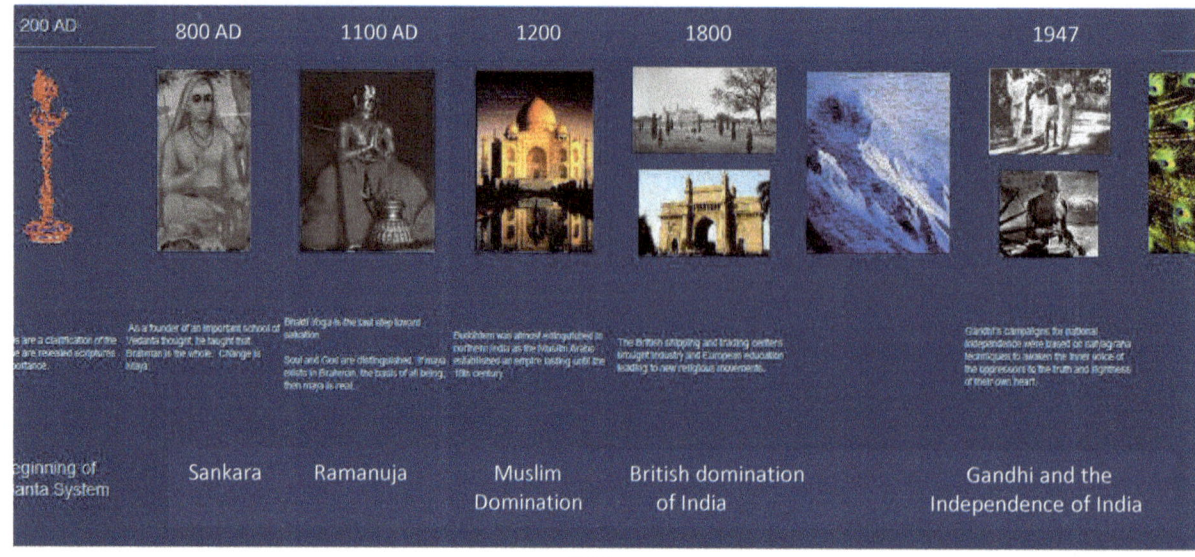

6.16

# 6.2.5 Light persists: a lifelong quest for truth and justice

*In India, light is not an abstraction in which the senses delight. It is a daily part of the struggle for survival.*

**In** India, as everywhere else, light comes from the sun. However in India, the meaning of light is very much aligned with radiance. In India, it is a radiance with a depth of patina that has been refined and consciously maintained over millennia. This radiance has been bestowed by virtue of a conviction to seek and manifest the truth. The radiance can be in a person, a garden, or a place. It may manifest from the morning mist as a vision - as the Taj Mahal does for those who rise early enough to see it. It also has a vigour that is undeniable and not necessarily pretty.

In India, light is not an *abstraction* in which the senses delight. It is a daily part of the struggle for survival. A discourse about light in terms of abstract design concepts inevitably crumbles when discussed in the context of India. It must step aside in favour of India's more robust and compelling debate about justice, empowerment of the people, democracy, self rule, and the unfolding manifestations of the words of the sages.

For example, Vincent Van Gogh may have exclaimed *Jeune Magnifique,* as his heart and senses delighted in the magnificence of the light upon the yellow cornfields and sunflowers that he painted in the south of France. Gandhi, however - in the midst of his life long struggles for freedom, justice and personal responsibility - referred to light in a more visceral sense:

*"In the midst of darkness, light persists."* (10)

The influence of Gandhian philosophy is still playing out, despite being resisted during Gandhi's lifetime by the Indian Prime Minister Nehru, who regarded it as impractical to implement in a national political context. (11) Its global reach and all-embracing principles are still inspiring people around the globe as the message spreads.

Underlying this, the celebration of light and life light is so tightly embedded in Indian culture it is liable to burst forth with vibrancy at any time of year.

The festival of Diwali (The Festival of Light) is a good example. Drawing upon the ancient Vedic scriptures, (with centuries of time-honoured meaning bestowed in the symbology of light and darkness), it celebrates the triumph of good over evil. (12) It is one of the most popular and widespread annual festivals in India and is described in more detail in Part 5 of this chapter.

*Below* Image credit 6.17.1 *Gandhi's words about light*

# 6.2.6 Gandhi's principles live on

*Although Gandhi's focus was not on biophysics or the natural world, since his assassination in 1948 the principles that he established for participatory democracies continue to be taken up by many groups. This groups are actually a strong guiding force behind the biodiversity civilisation in India and elsewhere, so it is worth considering the principles behind it.* (13)

For example, when people come to live and work at the Indian property *Navdanya*, they are given a *Visitor's Guide* which refers to Gandhi's principles. (14)

Whilst this may seem simple enough in concept, for many people from Western cultures it is a deep culture shock to travel to India and witness people who gained their post doctoral qualifications at the world's most prestigious universities and who are renowned as international speakers but who choose to live in communities such as *Navdanya*.

They chose to live simply and happily by adhering to these principles and serving their people, rather than pursuing individualistic Western lifestyles. The Navdanya principles include Satyam, Ahimsa, Brahmacharya and Swadesh, as briefly described below:

**Satyam (Truth)**

> "The pivotal and defining element of Gandhism is Satyam, a Sanskrit word usually translated into English as 'truth'. The literal meaning is 'what actually is'. Gandhi believed that the principle of Satya should pervade all considerations of politics, ego, society and convention."
> (15)

Gandhi believed that each person had to seek their own version of Satyam, whilst adhering to the spirit of the concept and all the other principle as well. Therein lies one great difference between Indian civilisation and other simpler Western lifestyles, which are more focused on individuals.

**Ahimsa (non-violence)** . . . Gandhi . . . held that total non-violence would rid a person of anger, obsession and destructive impulses.

**Brahmacharya** (self perfection through self-control and contentment) . . . meant control of the senses in thought, word and deed. It also means the pursuit of virtue and to strive for excellence in all domains of activity and relationships.

**Swadeshi** (self-reliance) began as a concept with which Gandhi galvanised masses of the Indian population to abstain from cloth that was not made in India during the time of the British Empire in India. In later years, the term came to have a wider meaning, associated with the self reliance of local economies, communities and systems of government. (16)

It is interesting to speculate whether Greta Thunberg thinks application of these principles would help solve the climate crisis in 2019. Greta was a 15 year Swedish schoolgirl in 2018 when she started the world-wide School Climate Strike movement. Invited to speak at the World Economic Form in Davis the following year, she said to the adults of the world: *I want you to act as you would in a crisis. I want you to act as if our house is on fire. Because it is.* (17)

# 2.7 Baskar Save "the Gandhi of natural farming" (18)

*Inspired by the writings of Gandhi and Vinoba Bhave, in 1956 Baskar Save decided to begin experimenting with reverting back to an organic farming system on his family's farm in the state of Gujarat, India. It is interesting to examine from first principles how Baskar works with the natural resources available to him, including sunlight.*

**Using** an awareness of light that is relevant to the theme of this book, Baskar developed ways to optimise the use of the *available sunlight* on his farm. In the early years, he planted short-lived crops such as vegetables, legumes and rice between longer-lived tree species of coconut and chikoo. Later he introduced medium life-span crops such as bananas and papayas.

Sixty years after he began in 1956, Baskar lived to see the family farm as a stable and profitable enterprise, with 90% of the income earned from the long-lived chikoo and coconut trees. (19)

The principles that Baskar developed for organic farming recognise the centrality of working with sunlight and other natural resources to create a prosperous, living, biodiverse economy. His **first principle is very similar to Gandhi's Ahimsa principle:**

> *"all living creatures have an equal right to live."*

His second principle recognises that *"everything in Nature is useful and serves a purpose in the web of life."*

Baskar's **third principle is:**

> *"farming is a dharma, a sacred path of serving Nature and fellow creatures; it must not degenerate into a pure dhandha or money-oriented business. Short-sighted greed to earn more – ignoring Nature's laws – is the root of the ever-mounting problems we face."* (20)

**Baskar's fourth principle is for on-going regeneration of soil fertility.** It recognises that the energy of sunlight, (as described in the 'Light Garden' model of this book), can, like other natural resources, can be cycled back through soil and water to maintain ecologically sound and balanced systems.

After harvesting products, trees should be retained and the balance of the biomass, (85% to 95%), should be returned to the soil to replenish the fertility. This can be done through direct composting of vegetative matter, or through feeding plants to animals, which then produce manure for composting back into the soil. (21) This system is consistent with the *'Light Garden'* theme and the centuries old farming practices of the Amish, which are described in Chapter Nine.

**Below** Image credit 6.19.1 *Coconuts have been a big part of Baskar Save's organic farm*

# Part 6.3
# Traditional villages

6.3.1 Ziro Valley

- Map of the Indian Himalayas

- The Himalayas – traditional life and worship of the light

- UNESCO & traditional gardens

- Ziro Valley: new ways of seeing the light

# A village in the Himalayas

*Although they may have many things in common, there is no typical village garden found in the great diversity of places that occur in India and Bangladesh. In addition, due to outside influences since 1950, many villages have experienced changes to traditional practices that had previously endured for centuries.*

**However** I have chosen to describe one group of traditional villages that has been preserved, despite outside pressures.

Considerable documentation of the authenticity of this culture has been compiled in the process of nominating the village-based way of life in the Ziro Valley of the Himalayas for inclusion on UNESCO's World Heritage list. The culture of the people who live in Ziro Valley is also an example of a culture where *light* is consciously revered as part of spiritual, social, garden and landscape management. Hence it serves to illustrate the theme of this book in more depth. The World Heritage listing documentation provides much of the material to which I refer in describing the role of light in this culture.

As shown by eight ★ symbols on the map below, there are eight Indian States in the Himalayan region: Jammu and Kashmir, Himachal Pradesh, Uttarakhand, Uttar Pradesh, Sikkim, Arunachal Pradesh and the hilly parts of Assam and West Bengal. The Ziro Valley lies in the state of Aranchal Pradesh, in the north east of India.

**Below** Google Earth image credit 6.21 **Himalayan States of India**

*Indians love these peaks because they are a part of every Indian's life. Indians revere the mountains, as they would, the father. Even today, when urban India is racing against time, in the caves of the snow-clad peaks, live hermits - seeking the divine. Not a surprise when you consider that even this century has seen some great philosophers like Ramana Maharishi, Swami Vivekananda, Ramakrishna Paramhansa and u. Krishnamurti.* (1)

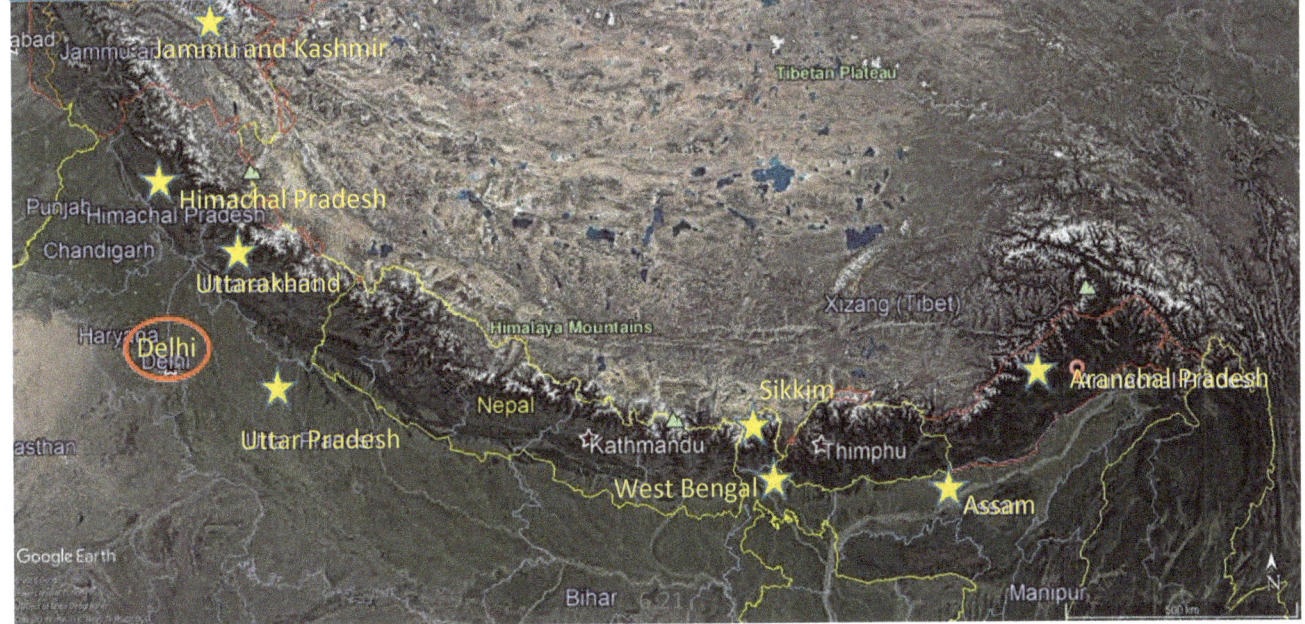

# The Himalayas – traditional life and worship of the light

*For centuries, the Siang River, (otherwise known by the Tibetan name of Yarlung Tsangpo), has also been known as the Brahmaputra River, once it flows south across the Himalayans into India. To the north of the Himalayas, it flows for 1600 kilometers before reaching the border with India. (2) Ziro Valley is marked by the symbol ⭐ on the map below.*

**Above** Image credit 6.22.1 *Location map for Ziro Valley*

**The** river Yarlung Tsangpo originates in the Angsi Glacier near Mount Kailash. Flowing to the east, it reaches the "Great Bend" between Namche Barwa and the Gyala Peri mountains. Among the gorges of this north eastern extremity of the Himalayas, as the river flows south into India as the Brahmaputra, is the spot where I have chosen to begin this description of the role of light in the traditional gardens in India.

Ziro Valley lies in the Indian state of Aranchal Pradesh on a tributary of the Brahmaputra, less then 200 kilometers south of the Himalayan border with China. It is some 2,000 kilometers to the east of New Delhi, the capital city of India. The indigenous religions of the Tibeto-Burmese peoples of Aranachal Pradesh are known as *Donyi-Polo*. (3)

As an example of how integral the concept of *light* is to the cultures of these peoples, the term *Donyi–Polo*, translated to English literally means *sun – moon*.

The practical expression of the faith in Donyi-Polo can be found in the daily life and actions of people: they call themselves "Donyi O, Polo Ome", meaning "children of the sun and the moon". (4) In more depth, *Donyi–Polo* is an analogy for describing God:

> " representing the way in which the divine principle manifests itself, that is: eternally veiling, unveiling and then revealing himself in nature; providing harmony and balance to the universe, for example in the alternation of light and darkness . . . " (5)

As described in more detail on the following page, **this belief system around the concept of light underpins the practical organisation of tasks in the traditional village life of the Donyi Polo people.** It also is recognised as being a significant contributing factor to the nomination of the cultural landscape of the Ziro Valley on the United Nations Education, Scientific and cultural Organisation's (UNESCO's), World Heritage List. (6)

# UNESCO & traditional gardens

*It has been their ability to maintain their traditional agricultural and belief systems, despite pressures from outside influences, that makes the Apatinai unique. (7) In order to better understand how this has been achieved, it is worth considering some of the history and detail of their gardening and agricultural systems.* Note: All information on this page from refs (7), (8) and (9).

*Above* Image credit 6.23.1 *Wet rice cultivation.*

**The** Apatani tribes of *Ziro Valley* inhabit an area of 1058 square kilometers and in the 21st century, the population is estimated as being between 20,000 – 40,000 people. They consciously worship sacred groves, forests and light, in the form of the sun, moon and nature. The religion is called *Donyi-Polo,* which literally means *sun – moon*. Religious rituals and agricultural practices are synchronised with lunar phases.

This belief system that reveres all forms of life, has underpinned the Apatani's ability to maintain the forested watershed of Ziro Valley, ensuring some biodiversity and a clean flow of water into their fields, gardens and villages. Unlike many parts of Asia where pesticides are now used, the Apartani developed a unique system of organic, wet rice and fish cultivation (Aji-ngyii). Based on estimates of village elders, one hectare of land produces about 200kg of fish, in the size range of 140 – 200 grams each.

The Apartani system of governance through village councils called *bulyañ* has helped maintain their traditional communal agriculture and belief systems, despite pressures from outside influences. That is what is recognised as unique, in the UNESCO World Heritage listing citation for the cultural landscape of Ziro Valley.

Tibetan and Indian sources indicate that the Apatani and other tribes of the Arunachal mountains have probably inhabited the areas since about the 8th century CE and certainly since the 15th century CE. Until very recently, traders travelled between Tibet and Assam, through the Aranchal mountain passes.

The Apartani, along with other Himalayan hill tribes, were accustomed to negotiating treaties for co-existence with the Indian Ahom kings of the Brahmaputra valley. The tribes resisted the undermining of their local tribal authority and way of life when the British colonial government of the 19th century ousted the Ahom kings and tried to force the hill tribes to be porters for them and to work as plantation farm labourers.

Such activities meant the Apartani were forced to leave their own farms and community responsibilities for extended periods. The Apatanis were brought into this colonial conflict situation relatively late, (in 1897), due to the relative isolation provided to Ziro Valley by it's elevation of 5,000 metres. *(7), (8) and (9)*

# Ziro Valley: new ways of seeing the light

*The landscape of the Ziro valley homeland of the Apatanis has some similarities with other Himalayan valleys such as the Imphal valley of Manipur, the Kathmandu valley of Nepal and the Paro valley of Bhutan.*

**Urbanization** has completely changed the landscapes of the Imphal and Kathmandu valleys. Though Paro valley still retains its charm, agriculture is minimal and mainly due to individual efforts rather than the type of community activity that still occurs in Ziro valley. (10)

Looking downcast, perhaps the Apartani woman depicted below right is thinking of the loss of traditional values and peace amongst the younger generations who come and go through the Ziro Valley in the 21st century.

Despite the sublime natural landscape and great diversity of sustainable, traditional local cultures in the Himalayas, one can see why there are tensions and despondency, as neighbouring countries seek to gain control of resources and climate change causes melting of the glaciers, flash flooding and uncertainty over water supplies for the millions of people, farms, ecosystems and gardens the along the rivers fed by the Himalayas.

For millennia, the Brahmaputra has been known as the crystal clear, *lifeblood* water for gardens and villages in the north eastern part of India. However, as reported by *The Hindu* newspaper in December 2017, the Indian Government at that time was investigating why the river had turned black. The water was unfit for consumption. Natural causes such as earthquakes were suspected. (11)

In November 2017 *The Times of India* had carried similar reports with photographs of the river sludge. It quoted local people saying they had seen the river turn dark before after mudslides, but never before had it been like this. This prompted speculation that the cause was Chinese activities upstream, leading to release of large quantities of cement into the river, probably in conjunction with underground tunneling and redirection of the natural flow of rivers away from India and into the dry parts of China. (12)

In spite of this, the Himalayas continue to draw many gardeners, pilgrims and visitors, many of whom are seeking to create in their own lives a reverence for nature and for light, such as has been kept alive by the Apartani people.

*Left* Image credit 6.24 In a concession to the modern age, well as the traditional nose plugs and facial tattoos an Apartiti woman wears spectacles and some factory made garments.

# Part 6.4
# Famous gardens

There are a number of internationally famous gardens in India, many of which were constructed in the Moghul style of Islamic Paradise Gardens. I have therefore chosen to consider one of these in relation to the theme of this book, rather than consider several sites which have similar features.

The Taj Mahal is the most well known of the gardens of India and Bangladesh and it is the one I have chosen to review.

In addition, Vastu Shastra is a body of knowledge with ancient origins in India. It predates Islamic influences. As it lends a particular presence to the gardens and sites of India, I have briefly reviewed it at the conclusion of Part 4.

6.4.1 Taj Mahal.
- Rivers of pilgrims
- Shah Jahan foresaw the vision
- Light and Space: the Taj Mahal

6.4.2 Vastu Shastra

# 6.4.1 The Taj Mahal - rivers of pilgrims drawn to the light

*Light in a garden in India is not an abstract concept. It is a radiance, a presence - something of awe. Perhaps that is why the Sanskrit and Arabic languages are so rich in terms for such phenomenon, which are not easily or simply translatable.*

**Above** Image credit 8.26.1 *The Taj Mahal. The plan for this 17 hectare site has five main parts as listed below:* (1), (2)

1. The *Taj Ganji*, or paved bazaar forecourt, which has wall boundary adjoining the dense urban area to the south.

2. The large, brown coloured *Jilaukhana*, or front of house area. This was built as an arrival hall for guests with sizeable entourages, including elephants.

3. The Charbagh. This is the flat, enclosed garden with trees, flowers, lawns and intersecting water channels.

4. The riverfront terrace, upon which the domed, white marble Mausoleum (4a) and Kau Ban Mosqe (4b) stand. An image looking north across the garden towards the mausoleum (4a) is shown above left.

5. The Yamuna River, plus the moonlight garden on the far bank of the river. The far bank of the river is out of view, to the right hand side of the photograph.

**4b Left** Image credit 6.26.2 **Women at the Kau Ban** Mosque of the Taj Mahal. Refer also to Chapter 4, page 4.9.
**4a Above left** Image credit 6.26.3 **View across the Charbagh (garden)** towards the mausoleum at the Taj Mahal.

# Shah Jahan foresaw the vision

*Popular culture holds that the Taj Mahal celebrates the love of Shah Jahan for his wife Mumtaz Mahal. The Taj Mahal is India's most well known international icon. What could be more appropriate in one of the world's most successful and enduring matriarchal societies, where the divine light of women and Goddesses is still venerated in daily life ?*

*Top left* Image credit 6.27.1 ***Gardeners in their daily finery***, at work in the paradise gardens of the Taj Mahal.

*Centre Left* Image credit 6.27.2 Although eight million visitors per annum come to the Taj Mahal and in 2018 the Indian Government introduced a limit of 40,000 domestic visitors per day to the site, the triumphal mystique remains.

*Bottom Left* Image credit 6.27.3 As illustrated here, one of the brilliant features of the landscape design is that no matter how large the rivers of people grow, the mausoleum is always visible from all parts of the garden.

Just as Jorn Utzon would have nothing but white ceramic tiles upon the curved sails of the Sydney Opera House, so too did Shah Jahan foresee the incomparable reflection of light from the finest of white marbles on this structure.

# Light and space: the Taj Mahal

*The Taj Mahal is not only a masterpiece in its own right, it offers an insight into the wonderful visions and lights of paradise that bejewel the world of Muslim art, philosophy and religion.*

**According** to Islamic beliefs, Paradise consists of a garden and four rivers with lush green trees, beautiful flowers and plants. The plan of the Taj Mahal was designed to reflect this. (3)

As briefly described on the preceding page, the story of the Taj Mahal illustrates how discussion about gardens, farms and landscapes in India, (both ancient and modern), needs to proceed with an **awareness of concepts of light, colour and space. These will be inseparably paired with solid, practical site planning.**

Shah Jahan went to great lengths to chose the site of the Taj Mahal on the banks of the Yamuna River, it being some eight hundred kilometres from where his wife Mumtaz died. The site originally planned for mausoleum was found not to have foundations solid enough to bear the weight of the great marble structure that Shah Jahan envisaged. Nor did the original site have a river wide enough to adequately reflect the glory of the structure within its waters. **So right from the beginning, we see the importance placed upon the pairing of concepts of light with practical site works.**

The Taj Mahal was built near Agra between 1631 and 1648. It is described in the UNESCO World Heritage Listing of the site as

> *" the jewel of Muslim art in India and one of the universally admired masterpieces of the world's heritage."* (4)

> *" Charbagh or Chahar Bagh is a Persian and Islamic quadrilateral garden layout based on the four gardens of Paradise mentioned in the Qur'an. . . . In Persian, "Chār" means 'four' and "bāgh" means 'garden' ."* (5)

The Char Bagh, or central garden area of the Taj Mahal, covers an area of three hundred by three hundred metres. Four symbolic rivers of paradise separate the garden into quadrants. The rivers are of water, milk, honey and wine. Multiples of the number four are considered to be most holy of numbers in the Islamic religion, so the four garden quadrants were further divided into sixteen flowerbeds. The tree species used in this garden are Cyprus, (which symbolise death) and fruit trees, (which symbolise life). (6)

**The design of the Taj Mahal site has been analysed in terms of Vastu Shastra, which is the traditional Indian science of construction or architecture.** This science is concerned with creating a central space surrounded by zones where particular activities occur and the flow of energy and sunlight is carefully considered. (7)

Thus we see that a central space with openness to sunlight is one of the basic principles of Vastu Shastra that is found at the Taj Mahal. Other features that align with Vastu Shastra principles include open space in the East and North of the site; the presence of the Yamuna River in the East and North and the flow of the river from West to East across the site. (8)

# 6.4.2 Vastu Shastra

*Underlining the significance of light in Hindu design, is none other than the Lord Brahma, Creator of the Universe. He is responsible for bringing light upon the surface of the Earth, in an alternating sequence of day and night.*

**It follows that an uncluttered space for Lord Brahma and light must always be reserved in the centre of a design, whether it be indoors or outdoors.** (10)

**The peaceful existence of humans is guarded by nine Hindu Gods of Nature, the *Ashtadhik Balakars'* or *Guards of Directions*. The Vedas contain much scripture dedicated to these Gods.** One of the earliest poems in the vast Hindu collection of the Rigveda, describes the desire for alignment with the dawning of light.

> *"An unshaped consciousness desired light*
> *And a blank prescience yearned towards distant change"* (9)

In turn, such concepts underpin Hindu design principles and remain as powerful influences in the contemporary practice of Vastu Shastra.

The surface of the Earth is represented by a square in Hindu cosmology. The four sides of this square are defined firstly by the two positions where light rises at Sunrise (East) and sets at Sunset (West). The other two sides of the square are defined by the directions of North and South. This geometry provides a tangible indication of how important the concept of light is in the design of Hindu sites. (11)

Hindu sites are designed on a mathematical basis, which is encoded in the *Vastu Shatra, including the Purusha Mandala*. A *Mandala* is a plan or chart that symbolically represents the universe. The term *Purusha* refers to humankind's cosmic nature – to our energy, soul and power. An analogy may be made with the game of chess, which originated at least 1,500 years ago in India. *The chessboard symbolises our existence as a field* of action on which the Gods engage in combat, each with their own role within the eternal battle between power - seeking asuras and benevolent devas. (12)

The design of Hindu sites, (cities, temples, gardens, offices, homes and so on), is guided by specific activities which should be conducted in each direction. For example, in a home, the pooja or prayer room should be located in the east because that is the direction from which daylight first touches a site. A pooja room is separate from a bedroom, office or lounge room, as commonly understood in Western culture.

Kandariya_Mahadeva_Temple in the city of Ahmandabad is an example of an 11th century Shiva temple designed according to Vastu Shastra principles. (13) Larger scale application of these principles is described in Part 5 of this chapter with reference to the city of Madurai in the south of India.

Image credit 6.29 **Lord Shiva**

6.29

# Part 6.5 Temple, festival and pilgrimage gardens

6.5.1      Temples as places of pilgrimage

6.5.2      Diwali, the festival of light

6.5.3      Trees and gardens in the life of Gautama Buddha

6.5.4      Meenakshi Amman temple in Madurai, Tamil Nadu

6.5.5      The temple, city and light.

# Part 6.5.1
# Temples as places of pilgrimage

*To understand the nature of how Light is incorporated in Indian and Bangladeshi Gardens and landscapes, an appreciation of the prevailing and historical Hindu and Islamic religions that underpin these societies is necessary. A brief introduction to this subject is included on the following pages.*

> **"** The gods always play where groves are near rivers, mountains and springs, and in towns with pleasure gardens. Temples are therefore sited in relation to rivers and groves. They are places of pilgrimage, not places of congregational worship. (1) **"**

**Almost** all the Mughal gardens of India that relied upon open channels and displays of water are dry and derelict today. Some, such as the Taj Mahal, are maintained by a paid workforce. In contrast, the innumerable smaller Hindu gardens throughout the land are still used and maintained by the local people. The images above were taken at Varanasi on the Ganges.

*Above left* Image credit 6.31.1 **Varanasi**
*Above top right* Image credit 6.31.2 **Hindu women** at a Diwali ceremony. Diwali is the festival of light.
*Above lower right* Image credit 6.31.3 **Sunrise** bathing in the Ganges at Varanasi

# 6.5.2 Diwali, the festival of light

*Of the many festivals celebrated in India, the festival of light is perhaps the most widely followed. Known as Diwali, it occurs over a period of five days.* What better symbol to signify how important the concept of light is within Indian culture than this event?

**Diwali** is celebrated at the time of the Hindu New Year, during the lunar month of Kartika (October and November). Millions of Hindus, Sikhs and Jains across the world join in the festivities. Diwali is a time of gift giving and visiting friends and relatives. Fireworks and lamps are lit; prayers are said and special community events organised. Diwali is equivalent in significance to the celebration of Christmas in Western culture. (2)

While each faith has its own reason to celebrate Diwali, the central theme is the triumph of light over darkness and goodness over evil. The legend of Lord Rama and his wife Sita returning victorious to their kingdom in northern India after defeating the demon king Ravana is one that people of all ages can relate to. It is the 15th century historical story behind present day Diwali celebrations. (3)

The Sanskrit word Diwali means "rows of lamps" and these can be seen in all the homes and shops. As illustrated at right, Rangoli's are traditionally made from flower petals, coloured grains of rice and similar granular materials on the floors of peoples' homes. Unlike the Christian celebration of Christmas which has a strong church focus, Diwali is traditionally a home based festival. Indian temples are not designed as places for congregational worship but rather as places of pilgrimage. (4)

Both Christmas and Diwali are times when people visit and entertain their friends and relatives, deriving joy from the beauty of decorations, good food, celebrations and the lamps and candles that they light.

In contrast to Diwali, when Buddhists light candles, if is often as an aid to silent and solitary concentration and meditation. I shall now turn to the subject of Buddhism, which arose in north eastern India in the 6th century BCE.

*Below* Image credit 6.32.1 *Preparing a rangoli*

*Below* Image credit 6.32.2 *Celebrating Diwali* with a traditional Rangoli (pattern drawn on the floor)

# 6.5.3 Trees and gardens in the life of Gautama Buddha

*In contrast to the bright lights, crowds and family events of Diwali, the life the Buddha, (Guatama Buddha) was characterised by taking refugee and teaching outdoors under the shelter of trees. Pilgrimage trees have also became associated with his significant life events.*

The life of Gautama Buddha was spent not in the deserts of Rajastan, the beaches of Kerala or the snow clad peaks of northern India but in the fertile plains of the Ganges and the foothills of the Himalayas. Trees, gardens, flowers and forests abounded in those parts of India. No wonder they are interwoven not only through the imagery of Buddhist texts, sculptures and tankhas but also through the course of Gautama's actual life.

Historical accounts indicate that he was born about 550 BCE at Lumbini, in a garden under a sal tree. At the time, his mother was journeying back to her father's kingdom to give birth. Making such a journey was the custom at the time. Buddha's birth en route is somewhat comparable to the birth of Jesus in a stable, when his parents were travelling to Bethlehem.

**Below** Image credit 6.33.1 *Bodhi Tree leaves*

Guatama Buddha gained enlightenment under another tree: the Bodhi Tree. This tree is also known as the Peepal Tree. Realizing that he was close to attaining enlightenment, Buddha chose to trek to this tree and sit in meditation until attaining full enlightenment.

Today the Bodhi Tree is a large and sacred fig in the Mahabodhi Temple at Bodhgaya. It has been maintained through propagation of successive fig trees from the time of Buddha's enlightenment in about 585 BCE up to the present day. It has large and appealingly heart-shaped leaves, symbolic of the heart felt sentiments necessary for successful and sustained Buddhist practice.

Multitudes of pilgrims now visit these sites in Lumbini and Bodhgaya each day. As a sign of how important the living trees are to the experience of Buddhism, walls have been erected around them to protect them from physical damage by the crowds.

Buddha also chose to pass away under a tree in the forest outside the town of Kushinagar. Buddhism itself became almost extinct as a movement in India by about the 12$^{th}$ Century CE but in the mean time, it had spread to many other Asian countries, where it still prevails today. (5) (6) and (7). Trees are not as prevalent in some of these regions, (such as the Tibetan plateau), but the imagery of trees and flowers remains in the rituals.

# 6.5.4 Meenakshi Amman Temple

*This temple is located in the southern Indian State of Tamil Nadu. It attracts over a million pilgrims and visitors during the annual 10-day Meenakshi Tirukalyanam festival, which is held during the Tamil month of Chittirai. Chittirai usually coincides with the month of April in the calendars of 21st century Western cultures. (8)*

**The** ancient temple site was built without walls. It is said to have been first constructed in the 6th century BCE in the city of Madurai. The city itself is dated as 2,500 years old. (9)

The temple has always been at the heart of the city. Hindus rebuilt the city in the 16th and 17th Centuries, after Muslim invaders sacked and looted the temple in the 14th century. The Muslims also subsequently demanded tribute from the Hindus for centuries but the Hindus remained in control of the city none the less.

The city was rebuilt it to incorporate Hindu and Vastu Shastra principles, such as having the city face East to greet *Surya*, the Sun God who rises in the East. (10) The street layout of the old city is illustrated below right, with yellow coloured line work overlaid to the Google Earth 2019 aerial photograph. The original concentric squares and streets opening to the East can be seen. This street layout contrasts with the surrounding streets of the modern city which surround the ancient city.

For example, a large transport corridor can be seen running just to the west of the old city in the aerial photograph.

**Right** Image credit 6.34.1 **Meenakshi Amman temple** in the centre of the lavender coloured street overlay diagram. The aerial photograph is a Google Earth 2019 image of part of the city of Madurai.

Streets in the original city were named after the months of the Tamil Hindu calendar, such as Masi, Adhi, Avani-moola and others. (10)

The tradition of festively parading bronze statues from the temple through the streets of the city continues today at religiously auspicious times. This tradition developed centuries ago. (11)

Not surprisingly, the rebuilding of the temple included the addition of courtyard walls to protect the inner shrines. The shrines are dedicated to the Hindu Goddess Parvati, (also known as Meenakshi), and to her consort, Shiva. The shrines are housed in buildings constructed according to Vastu Shastra principles that enhance the experience of the many pilgrims to the shrines. (12)

# Meenakshi Amman Temple

*Madurai is one of the many temple towns in the state of Tamil Nadi. The name Tamil Nadi is derived from the groves, clusters and forests which are each dominated by a particular variety of a tree or shrub. Each variety of tree or shrub is believed to shelter a presiding deity. (13)*

**Despite** the huge crowds who visit the site, it is interesting to see in the aerial photographs below that there is a ring of large shade trees around the perimeter of the site. These trees help to retain something of the character of the groves after which Tamil Nadu was named.

The significance of *light* in the rebuilding of the temple and of the whole city has been described by Susan Lesandowski:

*"The Nayaka rulers followed the Hindu texts on architecture called the Silpa Shastras in redesigning the temple city plan and the Meenakshi temple. The city was laid out . . in the shape of concentric squares and ring-roads around them, with radiating streets culminating in the Meenakshi-Sundaresvara temple."* (12)

As illustrated below, in the 21st century the Meenakshi Amman temple is surrounded by vast walls and a series of towers. Like the Taj Mahal in the north of India, the Meenakshi Amman temple attracts tens of thousands of visitors per day. Why is it so popular? The timeless appeal of the non duality of human and divine romance may provide an answer:

*" The wedding of the divine couple [Meenakshi and Shiva] is regarded as a classic instance of south Indian marriage with matrilineal emphasis, an arrangement referred as "Madurai marriage."* (16)

In further analysis of the temple it has been noted:

*" this may reflect the matrilineal traditions in South India and the regional belief that "penultimate [spiritual] powers rest with the women", gods listen to their spouse, and that the fate of kingdoms rest with the women."* (15)

**Above left**
Image credit 6.35.1

**Left** image credit 6.35.2
**Meenakshi Amman temple**

# Part 6.6 Gardens of the 21st century

6.6.1      Planning for refugee resettlement as Light Gardens

6.6.2      Bangladesh's floating gardens

6.6.3      Jaipur's Rooftop terraces & organics

6.6.4      Chapter Summary

# 6.6.1 Planning for refugee resettlement as *Light Gardens*

*What role do light gardens and landscape planning have in the daily lives of the millions of refugees in India, Pakistan and Bangladesh, where survival on a day to day basis is the chief concern?*

**Muslim** refugees, driven from their homes in the neighbouring country of Myanmar by years of unrelenting violence, have flooded into Bangladesh in recent years. Some enter Bangladesh by wading through the Naf River delta at night, trying to avoid Myanmar solders before landfall.

The United Nations Humanitarian Commission for Refugees (UNHCR) Global Trends report of 2017, presents data which shows that 85 per cent of refugees live in developing countries. [1] Many of these countries are desperately poor and receive little support to care for refugee populations.

In addition, there are often flow-on effects such as serious environmental and social problems in the host countries. For example, over 4,000 hectares of forest near the refugee camps in Bangladesh has been stripped bare by refugees seeking firewood. Even the tree roots have been dug out. [2]

The sheer scale and population density of the Kutupalong camp that houses 900,00 refugees in Bangladesh necessitates and actually facilitates such planning. The area of the camp is at least 3 kilometers by 3 kilometers, or 9 square kilometers, if one calculates this using the bar scale provided on the Google Earth image shown on the following page. [3]

The population density of this camp may thus be calculated as about 100,000 people per square kilometre. (900,000/9 = 100,000). This density is at least twice that of the most densely populated city on Earth, which is Manila. The urban density in Manilla is 43,079 inhabitants per square kilometre. [4] In comparison, the density of Beijing in 2016 was 1,146 people. In Shanghai it was 3,816 inhabitants per square kilometer. [5]

**There is a strong case for refugee camps to be internationally funded with no interest, long term loans and the goal of creating self-contained, zero carbon local economies that grow their own food; create their own employment; plant trees; collect and store their own water requirements; and generate their own fuel through a suite of sources such as solar power, gas from waste composting and wind power.**

*Below* Image credit 6.37.1 *A refugee*

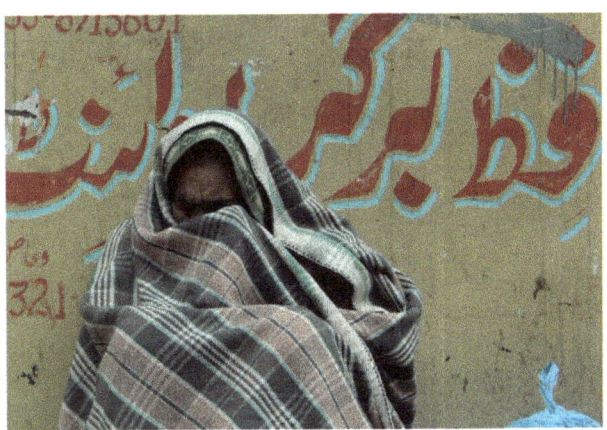

6.37

## 6.6 cont.
## Four out of five refugees remain in countries next door to their own (6)

In one of the ironies of the 21st century, we now have the technology to plan this type of low carbon economy in accordance with the *Light Gardens* concepts described in this book and rather than costing the international community money, it would save money by not generating greenhouses gases and thus not further exacerbating the costs of international climate change management.

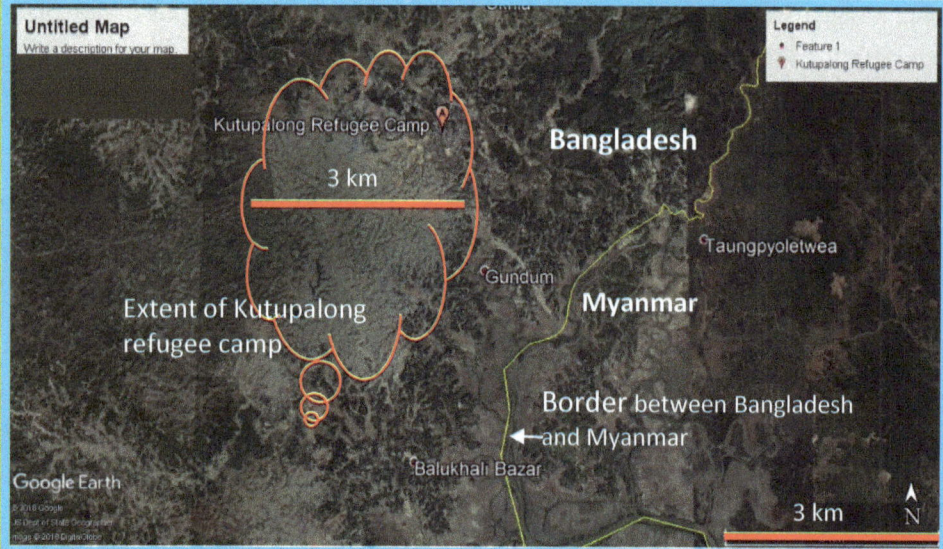

*Left* Image credit 6.38.1 *Google Earth* copyright photographic image of Kutupalong Refugee Camp with notes and graphics added by A. Whittingham.

*Below* Image credit 6.38.2 *One of the camps in Bangladesh*

**Tolerance of other faiths is a consciously cultivated virtue of the inclusive belief system of the Hindu people.**

This is exemplified by the willingness of India to host Buddhist refugees who fled Tibet in the years following 1959. Similarly, in the second decade of the twenty first century, Bangladesh has hosted nearly 900,000 Muslim refugees, who fled for their lives from violence, persecution and death in their neighbouring homeland of Myanmar. (7)

**While Buddhist-majority Myanmar does not recognize members of the Rohingya Muslim minority as citizens, referring to them pejoratively as "illegal Bengali immigrants," government officials on the other side of the border refuse to classify them as refugees.**

Instead, Bangladeshi authorities consider them as *"forcibly displaced Myanmar citizens".* (8)

**The predominant religions that co-exist in both India and Bangladesh are Islam and Hinduism. By 2018, 80 % of India's population was Hindu. (9) By 2015, 90% of the Bangladeshi population was Moslem. (10)**

## 6.6 cont. Refugees grow vegetables on land around their shelters

*Given the particularly dense and challenging environment, the United Nations International Organisation for Migration (IOM) has put the case for gardens and landscape planning utilising some new technology at Kutupalong and the surrounding communities so well that I have included their description in full below.*

**Above** Image credit 6.39  **A Rohinga woman with her micro gardening kit in her camp**

"**IOM,** the UN Migration Agency, and the UN Food and Agriculture Organization (FAO) are distributing 50,000 vegetable gardening kits to tackle malnutrition and improve the diet of people affected by the Rohingya refugee crisis in Cox's Bazar, Bangladesh. . . .

" Many were already suffering from malnutrition due to poverty and discrimination in Myanmar. Now reliant on basic food rations of rice, lentils, cooking oil and spices distributed by aid agencies every two weeks, the refugees, particularly children under five years old, urgently need to diversify their diet. Local families also need access to more diverse and nutritious food.

" The micro gardening initiative, which will provide seeds and tools to 50,000 families – 25,000 in the refugee camps and 25,000 in host villages in Ukhiya and Teknaf sub-Districts – is part of a USD 3 million programme to promote home gardening and larger-scale production among local farmers. The initiative is funded by the US State Department's Bureau of Population, Refugees and Migration (PRM). Almost half of the households receiving the kits are female-headed.

"In the coming months, we'll be able to have leaves and vegetables regularly," said 27-year-old Hamida, a young mother living in the Kutupalong-Balukhali mega camp with her husband and two children, who recently received a micro gardening kit. "Now we only eat them when we have money to buy them in the market. Otherwise we just eat rice and lentils or sometimes just rice with some chili and salt," said Hamida.

"The kits mean that they (the refugees) can grow leaves and vegetables on whatever land they have around their shelters. They can also sell the extra produce," said Mohammad Abul Kalam, Commissioner of Bangladesh's Refugee Relief and Repatriation Commission (RRRC) in Cox's Bazar, who handed over the first kits in the Ukhiya sub-district complex. "This will enable people to live better," he added.(11)

"Local day labourer Rashid Ahmed, 48,

# 6.1 concluding remarks: micro gardens & new technology

The refugees are not allowed by law to work in Bangladesh but many escape the camps and find jobs, forcing down wages for the long term local Bangladeshi population. This creates angst. (11)

**Above** Image credit 6.40 Rohinga **workers on a fish farm near Cox's Bazaar in Bangladesh.**

**(cont)**

**agreed** "Buying leaves and vegetables regularly from the market isn't possible. But we can have it almost every day if I grow it myself." said Rashid, who is the only person earning money in his seven-member family. "It will bring in some money as well. I can earn at least 100 taka (USD 1.19) a week selling the extra produce," he added.

As part of the kits, families received red amaranth, high-iron spinach, lady fingers, long yard beans and pumpkin seeds. They also got compost, a spade and a watering can. The kits include a watertight, 60-litre food storage drum to prevent mould and infestation of food stocks, which will be essential in the coming wet season. Local families received a slightly different kit, as most have bigger kitchen garden areas than the refugees. All the beneficiaries received basic training in micro gardening techniques.

"The initiative mainly focuses on providing high quality, nutritious food to improve nutrition at the household level, but also focuses on production capacity and farm-to-market strategies for farmer groups," said Peter Agnew, FAO's Emergency Response Coordinator in Cox's Bazar.

"We're also introducing new technology to the communities, as it's been successful in producing high-nutrition vegetables for the refugee population and providing some income generation for the host community." FAO is implementing a five-year project with Bangladesh's Department of Agricultural Extension (DAE).

"Seven months into the crisis, it's not only the refugees, but also the host community that needs assistance," said Manuel Pereira, IOM's Emergency Coordinator in Cox's Bazar. "The speed of the influx of refugees put huge pressure on local agriculture and the food supply chain.

There are 400,000 people among the refugees and host communities who currently need nutrition support. This initiative will improve their nutritional status. It will also contribute to mitigating an expected 50,000 metric tonne annual food deficit in Cox's Bazar," he added. (12)

# 6.6.2 Bangladesh's gardens

*"... these areas have been repeatedly affected by cyclones, heavy rainfall, flooding, salt damage caused by sea level rise and snow melting from the Himalayas, resulting in extremely low agricultural production."* (13) Such is the plight of many in Bangladesh as climate change takes hold in the 21st century.

**Despite** these afflictions, the people of the coastal deltas of Bangladesh have not suffered any loss of the freely available sunshine and light. Utilizing that as the energy source, (plus their hard work), they make Dhap, or floating, soil-less gardens of tightly packed hyacinth plants, (which are regarded as weeds).

Water Hyacinth is extracted from the vast quantities that accumulate in the Ganges delta. It is then labouriously packed onto rafts to make the Dhaps. This work tends to be done by local people who do not own land on higher ground. The nutrient rich waters of the Ganges Delta mean fertilisers are not required.

As part of their coping strategy and motivation for making dhaps, Bangladeshis have a term for seasonal hunger: *Mongo*.

> " Local communities didn't chose the way to conquer this severe environment, but chose the way to cope with the surrounding nature." (14)

In 2015 the floating gardens were declared by the Food and Agriculture Organization (FAO) as one of the world's 34 types of *"Globally Important Agricultural Heritage Systems."* (15)

**Right** Image credit 6.41.2 **this floating garden includes a fish** enclosure and a shed for ducks.

Fish are harvested from the water before it recedes in the winter. If storms or waves have not destroyed the rafts, they are then left in situ, or moved to higher ground, where they form compost for winter crops.

It is reported that although small farmers face competition from commercial landowners for the best spots to anchor the dhaps, for 60 – 90% of the population, this form of gardening is their major and best livelihood option. (16)

Image credit 6.41.1

# 6.6.3 Jaipur's organic gardens

*As an example of innovation with sunlight and 21st century technology in India, a Jaipur based company developed an innovative rooftop organic farming system. By 2020, twenty five percent of households in Jaipur are expected to be participating in the system. (17) Six million people live in Jaipur and the government's water management program provides subsidies for drip irrigation systems. The motivation is tackle the city's dropping water tables as well as climate change.*

**As** an example of the spreading urban organic movement in India, one company has set itself three goals to achieve by 2020: Firstly to create one million organic homes; secondly to cover one million square feet with living green walls and thirdly to become the largest urban farming company in the world.

The company states that with government subsidies for drip irrigation systems, each household can produce around 100 – 120 kilograms of food per year. (18) As one of the participants said:

> " It's really very simple. Nature comes back with a force but we just have to give it a little bit of space and a little bit of time . . ." (19)

That sentiment is very much in accord with the second '*Light Garden*' principle that is described in Chapter 10 of this book: **Allow ecosystems the *space & time* they need to rejuvenate.**

**Top left** Image credit 6.42.1 *A father and son* proudly stand by their rooftop garden in Jaipur.
**Centre left** Image credit 6.42.2 *Close up view of a productive rooftop garden.*
**Botton left** Image credit 6.42.3 *A newspaper in Bangalore, India presents information* about common food items containing banned pesticides in "*quantities a thousand times higher than permissible*".

6.42

# 6.6.4 Summary

*In the 21st century many media images depict the rapidly expanding urban areas of India, where there are plenty of lights but hardly a tree to be seen. However to imagine that India has ever separated from its farms and gardens - and its celebration of light and colour - would be as unlikely as India ever separating from its history.*

**As** Dr Vandana Shiva said in 2018,

*" The Holi Festival is a festival of colours. It has been made toxic. Come to Navdanya and celebrate a toxic free Holi . . . Make Holi a Festival of the real colors of nature!"* (19)

In recent decades there has been a tendency for toxic, factory-made powders to flood the market in India and supplant these safe, natural alternatives. However, as illustrated below at Navdanya, they have produced the traditional, natural plant based colours used for sprinkling coloured powders at the Holi Festival. (20)

As part of the wider program at Navdanya the gardeners and farmers, like millions of others across the nation, are harnessing ancient knowledge, new technology and the power of sunlight to help preserve biodiversity and enact their vision for India to become a modern, biodiverse, organic civilization.

Supporting this vision are the innumerable temple gardens where the flames of faith and pilgrimage burn bright. Irrigated rooftop terrace gardens are greening the cities. Famous gardens such as the Taj Mahal are more popular than ever.

Rivers of refugees pour into Bangladesh. Using micro-garden technology provided in the refugee camps, these people too are harvesting the energy of sunlight to grow food plants in whatever space they have available.

They are all part of non-violent green revolution that continues to evolve in India and Bangladesh during the 21st century.

**Right** Image credit 6.43.1 ***Dr Vandana Shiva: physicist, activist, international speaker and gardener,*** demonstrating how to make the plant based colours of Holi.

# Chapter 7
# Europe

Previous page Image credit 7.1

# Table of Contents Chapter 7

| | |
|---|---|
| Introduction: Welcome to Europe | 7.4 |
| Europe in the 21$^{st}$ century | 7.5 |
| Paris, City of Lights | 7.6 |
| Flowing reflected light | 7.8 |
| Translucent petals and seeds | 7.9 |
| Beauty and the Bulb | 7.10 |
| Tulips and Turnips | 7.11 |
| Harvesting the lux | 7.12 |
| Keukenhof Pools of Light | 7.13 |
| More starkly defined design | 7.14 |
| Keukenhof - plan | 7.15 |
| Keukenhof – simplified plan | 7.16 |
| More gardens of light and shade – transition zones | 7.17 |
| Flowers in light and shade | 7.18 |
| Keukenhof – light transitions | 7.19 |
| The infinite light of Versailles | 7.20 |
| Concluding poem: stones and streams | 7.21 |

# Europe

**Like** all the continents, Europe is a diverse place. In this chapter I can only touch upon a few examples of European life, with the aim of highlighting yet another aspect of the *'Light Garden'* principles that underlie design with light. Much as I would like to highlight the initiatives of Europe in addressing the global sustainability agenda of the 21st century through innovations such as strong achievements in limiting carbon emissions, I have chosen in this chapter to focus more on techniques of working with light at the scale of gardens for human use.

The simple rural scene below illustrates a hillside with abundant sunlight. The people who live here do so with time honoured customs that inherently exercise some restraint on the way in which natural resources, (including light), are used. For example, unlike the urban sprawl of so many contemporary urban settlements, there is a clean-cut edge between the agricultural landscape and the urban footprint of the village. This is a positive sign of a culture that values the natural resources of the land and exercises restraint in how they are used.

Restraint also is apparent in the containment of the road corridor within the landscape, so that the view across the landscape is not dominated by the road, as often occurs with roads constructed in the 21st century. Restraint in the use of building materials is also evident. The light we see reflected off fields, walls and roofs is not in the large, bright, shiny expanses that are often seen in 21st century towns with warehouses and shopping centre car parks.

Instead, the reflected light is controlled by a limited colour palette and the limited scale of the building units and fields. The outcome of this creates a place that attracts visitors. This in turn enhances the wealth of property owners and local residents, who welcome visitors but none the less limit the number who can come to share their hospitality.

In contrast to this culture of restraint, at the conclusion of this chapter there is reference to the mid 17th century Palace of Versailles. Historians have noted that the design principles used at Versailles were perpetuated for centuries, through to the redesign of Paris in the 19th Century. Perhaps in comparing the cultures of restraint and indulgence, we shall find the presence of more Light Gardens!

**Below** Image credit 7.4 ***The abundant light on this hillside is transformed into the wealth of vineyards.***

# Europe in the 21st century

*The map below shows the extent of Europe in the second decade of the 21st century. There were about 50 countries in Europe at this time and some of the are labeled for ease of reference.*

**Below** Map Image credit 7.5.1

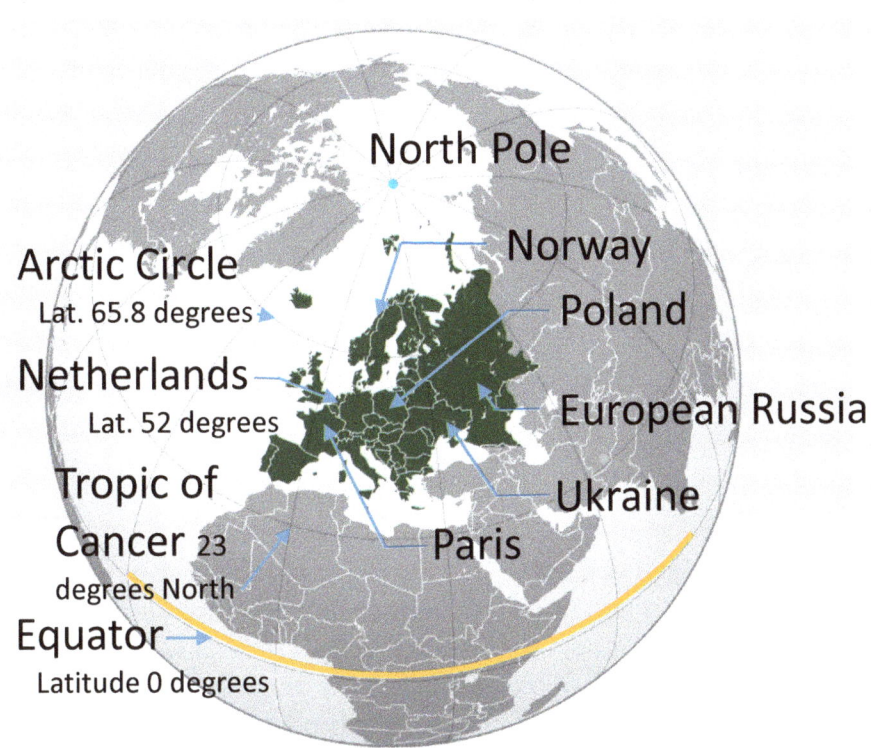

**Throughout** Europe and in many other parts the world, *travel and tourism* is classified as a significant sector of the economy. For a number of years it has accounted for about 10% of global gross domestic product and for one in ten of jobs globally. (1)

In addition, about 4.4 % of jobs in the European Union are in the agricultural sector. This includes food gardens, farms, the flower trade and horticultural activity. (2) Thus in Europe, the combined economic importance of agricultural, gardening, horticultural, tourism, landscape management, nature conservation and similar activities accounts for about 20% of employment. All these occupations rely upon *equitable access to sunlight* as the power source that drives plant growth and creates attractive, liveable places where people want to be. Let us now look at one of those places: Paris.

*Below left* Image credit 7.5.2
*Below right* Image credit 7.5.3

# Paris, City of Lights

*From the earliest years of the 19th century, Napoleon Bonaparte set the goal of making Paris the most beautiful city in the world.* (3)

**Below** Image credit 7.6.1 **Paris. The cluster of high rise buildings** on the skyline is consciously located away from the precinct of the beautiful 19th Century boulevards and Eiffel Tower.

**Below** Image credit: 7.6.2 **Paris by night**

**Below** Image credit: 7.6.3 **A light filled, people friendly, tree lined boulevard of Paris**

**This** work continued in the mid 19th Century under Napoleon Bonaparte's nephew, Emperor Napoleon III. He appointed Baron Haussmann to redesign Paris with a new level of city infrastructure.

Continuing in this genre, the Eiffel Tower was constructed for the Paris World Expo in 1889. Due to its sound engineering, appropriate location and beautiful fractal proportions, it was an immediate popular success. However, it has endured as a centre-piece in the skyline because the citizens of Paris have been willing and able to exercise restraint to avoid more recent structures blocking views to the tower. This is an example of the application of *'Light Garden'* Principle 9: *Human Use within a culture of intelligent restraint.*

As illustrated above left, the cluster of high rise buildings in Paris is located at a sufficient distance away from the tower that they do not interfere with views around the tower. The Eiffel Tower is the most visited, paid-entry landmark in the world and draws the endless admiration of some seven million tourists each year. (4)

The work that Baron Haussman commenced in Paris in the 19th century included firstly the introduction of underground railway stations, which were new technology at the time. They required significant re-design of relevant parts of the city. In conjunction with this, streets were redesigned so that they were wide enough to be tree lined boulevards which accommodated pedestrians, cyclists and vehicles. Thirdly the work (continued from previous page), **included** efforts to eliminate the epidemics of disease that had plagued the city for centuries. This was done through the provision of a safe and healthy system of underground water, gas and sewerage. (5)

**Paris soon became known as the City of Light for several reasons**. Although Haussmann's vision was criticized by some residents because it involved the removal of old, low cost housing in poorly drained alleyways where people had lived for centuries, in effect the enlightened approach inherent in the new city design benefited all citizens. This was through provision of features such as illuminated boulevards where all people could walk in safety; new public parks and the integrated water, gas and sewerage system that was safe, clean and accessible to all.

A second reason for Paris becoming known as the City of Lights was that the French Impressionist movement, (which started in 1874), coincided with Haussmann's' work. The impressionist artists such as Monet and Degas celebrated and consciously painted light, whether it was in the city or the country.

In 2015 Paris was host city for the *United Nations Framework Convention on Climate Change,* which led to signing of the Paris Agreement in 2016. This agreement was first international effort by signatory nations to combat climate change and added a new layer of meaning to term *The City of Lights.*

Just as the Eiffel Tower is a distinctive urban landmark, so too the horticultural practices of Europe form distinctive landscapes. They illustrate conscious management of the Earth's resources to achieve the combination of light and temperature that people and plants need in order to flourish.

There are many traditions of European sustainable farm, garden and landscape management practices. Bearing that in mind, in the remainder of this chapter I refer to the cultivation of the humble tulip as an example of a typically European way of managing '*Light Gardens"* and using plants to harvest light.

*Below* Image credit 7.7 ***The city of Paris.***

# Flowing, reflected light

*Thousands of tulips may be closely planted in European gardens such as Keukenhof in Holland but as illustrated below, although this takes careful planning and great precision, there also is a cultural sensitivity that lends a sense of free flowing, natural forms in the landscape, rather than the flowers being merely showpieces.*

## Tulips at Keukenhof

**These** flowing bands of flowers beside the lake create a feeling of the abundance of nature. The human eye has grown accustomed to seeing green foliage in such views but why is foliage coloured green, whilst flowers come in so many different hues?

That question takes us back to the process of photosynthesis. Plants use sunlight to create food. Of all the wavelengths of sunlight, the green frequency is the least useful to plants in the process of photosynthesis. So the green wavelengths are reflected back off the surface of the foliage, rather than absorbed as an energy source for photosynthesis.

Let us now look more closely at the human intervention that has used light in creative ways to structure this garden at Keukenhof. Thousands of tulips have been planted in a band of sunlight beneath the trees. There is consistent, careful attention to the spacing between each plant, so each one obtains suitable sunlight, airflow and nutrients.

The nutrients flow first to roots and leaves, before the flowers that bloom. Just as in a mixed vegetable garden, different types of plants not only have different colours, they also grow to different heights and grow best in combination with certain other plants and organisms such as the soil mycorrhizae.

***Below Keukenhof. Figure 7.8*** Image credit 7.8

# Translucent petals & seeds

*By considering these details, we can see that tulip cultivation in Europe embodies several of the 'Light Garden' principles outlined in Chapter One. For example, there is careful measurement and sophisticated awareness of human perception in how the bulbs are planted out. This reflects application of principle number seven: Measurement and Perception.*

**There** is also restraint exercised in the human use of these gardens, which are open to the public for a limited season each year. *'Light Garden'* principle number 9 refers to *Human Use* that is appropriately constrained in partnership with other *"Light Garden'* principles such as *Context and Environment,* (principle number 8).

Gardeners cultivate *Context and Environment* conditions in the soil of their gardens over many years to ensure the long term viability of the garden and the wider environment in which the garden and all other creatures exist. This occurs not just in Holland but all around the world. Refer for example to the plan of the cultivated area tended by Jorama Onjimbo in Kenya, Africa, (Chapter 5) and to the photographs of the biodiverse gardens of Bali in Chapter 2.

**In addition to space and light**, tulip bulbs need eight to 15 weeks of chilling at 35 to 55 degrees Fahrenheit, or they will not produce shoots and flowers. For each plant variety, there is an optimal temperature for vegetative growth, with growth dropping off as temperatures increase or decrease. **Similarly,** there is a range of temperatures at which many plants will produce seed. For example, corn will fail to reproduce at temperatures above 95 °F (35 °C) and soybeans above 102 °F (38.8 °C). (6) .

In the cut - away view below of the translucent petals of a tulip, we see a ring of golden stamens as they prepare for launch. As the petals unfold, the stamens move up towards the sun, then release pollen. Centuries of human intervention and breeding of tulips has not deterred the stamens from this essential task.

A tulip garden may be a thing of beauty to the human eye but to the tulip, it is a chance to produce seeds and propagate with the help of sun, wind and insects. When planning for the preservation of the natural world we need to bear this in mind. Don't crowd things. We need to leave space for flowers to catch the light and to wave gently in the breeze.

This is an example of 'Light Garden' principle number 2: allow the space and time that is needed for life processes and ecological systems to co-exist.

***Below*** Image credit 7.9 ***Tulip stamens and petals***

# Beauty and the Bulb

*What is it about a flower that means people will pay a lot of money for some flowers, such as tulips and roses, but dispose of others that may be similar, such as wild turnips?*

**Once** it reaches the flowering stage, the wild turnip, *Brassica rapa* ssp sylvestris, is *a tall competitive annual weed, capable of causing large reductions in crop yields due to competition for light, nutrients and water.* (7)

This statement emphasises the competitive environment in which cultivated plants and weeds grow. For example, a tulip bulb, (depicted below right), is similar to a turnip bulb, which is depicted below left. Similarly, as it swells with age, the root system of a wild turnip forms a storage organ that is similar to that of the crop species turnip bulb, but much smaller in size.

This may point to the answer to the question about why tulips are considered beautiful.

Tulips and turnips have been cultivated from Wild species to be what humans desire over hundreds of years.

Turnips have been cultivated as useful food plants and tulips have been cultivated for their perceived beauty, which not least of all arises from how the flowers interact with light.

*Top left* Image credit 7.10.1 **A yellow tulip.**

*Middle left* Image credit 7.10.2 **A wild turnip flower.**

*Bottom left* Image credit 7.10.3 **Turnip vegetable bulbs**

*Above right* Image credit 7.10.4 **Tulip bulb**

# Tulips and turnips

*Tulips petals have a translucent quality that allows sunlight to shine through them. Is this just so that they appear more beautiful when we look at them, or are there other reasons?*

*Having considered tulip cultivation on the previous pages and how it incorporates a number of 'Light Garden' principles, we can begin to glimpse how it also incorporates principle number five: 'Multiplication effects and scale'. This is a natural phenomenon that tulip growers are aware of. They plant vast drifts of flowers that capture the human imagination, beyond (and as a multiplication effect of) the beauty of each flower.*

**As** we have seen, the form of flower petals is highly relevant to whether we will find two otherwise quite similar flowers, (such as tulips and turnips), either irresistibly attractive (and something that we are willing to pay for), or as something to be disregarded.

Millions of people each year go to gardens to experience the tulips. Millions of people do not go to gardens to look at turnip flowers each year. However they may be glad to eat turnips. Hence the concept of *Light Gardens* is relevant to all these people, whether they are surviving by eating turnips in the freezing conditions of Uzbekistan, (which has by far the highest per capital consumption of turnips in the world), or whether they are planning a holiday to enjoy the tulip gardens of Holland.

Turnips that have been cultivated as crop vegetables from wild species are amongst the top ten vegetables, in terms of global annual consumption of vegetables. Available statistics tell us that 42.7 million metric tons of carrots and turnips combined were produced in 2016. (8) This may be compared to the annual global production of about 119,066 tons of tulip bulbs. (9)

According to NASA statistics, The Netherlands is the largest grower of tulip bulbs in the world, producing 4.2 billion annually and exporting half of these. (10) So we are talking about big business when it comes to this type of Light Garden, powered by the sun and human labour.

We cannot take the space and light needed for gardens and landscapes for granted. Already in the second decade of the 21$^{st}$ century we are seeing Governments auctioning off the planet's airspace. For example in 2018 the United States Secretary of the Interior announced that the Bureau of Ocean Energy Management was planning to auction off the offshore wind farm rights for an area near Massachusetts. (11)

As with all other natural resources on this planet, such as fresh water and clean air, there will be competition for the resources of light and space, unless we can learn new ways to coexist with the growth of living creatures in *'Light Garden'* places and landscapes. What is being done to ensure that there *will* be light and space for flowers, people, bees and other creatures to turn their heads towards? One approach is the work of the Intergovernmental Panel on Climate Change (IPCC), which in October 2018

*" issued its bleakest report yet this week, saying that without drastic changes, the world doesn't have a hope of avoiding uncontrollable climate change. Unless*

# Harvesting the lux

*Horticultural products, including flower bulbs, are a significant part of the Dutch economy. 77 % of bulbs traded internationally come from the Netherlands.* (13)

*emissions are halved within 12 years and virtually eliminated by 2050, temperature increases will likely exceed 2 degrees Celsius."* (12)

That same report refers to "tipping points" such as melting of the permafrost. Once tipping points are past, global temperature increases are likely to continue to grow exponentially. (14)

In my native country of Australia, in the summer of 2018 – 19, we officially recorded an average 2 degree increase in temperature, which is more than the IPCC target of limiting increases to 1.5 degrees Celsius. (15) **Such temperature increases have rapid economic impacts. For example, imagine the impact on the Dutch economy if temperatures rose to the extent that winters were not cool enough for tulip bulbs to sprout and artificial chilling was not viable.**

Continuing with this example in more detail, I would now like to describe how light is used as part of the design of Keukenhof, a famous garden in Holland, where the beauty of the flowers boosts the local economy. Over a million tourists come to visit the gardens of Keukenhof during just two months of Spring each year. For similar reasons, even larger numbers of tourists visit famous gardens in Asian centers such as Kyoto and Hangzhou. More detail about these North Asian gardens is provided in Chapter Three.

In the Netherlands, Keukenhof gardens cover an area of 32 hectares ( 79 acres). Each year they are planted with 7 million bulbs. (16) On a bright sunny day in maximum sunlight, up to 100,000 lux of illumination may fall upon a garden as the flowers burst forth. In the shaded parts of the gardens on the same day, the illumination is more likely to be about 20,000 lux.

In contrast, on a cloudy, overcast day, 1,000 – 2,000 lux may be present. During a storm, the illumination may drop to less than 200 lux. One lux is equal to one lumen of visible light, which is otherwise known as *luminous flux*. Illumination measures the intensity of light falling upon a surface. Hence the intensity of light falling upon a flower in full sun on a bright, clear day (say 100,000 lux) is 5 times more intense then the intensity of light falling upon a flower growing in the shade on that same day, (say 20,000 lux). (17)

While light intensities are low, the rate of photosynthesis increases proportionately with increases in light intensity. *The more photons of light that fall on a leaf, the greater the number of chlorophyll molecules that are ionised and the more ATP and NADPH are generated.* (18)

However, above an optimum temperature, the rate of photosynthesis begins to decrease, as the enzymes involved lose their structure and cease to function normally. (19) Tulip growers and all agriculturalists will thus keep a close eye on the weather while trying to maintain optimal growing conditions for their crops, as they plan to coincide with peak tourist seasons, festivals, big sale orders and so on.

# Keukenhof pools of light

*Keukenhof gardens in Holland, (the Netherlands), are famous for the beauty of the tulips. However the beauty and economic viability of the gardens does not exist in isolation and is the result of a diverse range of teamwork skills passed down through the generations.*

**At** Keukenhof, In addition to the flowers, the garden designers skilfully play with pools of light on lawns, streams and foliage. As shown in the plan on the following page, a system of streams and pools threads through the site. There are many layers of meaning to the concept of "Pools of light" that meander as dappled light through this garden.

Try to imagine the view depicted below on a cloudy day, when the pools of light would be absent. What a difference it would make if there were no bright patches of light upon the lawn and flowers to contrast with the darker shades of trees and shrubs.

The molten, reflective surface of the water forms another pool of light, with gentle ripples from the fountains making their way towards the viewer. These features of the design help to develop a sense of depth, perspective and tranquility. Following the light, our eye tends to meander peacefully from the blue, pink and white flowers in the foreground, on to the tree trunks and the line of tall red tulips in the background shrubbery.

***Below*** Image credit 7.13

# More starkly defined design

*Pools of light can be molten, like in the water. They can be meandering, as through the lawns and flowers . . . and they can be more starkly defined in multiple patches, as illustrated below.*

**Below** Image credit 7.14 ***Keukenhof***

**Changing** the contrast of the photograph helps us appreciate the "pools of light" concept as applied in this garden.

Here the design is made to look more like what you might see in a colouring-in book. There are primarily black outlines for shapes, with some shading added. It is easy to see that the structure of the design remains the same but the impact is quite different. Explore the different impact of different colours of light by adding your own

.

"pools of light" with colouring pencils, or paints over the image on this page.

If you are not sure where to start, make a few copies of the image and try out different colour themes. You might also like to look back over the previous page where we talked about pools of light on the lawns, flowers and water. Try to also develop a sense of perspective and distance with the colours that you choose for your design.

# Keukenhof – plan

*The Master plan of Keukenhof gardens is shown below. Wherever there is blue water, larger open green lawns or pathways, we know there is the chance for pools of light to enter the garden. The darker green trees and shrubs provide the framework for the garden.*

**This** plan illustrates how a garden that is consistently rated amongst the world's top ten most beautiful gardens, has been created with a mixture of some basic geometry to the plan layout, plus many meandering pathways. However when one looks at photographs taken by visitors to Keukenhof, it is the views of meandering flowerbeds and water that people chose to photograph. The garden pool illustrated on the previous page is an interesting example, where the shape of the pool introduces a formal geometric element into an otherwise meandering, informal layout.

*Below*: Numerous waterways offer opportunities for pools of light to enter the garden

*Below*: Open lawns, garden beds and paths offer more opportunities for pools of light to enter the garden. Trees are shown in dark green and buildings in grey

*Above* Image credit 7.15.1
*Below* Image credit 7.15.2

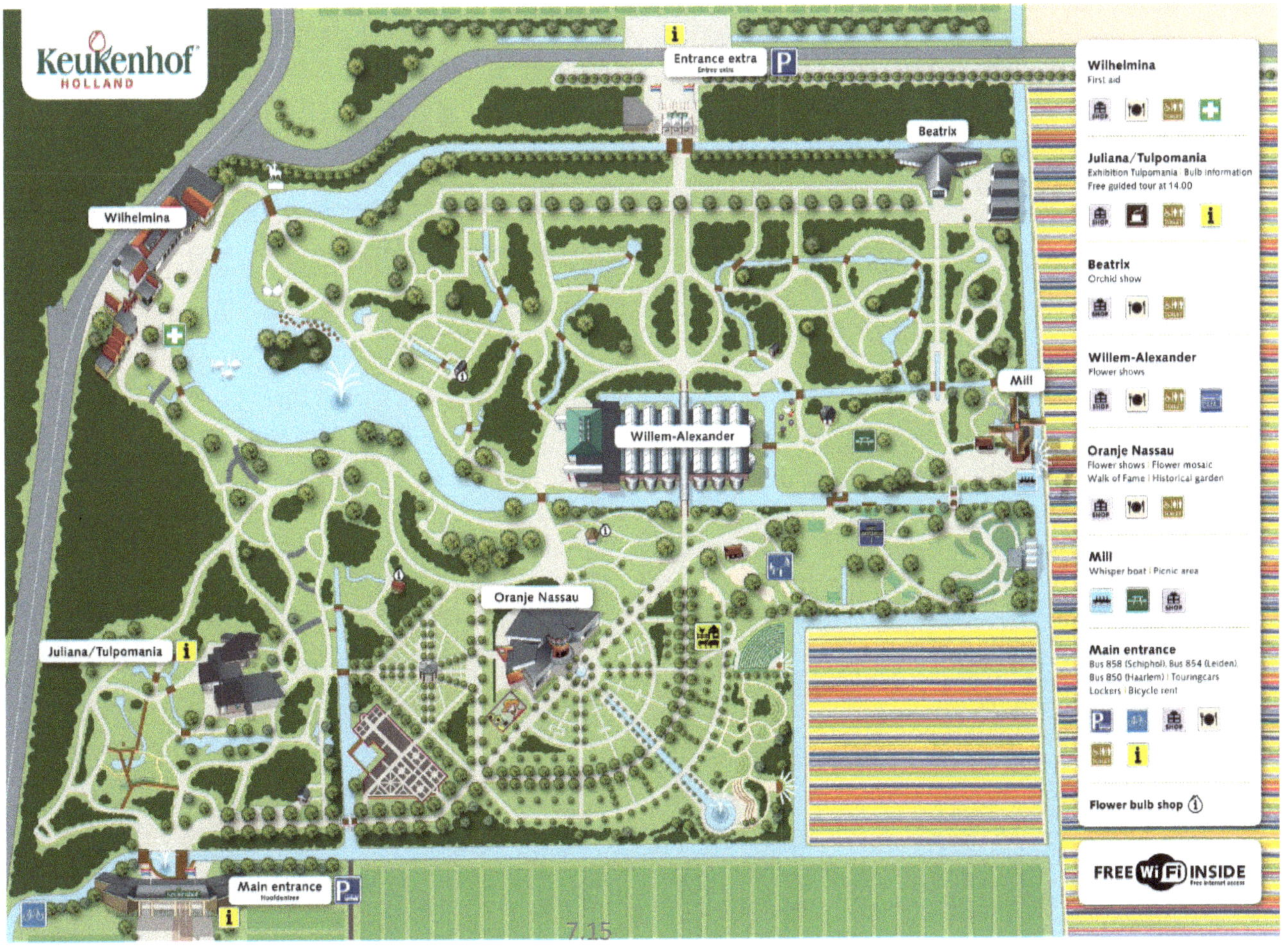

# Keukenhof – simplified plan

*Once again, (as was done earlier with one particular garden within the grounds of Keukenhof), the Keukenhof Master plan has been reduced to the simplified black and white drawing below.*

**Below** Image credit 7.16

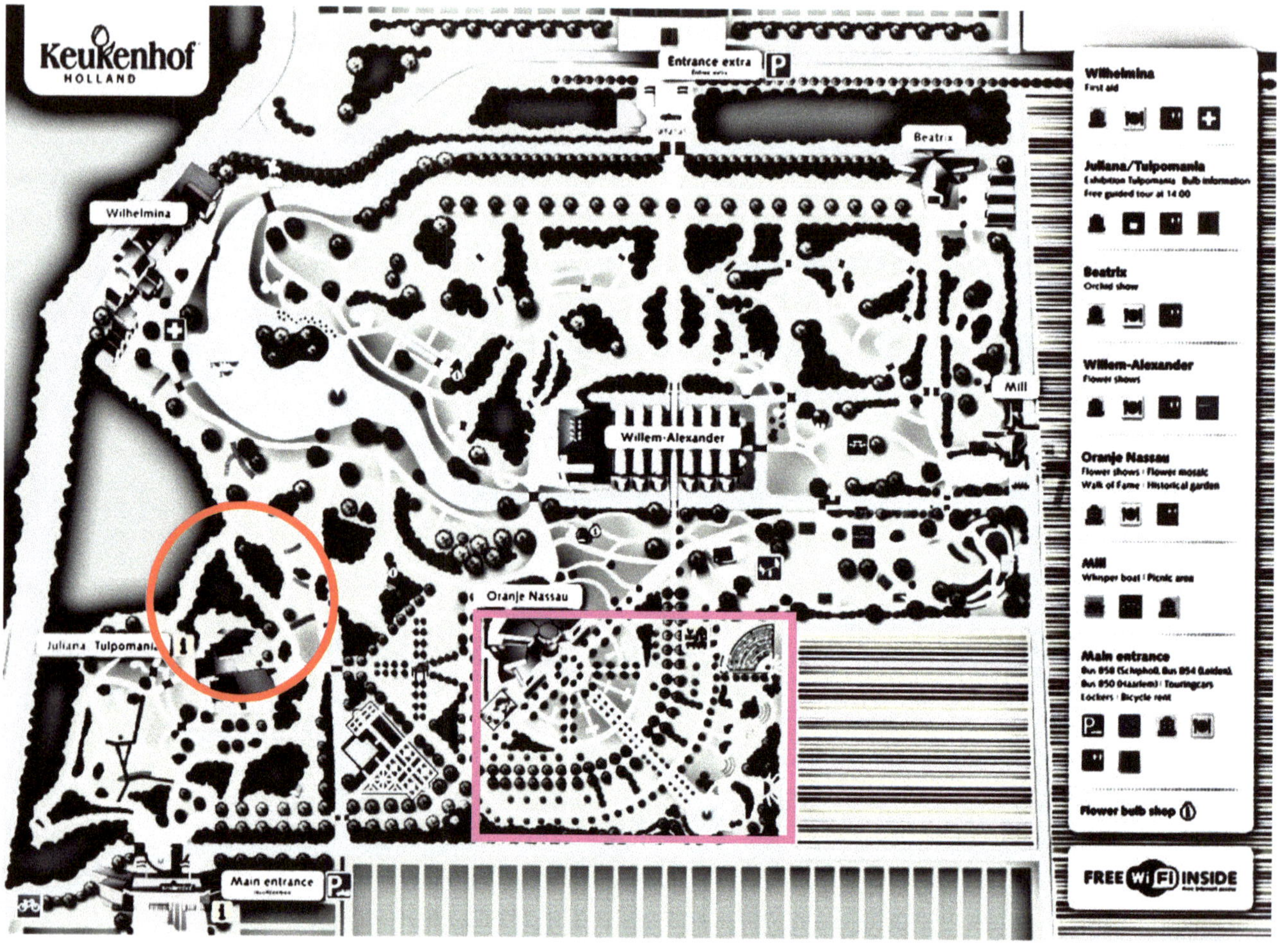

Massed vegetation on the plan is shown in shapes with crinkled black edges. The white areas between the crinkled edges represent open pathways and lawns. Wherever there is a crinkled green edge on plan, there is a zone of transition between sunlight and shade.

In addition to these irregular 'crinkled' edges, the formal gardens of the *Oranje Natasha* lie neatly within the shape of the pink golden mean rectangle that I have superimposed on the plan above. This reflects a common human desire for some geometry to aid in the legibility of a site. It also illustrates the relevance and common human desire for two more *'Light Garden'* principles: Numbers four *'Lines, patterns and probabilities'* and Six *'Entanglement and Focal Points'*.

# More gardens of light and shade – transition zones

*Designing effective transition zones between sunlight and shadow is a part of landscape and garden design. Looking at the photograph below one can see a quite clear-cut edge between the shade of the shelters and the full sun on most of the lawn, without the subtle transitions between vegetation, light and shade that we have looked at so far at Keukenhof.*

***Above*** Image credit 7.17.1

**In** comparison to the image above, the popular tulip gardens in the flowing lawns of Keukenhof have more dappled light and irregular edges between different areas. In keeping with a common human preference for the shelter of dappled light, the people in the two photographs at right have chosen picnic tables with nearly full sun when wearing winter jackets and nearly full shade when not.

***Above*** Image credit 7.17.2

The images on this page show typical public parkland settings, designed as recreation areas in the contemporary Western style. The combination of lawns and shade tend to attract teachers, parents and grandparents to bring children to what is generally a safe, pleasant and convenient setting.

***Above*** Image credit 7.17.3

Children growing up without adequate exposure to outdoor light has become an issue in the 21st century. Exposure to sufficient hours of outdoor sunlight each week is particularly important for growing children, as recent research has proved that without this, their eyes grow too long and they become short sighted. (19)

***Right*** Image credit 7.17.4 ***garden designs for sun and shade*** (Example designs by Anne Whittingham)

7.17

# Flowers in light and shade

**Take** a close look at the two photographs below. The garden in the upper photograph is in full sun, with virtually no pools of light and shadow. Although hardy blue salvia and golden marigolds have been planted, as climate change takes hold, these flowers might do better with a little more protection from the sun. The garden depicted in the lower photographs has a greater sense of light and shade – and of edges that weave in and out, in a somewhat similar way to how the dappled light plays in pools across the lawns and gardens at Keukenhof.

*Below right* Image credit 7.18.1  *Below left* Image credit 7.18.2

**By comparing these photographs, we start to see how working with an awareness of *moving patterns of light can* create more microclimates, biological diversity and resilience in a garden.**

This concept applies regardless of the purposes for which a garden or landscape is managed, such as growing food, rejuvenation of biodiversity, or for play and pleasure.

# Keukenhof – light transitions

*A photograph illustrating some typical garden transition zones between sunlight and shadow is overlaid to the Google Earth aerial photograph (2018) of Keukenhof below.*

**The** aerial photograph shows how many more trees there are on the Keukenhof site compared to the nearby urban area and car parks. It is interesting to compare the tree density at Keukenhof with the nearby urban area and with a new 'Light Garden' urban development: *Sustainability City* in Dubai, where thousands of trees have been planted and all the car parks and buildings are covered with solar panels. (Refer plan lower left).

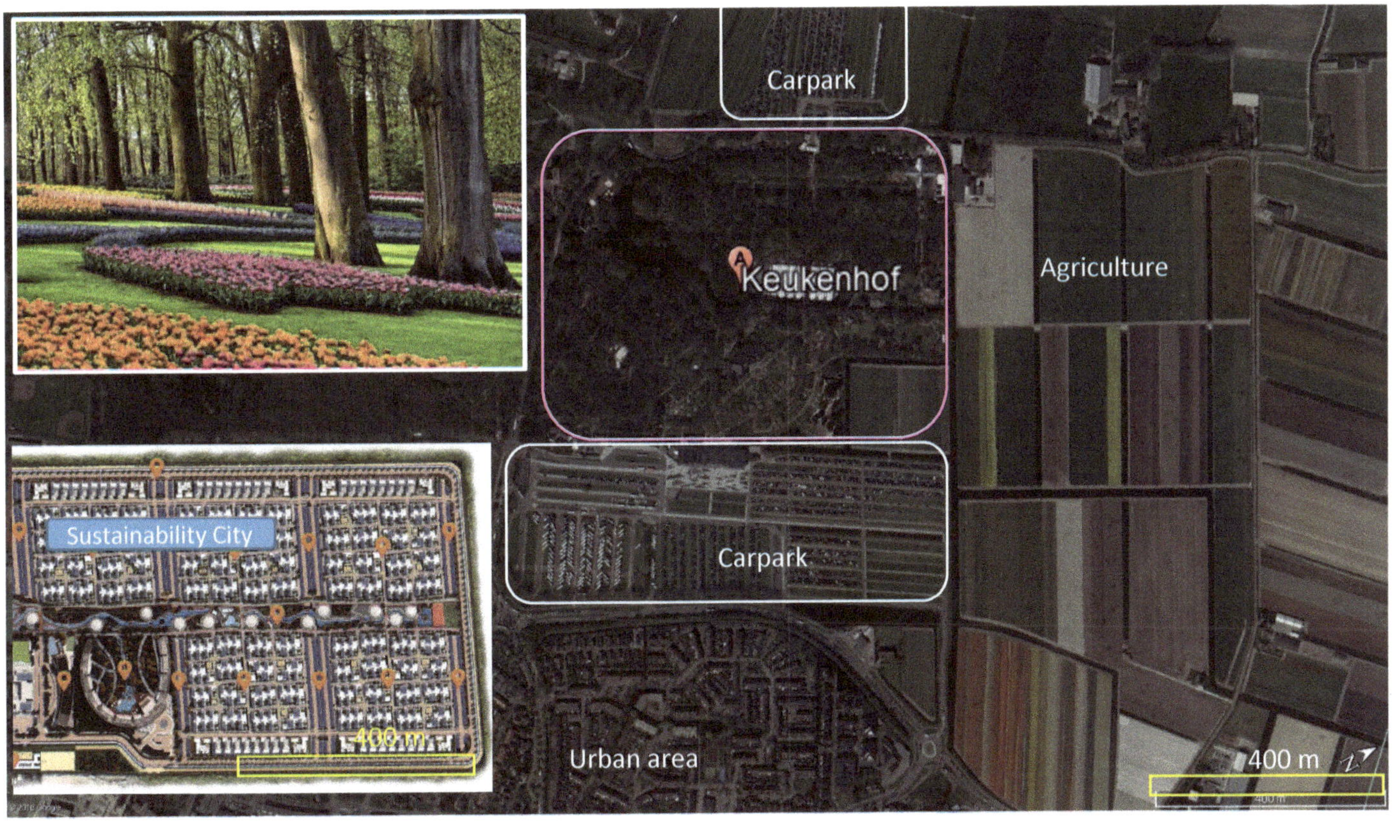

**Top above** Image credit 7.19.1 **Trees at Keukenhof.**
**Above left** Image credit 7.19.2 **the 46 hectare** site of Sustainability City in Dubai.
**Above aerial photo** Google Earth Image credit 7.19.3

**Right** Image credit 7.19.4. Although these gardens feature flowers, the design has many similar principles to food gardens, where intensively planted crops are interspersed with fallow ground. A mosaic of cultivated areas, within a larger framework of trees is developed. This is not unlike the central waterway spine shown above on the *Sustainability City plan.*

# The infinite light of Versailles

*In contrast to the tulip gardens, it is as though the 17th century French estates of Vaux - le - Vicomte and Versailles are expressions of a mindset that says all resources, including light, earth, water, air, space and manpower are unlimited and at the command of the property owner. The designs explore images of infinity, reflected light and vanishing points.*

**Top left** Image credit 7.20.1 **Vaux - le - Vicomte**

This landscape is the mid 17th century work of Landscape Architect Andre le Notre. The collaboration between Architect, Landscape Architect and Interior Designer on this project marked the beginning of what became known as the Louis XIV style.

> " To secure the necessary grounds for the elaborate plans for Vaux-le-Vicomte's garden and castle, Fouquet purchased and demolished three villages. The displaced villagers were then employed in the upkeep and maintenance of the gardens. It was said to have employed 18 thousand workers . . . " (20)

**Middle left** Image credit 7.20.2 **Versailles.**

Shortly after construction of Vaux – le Vicomte, King Louis XIV listened to advisers who spiked his jealously of Fouquet. The king sentenced Fouquet to life imprisonment. He then promptly commissioned Versailles, which was intended to be more grand than Vaux – le - Vicomte! (21)

**Lower left** Image credit 7.20.3 ***A more modest use of resources in a contemporary European village.***

Embodying many principles that are regarded as classical European style, gardens such as Versailles continue to attract tourists. However they are in stark contrast to the sustainability agenda of the 21st century, where attempts to rejuvenate planetary resources prevail, rather than allowing past practices that dissipated them to continue.

# Let all the children play 'midst Nature's stones and streams, with tales and treasures of the day, 'til nightfall brings them home to dreams.

In contrast to the 17th and 18th century monarchs of France, the contemporary Korean Royal Families chose to immerse themselves in gardens within natural settings. Their chosen activities, dedicated to the benefit of the nation, were ritual, study and contemplation. These were conducted around natural streams flowing through the palace grounds.

The aesthetic of such places contrasts strongly with that of Versailles. The natural flow of streams is nowhere to be seen there. Abstract expressions of light, water, space, vegetation and matter are patterned to create a sense of infinite human power. Beauty combined with power – or beauty combined with ceremony for community good and stewardship of the Earth: the choice is yours
– but which choice do you think will most benefit the Earth and the creatures thereon?

The whole concept of striving for beauty might be seen as a dualistic contradiction, if indeed beauty is conceived of an extraordinary phenomenon, rather than as the natural order of things, where natural environmental process are allowed to flow and human activity is restrained within the limits of nature.

Image credit 7.21

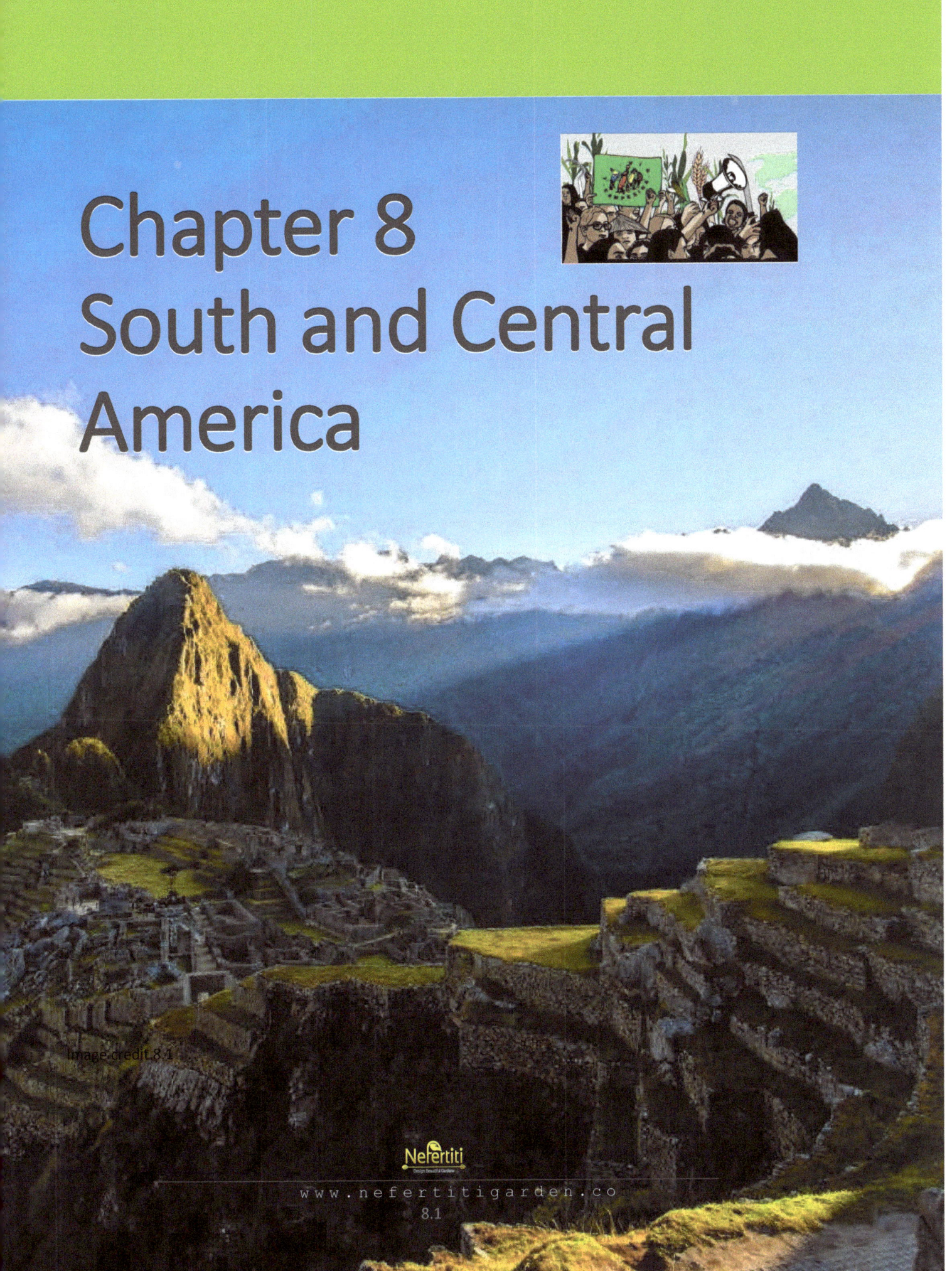

# Chapter 8
# South and Central America

Previous page Image credit 7.1

# Table of Contents Chapter 8

| | |
|---|---|
| South America in the 21$^{st}$ century | 8.4 |
| Sun Gods and access to Sunlight | 8.5 |
| Intensity of Light vs Latitude | 8.6 |
| Different intensities of Light | 8.7 |
| Light for the forests and fields | 8.8 |
| Timeline for Harvesting | 8.9 |
| The Incas and the Light Garden | 8.10 |
| The Incas: drama and longevity | 8.11 |
| The Incas: comparison to Bali | 8.12 |
| More Drama in the Landscape | 8.13 |
| Reflection and absorption of light | 8.14 |
| Colour, light and outline | 8.15 |
| A passionate heritage | 8.16 |
| Contemporary examples | 8.17 |

# South America in the 21st Century

*Below right* Map image credit 8.4.1 *The map illustrates how much of South America lies within the tropical zone of the planet.*
*Below left* Map image credit 8.4.2 *There are 12 countries in South America and those mentioned in this chapter are labeled for reference.*

**South America is a continent of contrasts.** Compare for example, the freedom symbolised by the Condor on the Bolivian Coast of Arms to the relative domesticity of a trout farm in Peru. Trout from farms, (rather than wild caught), is now one of the staple foods in the northern regions of South America.

*Right* Image credit 8.4.3 **Ceviche** is the national dish of Peru. The name comes from the indigenous quechua language word 'siwichi', which means fresh fish. (1)

*Below* Image credit 8.4.4 **The Bolivian Coat of Arms** on the National Flag. It features a condor at the top, plus the sun and an alpaca in the central motif.

*Left* Image credit 8.4.5 **Trout farms** are now an important source of fish in Peru.

# Sun Gods & access to sunlight

*The philosophical base underpinning the agricultural movements in Central and South America cannot be underestimated. In 1993, farmers' organizations in Central America were among the founders of La Vía Campesina. This group is now recognised by the United Nations as the world's largest family based, sustainable farmers' alliance group. It represents 200 million such groups globally and had been invited to make presentations to the United Nations Human Rights Council and the Food and Agricultural organisation (FAO).* (2)

As identified by La Via Campesina, in the 21$^{st}$ century "extractivism" has become widespread around the globe and includes activities firstly of land grabbing, where people who have lived in territories for centuries are forcibly removed by the governments of their own countries, who then allow foreign corporations to use or buy the land. This has been the experience of many people in South and Central America. Secondly it involves commandeering of access to other natural resources such as fresh water, oceans, seeds, soil and biodiversity *away* from local communities then r*eallocation* of them for use in large scale infrastructure projects such as dams, mines, large solar power plants or industrial scale farming, livestock raising and fishing.

> *" In many places, the people who defend themselves against and resist this "development" model face being demonised and criminalised, which in turn leads to prosecutions, imprisonment, violence at the hands of state or private security forces, and even murders. These are not random "incidents", they are occurrences reported by almost every organisation."* (3)

In 1993 at the Uruguay Round of the General Agreement of Tariffs and Trade (GATT) meeting, the *Trade Related Intellectual Property Rights* document and the World Trade Organisation's *Agreement on Agriculture* document were approved and signed by participating groups.

> *" These agreements caused backlash from many people around the world focusing on technical problems rather than the human right to access to food, especially for those living in the Global South. Globalization was under way at this time, affecting many industries including agriculture."* (4)

> *" **In South America,** Argentina lost more than one-third of its farms in the two decades from 1988 to 2008. Between 1997 to 2007, Chile lost 15% of its farms with the biggest farms doubling their average size, from 7,000 to 14,000 ha per farm. The United States has lost 30% of its farms in the last 50 years."* (5)

As reported by the United Nations in 2014, small farmers produce 70% of the world's food. However, in recent decades they now have access to less than 25% of the world's available farmland. This trend continues. (6)

As I write, I see access to sunlight developing as one of the next frontiers in this battle for resources. With access to light, comes access to food, good health, freedom of movement, recreation and the powerhouse of solar energy production. Also not to be underestimated is the blanketing effect of smoke from fires raging in the Amazon and elsewhere, as climate change takes hold faster than collective action to avoid it and resettle those people whose lives are endangered by it.

Image credit 8.5

# Intensity of light vs latitude

*On the previous page I talked about harvesting the abundant sunshine in South America but how we do measure sunshine and what exactly is being harvested? As illustrated in the graphs below, the intensity of light is measured in units known as lux. Plants harvest the energy of light to grow. The intensity of light at the equator is greater than at distances further away from it.*

**For example,** the graph at right illustrates how as latitude increases, (or distance from the equator increases), the amount of sunlight decreases. The amount of sunlight is measured in lux, as shown on the vertical bar on the left hand side of the graph.

**Below** Image credit 8.6.1 *Graph*

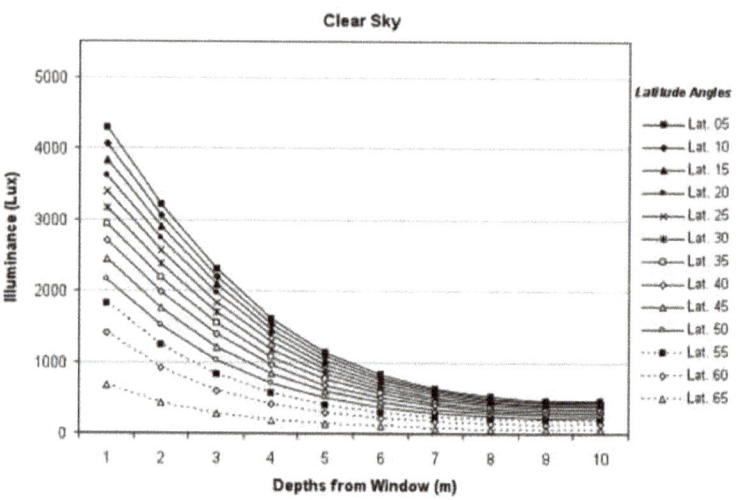

**Above** Image credit 8.6.2

**Above** The latitude is shown on the vertical bar on the right hand side of the graph. The amount of sunlight reaching a point indoors also decreases with distance from the window, as shown in the horizontal bar of the graph.

**Below:** Image credit 8.6.3 *Light, temperature, altitude and latitude* interact to affect the growth of plants. For example, low latitude maize is grown in South American countries such as Peru and is subject to global warming temperate changes. Fortunately, in South America there is a long history of experimenting with and developing multiple varies of maize that are adapted to different temperatures.

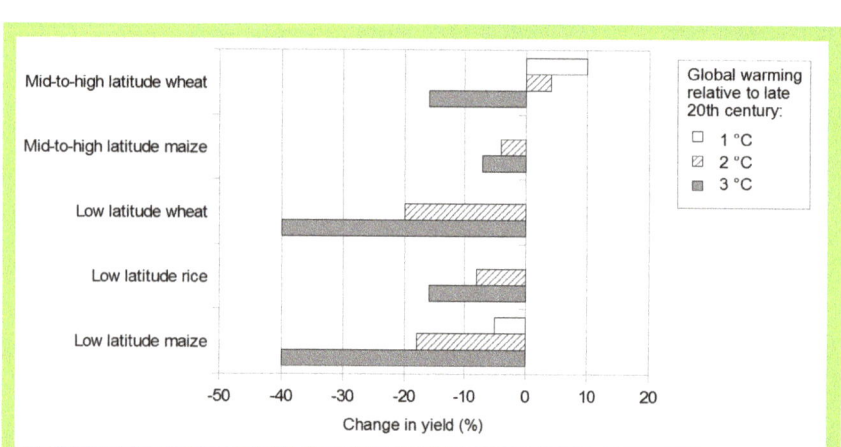

**Projected changes in crop yields at different latitudes with global warming.** This graph is based on data from several studies.

**Above** Image credit 8.6.4 *Corn*
For example as illustrated later in this chapter, the Incan site at Moray in Peru is one of several sites dating back to the 13th - 16th centuries where such innovation was carried out.

8.6

# Different intensities of light

In a moonlit garden, there is still enough light to see it but the intensity of the light is less than 1/100,000 of the illumination perceived by the human eye during the day. In addition, the intensity of sunlight in Central America (low latitude) is higher than at the southern tip of Argentina (higher latitude).

| Outdoor lighting conditions | Illuminance (lux) * |
|---|---|
| Brightest sunlight | 120,000 |
| Bright sunlight | 111,000 |
| AM 1.5 global solar spectrum sunlight | 109,870 |
| Shade illuminated by entire clear blue sky, midday | 20,000 |
| Typical overcast day, midday | 1,000 – 2,000 |
| Extreme of thickest storm clouds midday | < 200 |
| Sunrise or sunset on a clear day (ambient illumination) | 400 |
| Average general purpose indoor room lighting | 40 - 300 |
| Task lighting for close indoor work | > 1,000 |
| Fully overcast, sunset/ sunrise | 40 |
| Moonlight, extreme of thickest clouds | < 1 |

**Illuminance**

The definition of illuminance is: "*Illuminance is a measure of how much luminous flux is spread over a given area.*" (7)

**Above** Image credit 8.7.1 *Illuminance Table*
**Below right** Image credit 8.7.2

"One can think of luminous flux (measured in lumens) as a measure of the total "amount" of visible light present, and the illuminance as a measure of the intensity of illumination on a surface. A given amount of light will illuminate a surface more dimly if it is spread over a larger area, so illuminance is inversely proportional to area when the luminous flux is held constant. " (8)

# Light for the forests and fields

*The bright sunshine and natural beauty of the South American landscape is celebrated in local culture and surrounds the work of numerous smallholder farmers and gardeners, such as the Brazilian cotton farmers depicted below.*

**Reinforcing** the historic and present day significance of sunlight in South American cultures, the sun is an emblem found on the coat of arms of Bolivia. It is also part of the coat of arms of Ecuador and the historical flag of Peru. These three countries were part of the Incan Empire in South America.

In the Peruvian city of Cusco and many other parts of the continent, *Inti Raymi,* or the 'sun festival' is still celebrated each year at the time of Southern Hemisphere Winter Solstice. The festival originally was designed to celebrate the start of a new planting season. With tourism an important part of the 21st century economy of Peru, the festival in Cusco now attracts thousands of tourists each year to this ancient capital of the Incan empire.

Indicating the importance of light to the Incan civilization, the Inca ruler was believed to be a direct descendant of Inti, their primary God. Inti was the Sun God. Particularly in the highland parts of their empire, where the cool climate created more challenging growing conditions, sunlight also was valued because it was believed the heat of the sun caused rain, as well as powering the growth of food crops such as maize. (9)

**The** Inca dedicated many ceremonies to the Sun in order to ensure the Sapa Inca's welfare. During the rainy season the sun was hotter and brighter, while during the dry season it was weaker. The Incas would set aside large quantities of natural and human resources throughout the empire for Inti. Each conquered province was supposed to dedicate a third of their lands and herds to Inti as mandated by the Inca. Each major province would also have a Sun Temple.

Crops cultivated across the **Inca** Empire included maize, coca, beans, grains, potatoes, sweet potatoes, ulluco, oca, mashwa, pepper, tomatoes, peanuts, cashews, squash, cucumber, quinoa, gourd, cotton, talwi, carob, chirimoya, lúcuma, guayabo, and avocado. Livestock was primarily llama and alpaca herds. (10)

*" Incan priest-scientists experimented with wild vegetable crops to determine which should be disseminated for domestic production to farmers with fields all over the Andean region. Pollen samples found in Moray indicate that a huge variety of crops grew there – perhaps not surprising, since about 60 percent of the world's food crops originated in the Andes, including all known forms of potatoes, the most familiar types of corn, and, of course, the lima bean, named for the Spanish capital that succeeded Cuzco."* (11)

**Left** Image credit 8.8 **Harvesting cotton**

# Timeline for harvesting

*For thousands of years, South American people have known how to grow and weave cotton. However where the large cotton plantations exist today, previously there was usually a mixture of forests and villages where the indigenous people utilised a diverse range of traditional fibres, (such as cotton).*

**The** Indigenous people also harvested foods such as cassava, nuts and fruits. These foods added to the fish and other wildlife in the diet. (12)

From 1500 onwards, Europeans started taking control of the land in South America. The abundant sunshine and local population were harnessed with forced labour to establish cash crop plantations.

The pace of change in Brazil slowed during the period 1970 to 2006 but the number of large commercial farms still increased. The average size of farms in Brazil grew from 60 to 67 hectares during this period. However the number of small farms decreased, with the exception of gardens of less than one hectare in size. (13)

Since 2006 the trend to larger commercial farms has been balanced to some extent by many smallholders in Brazil and other South American countries choosing to join an international sustainable farming practice alliance. This alliance has a five year strategic plan based around four themes: good practices, sustainable landscapes, robust infrastructure and enabling policy environments. (14)

Turning now to a famous historical Peruvian site that in many ways was the antithesis of smallholder farming, let us consider Machu Pichu. The United Nations Educational, Scientific and Cultural Organization (UNESCO)'s World Heritage listing for Machu Pichu notes:

> "*The historic monuments and features in the Historic Sanctuary of Machu Picchu are embedded within a dramatic mountain landscape of exceptional scenic and geomorphological beauty thereby providing an outstanding example of a longstanding harmonious and aesthetically stunning relationship between human culture and nature.*" (15)

**Timeline for light harvesting and cotton harvesting in Brazil**

- \> 4,000 years BC the Incas, Brazilians and the Egyptians knew how to grow and weave cotton
- 1500 AD: the Portuguese arrive in Brazil. By 1530 they begin trading with local people to cut trees.
- Mid nineteenth century: cotton growing in north east Brazil becomes more widespread
- 2017: An international alliance of family based farmers, (including Brazilians), work with Solidaridad, the World Wildlife Fund and The Pesticide Action Network UK to launch the Sustainable Cotton Ranking Index. Many companies assessed with this Index were found to be in need of more sustainable practices.

Image credit 8.9

# The Incas and the Light Garden

*Let us now test how the Light Garden model applies on the Machu Pichu site*
*Column 1 scoring:* Was Machu Pichu built and operated on Light Garden principles ?
*Column 2 scoring:* Rating 1 – 5 from low to high for the extent to which the site reflected these principles

| Column 1: Was Machu Pichu built and operated on quantum biophysics *'Light Garden'* principles ?   Image credit 8.10 | |
|---|---|
| **1 ENERGY**: *To some extent.* The Incas had a highly developed knowledge of the movement of the sun and the site was a Sun Temple. The energy of the sun was used to grow food to sustain the population at Mach Pichu. However in the high altitude, wet and misty conditions, crop production and storage would not have been easy. | 2.5 |
| **2 SPACE and TIME:** *Probably not.* Although multiple theories have been developed as to the purpose of Machu Pichu, many scholars consider that it was built as a retreat for Inca rulers. Whilst the site is undeniably dramatic and suited to a temple, it was not operated as a place where the space and time supported the flourishing of life or a 'Light Garden'. Indeed the settlement was abandoned about 100 years after the herculean effort of establishing it. | 1 |
| **3. WAVES and PARTICLES:** *No.* To me the site is primarily symbolic of a *wave* of religious devotion, in which the individual *particles*, (the individual people who lived and worked there), were subordinated to the wave. I would not say that the site reflects the quantum theory that light behaves as both a wave and a particle. | 1 |
| **4. PATTERNS and PROBABILITIES:** *Mostly not.* Although this site demonstrates a mastery of stonework and solar astronomy which could be said to reflect patterns and probabilities within those realms, the decision to occupy this site was not based on the *probability* that ecosystems would endure and be rejuvenated . To the contrary, this site was a challenge to such concepts! | 1 |
| **5. MULTIPLICATION:** *Partially.* To the Inca mind this site probably rated very highly in terms of being a focal point for worship that was necessary to create religious multiplication effects for ongoing maintenance of life systems. Today we are unaware of how ecologically sound their broader system of management was but we do know that the site was abandoned. | 2.5 |
| **6. FOCAL POINTS:** *Partially.* As for item (5) in terms of creating a focal point for expression of Inca belief systems that included concepts of positive *entanglement* for ongoing maintenance of life systems, as well as other negative concepts such as human sacrifices to the Gods. | 4 |
| **7. MEASUREMENT and perception:** *Substantially.* This site functioned as a Sun Temple with ancillary activities, demonstrating a culture that valued *non-locality* and aesthetics in Perception. By non-locality, I mean the belief in the ritual role of religion in bringing about and maintaining the ongoing order and welfare of the empire . In addition, this site was certainly based on a culture of careful measurement and perception of astrological events, of stone masonry and of meticulously planned agriculture, in what was a physically steep and challenging environment. | 4 |
| **8. CONTEXT:** *Partially.* This settlement definitely considered the broader context in which it was established. It was concerned with **rejuvenation of the *living, biological*** aspects of the society and environment, through the role that religion played in those processes. | 3 |
| **9. HUMAN USE**: *Partially.* This site was and is a challenge to human use of natural resources within the culture of restraint that is part of the 'Light Garden" principles. It is not planned around the carrying capacity of the planet's living systems but around more inert concepts. | 1 |
| **10. STORAGE** of Information: *Partially.* The story of this site has been preserved in the stones. . | 2.5 |

# The Incas: drama vs longevity

*As illustrated below, sunlight steps down the terraces at the ancient Incan site of Machu Pichu in Peru. One of several sites where Sun Temples were constructed, Mach Pichu is world renowned for its dramatic impact. However, let us consider how it rates as part of the Light Garden concept.*

**As** described on previous pages, although Machu Pichu has dramatic impact and it rates relatively highly in two *Light Garden* concepts, (Number six, *Focal Points* and Number seven, *Measurement),* overall I would rate it as barely 2.5 out of 5 in terms of being a *Light Garden* site that enhances rejuvenation of Earth's life systems.

Supporting that relatively low rating, Machu Pichu was abandoned only one hundred years after it was constructed and it was never resettled. In contrast, another World Heritage site, (the Rice Terraces of Bali that were discussed in Chapter Two), has remained in production for hundreds of years.

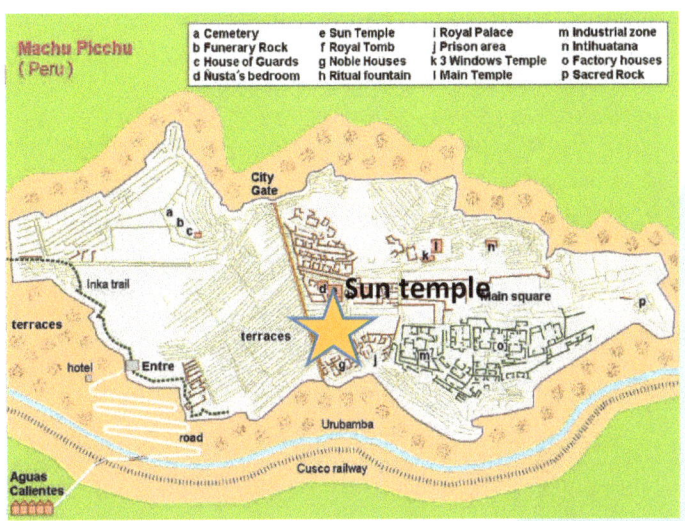

**Above** Image credit 8.11.1 *Machu Pichu Map*
**Below** Image credit 8.11.2 *Machu Pichu*

# Incas: comparison to Bali

*In order to better appreciate how the Light Garden concept directly applies to human management of natural resources, let us now consider how the 'Light Garden' model applies to Machu Pichu in comparison to the Rice Terraces of Bali site that was described in Chapter 2.*

In Table below: Column 1 scoring: Were the rice terraces built and operated on Light Garden principles ?
Column 2 scoring: Rating 1 – 5 from low to high for the extent to which the site reflected these principles

| Column 1: Were the rice terraces built and operated on quantum biophysics Light Garden principles ?  *Image credit 8.12* | |
|---|---|
| **1 ENERGY**: *Yes.* The Balinese have an integrated religious, social and agricultural system, including daily religious practices and *Lempuyang*, a temple to 'the Light of God' on the eastern tip of the island. The energy of the sun is used to grow food to sustain the population, but in a way that also includes responsible, sustainable stewardship of island environment. | 4.5 |
| **2 SPACE and TIME:** *Yes.* The traditional Balinese culture with the *Tri Hita Karana* philosophy includes a system of governance and organization that is derived from the philosophy and a landscape scale approach to natural resource management. This culture consciously values space and time not only for agriculture, but also for many other purposes such as for religious rituals, strategically places shrines, decision making base on participatory democracy, an inclusive approach to production of artwork and music by all members of the society and conscious management of resources such as water, soil and forests. | 4.5 |
| **3. WAVES and PARTICLES:** *Yes*. This landscape is a result of adherence to the wave of the *Tri Hita Karana* philosophy, plus the efforts and expertise of individual people. | 4.5 |
| **4. PATTERNS and PROBABILITIES:** *Yes.* This site demonstrates mastery of irrigated agricultural techniques that follow traditional patterns but it also reflects a culture in which the probability of sustaining the ecological viability of whole landscape ecosystem is high, if outside influences can be overcome. | 4.5 |
| **5. MULTIPLICATION:** *Yes.* The rice terraces landscape demonstrates the multiplication effects that arise in particular structures such as stone terraces and thatched shrines. It also demonstrated the multiplication effects that arise as social and environmental benefits when application of the *Tri Hita Karana* philosophy manifests as a cohesive society that is not prone to intertribal violence and as a system for natural resource management that is sustainable. | 4.5 |
| **6. FOCAL POINTS:** *Yes.* For example, water temples within the rice paddies act as focal points for religious and agricultural activity within the broader patterns of daily life. | 4.5 |
| **7. MEASUREMENT and perception:** *Yes.* This site demonstrates careful measurement of irrigated rice terraces, shrines and so on. It also reflects a culture that valued the quantum biophysics concept of *non-locality in perception,* through the daily rituals that establish the role of religion in bringing about the ongoing order and welfare of the society and nature. | 4.5 |
| **8. CONTEXT:** *Yes.* Management of this landscape was concerned with rejuvenation and maintenance of the living, biological health of the society and environment as described above. | 4.5 |
| **9. HUMAN USE**: *Yes*. This site is managed within the culture of restraint that is part of the 'Light Garden" principles. | 4.5 |
| **10. STORAGE** of Information: *Yes*. Cultural knowledge and religious rituals have been refined and passed down from one generation to the next for centuries. | 4.5 |

# More drama in the landscape

*Government intervention in forest management in Brazil in the 21st century currently bears little resemblance to the Subak system of Bali. As reported in the international media such as the British Broadcasting Corporation, (BBC) and as mapped by satellite imagery, in August 2019 there were 2,500 forest fires burning in the Amazonian region of Brazil. "Official data from Brazil's environment agency shows fines [for illegal forest destruction] from January to 23 August dropped almost a third compared with the same period last year. At the same time, the number of fires burning in Brazil has increased by 84%."* (16)

**In** earlier years (2012), the sentiment was different: the BBC captured the dramatic ethos of South America in an evocative narrative:

> " South America's 13 countries are home to dramatic landscapes, archaeological splendours from the past and a dizzying variety of wildlife. For the sheer awe factor, it is hard to top seeing the snow-covered peaks of the Andes, the world's longest continental mountain range, which stretches for nearly 8,000km from Venezuela to southern Patagonia." (17)

Despite this, how rare it is to find human cultivation that reflects the inspiration of a wild natural panorama in the detailed design of the foreground. However Juan Grimm, South America's most accomplished Landscape Architect of the early 21st century, has done this. He is known for his expertise in combining the vivacity and unique character of wild native South American native plants with the structure of man made elements in the landscape. Refer for example, to his work at Los Vilos, Chile below. All good visual dramatists work with lighting as one of their design tools. I will now discuss this in more detail with reference to Juan Grimm's work.

Image credit 8.13

# Reflection and absorption

*Comparison of two similar landscapes often helps us realize the qualities of the light in each. In the example depicted below, the light in a South American garden is compared to an Australian scene.*

**The** garden depicted in **A** below is found on the outskirts of Los Vilos in Chile. Garden **B** is located at a similar latitude on the other side of the Pacific Ocean, at Bodalla on the East Coast of Australia.

Bodalla has a latitude of 36 degrees south, whilst Los Vilos has a latitude of 32 degrees south. Bodalla is a small coastal village at a similar latitude to Australia's national capital of Canberra. So the qualities of the sunlight reaching these two coastal gardens should be fairly similar.

*Below A:* Image credit 8.14.1 *garden in Chile*
*Below B* Image credit 8.14.2 *garden in Australia*

## 1. Light reflection

The light reflective qualities of the tree canopies in gardens (A) and (B) are different. In Chile, the dark, dense, pointed forms of the pine tree canopies *absorb* a lot of light, whilst in Australia, the paler, olive green clumps of foliage in the Eucalypt trees *reflect* a lot of light.

## 2. Pools or lines of light

There is a bright pool of light at the center of the Australian garden (B) as highlighted by the white oval shape superimposed over the photograph below left. The pool of light is emphasized with a Xanthorrhoea clump growing as a focal point in the centre of the circular driveway.

In the Chilean garden (A) there is also a pool of light in the centre of this view of the garden. However in garden (A) the light from the central area meanders off into the distance through a landscape which has a definite structure provided by walls and hills. In garden (B) the landscape has a softer, less well defined structure and a softer less defined contrast of light and dark in the landscape.

Image credit 8.14.3

# Colour, light and outline

*Let us now consider how the design elements of sunlight, plus the man–made structures such as walls and paths, are combined in this South American garden.*

**To** illustrate this, let us compare the colour photograph of the garden at right with the black and white versions below it.

The black and white version at the bottom of the page loses none of the drama of the coloured landscape but the sense of light and shadow is more obvious. The dark foliage contrasts with the light reflecting off the meandering waterway and walls.

In the centre of the design are some rounded, fine- foliaged shrubs that do not catch the attention. I have drawn white circles around them on the central image at right. They act as a soft foil for the more dramatic pattern of light and dark in this landscape. Imagine if masses of bright orange flowers had been planted here instead. The whole focus of the view would change, as the bright colours would draw attention away from the meandering lines linking the foreground and the mountains.

I have highlighted these lines by adding blue lines over the central image. Complementing these lines of light, are the rounded shapes of mountains and the carefully chosen native plants in the foreground. These are hardy native shrubs that thrive in the high altitudes of Peru, and in this case grow in an urban garden.

**Below** Image credit 8.15 ***Urubamba near Cuzco, Peru:** design by Landscape Architect Juan Grimm*

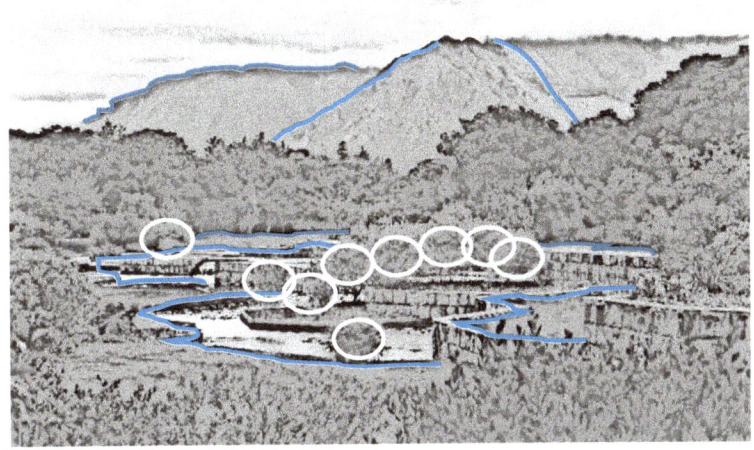

8.15

# A passionate heritage

*To the south of Peru and Bolivia, running along the Pacific Ocean coastline of South America lies the nation of Chile. It has a population of 17 million people. Whilst some have called Chile the land of poets, Chilean academic Oscar Galindo has noted that the concept of Chile as "a land of poets" is largely a foreign one that has been assigned to his native country.* (18)

**Regardless** of whether Chile is a land of poets, as we begin to think about the gardens, landscapes and places of South America in the language of South America, let us read a translation of one of the Chilean poet Pablo Neruda's poems from " Canto General":
'The Wide Ocean'

" Ocean, if you were to give, a measure, a ferment, a fruit
of your gifts and destructions, into my hand,
choose your far-off repose, your contour of steel,
your vigilant spaces of air and darkness,
and the power of your white tongue,
that shatters and overthrows columns,
breaking them down to your proper purity.
Not the final breaker, heavy with brine,
that thunders onshore, and creates
the silence of sand, that encircles the world,
but the inner spaces of force,
the naked power of the waters,
the immoveable solitude, brimming with lives.
It is Time perhaps, or the vessel filled
with all motion, pure Oneness,
that death cannot touch, the visceral green
of consuming totality." (19)

With such a passionate heritage as portrayed in Pablo Neruda's poem, it is little wonder that both ancient and modern sites in South America have become renowned for creative work that enhances human appreciation of the drama and human aesthetic connection with the underlying character of the natural world.

This type of appreciation is incorporated into the set of ten "Light Garden' principles proposed in this book through  principle number seven: *perception and measurement*.

For example, as illustrated at left and below, human perception of the landscape is enhanced by carefully measured and sensitively conceived  work that allows the natural drama of the landscape to be appreciated, whilst also facilitating restrained human use within that broader context.

**Above**  Image credit 8.16.1 *Incan site at Moray in Peru*
**Left** Image credit 8.16.2 *'The Wide Ocean' at Los Vilos*

# Contemporary examples

*As illustrated on the previous page, there is no sense that the grandeur of the ocean is tamed or domesticated in that Los Vilos garden. It is known as the Bahia Azul Garden by Juan Grimm. Native plants have been carefully fostered to colonize the rocky slopes. The surface finishes, shadows and colours reflecting from the water, timber and stonework are all chosen for dramatic effect to mirror and complement the light and colours of nature.*

**Also** renowned for its aesthetics and horticultural innovation, the irrigated stone terrace site illustrated on the previous page is thought to be an agricultural experimentation station from the Incan empire, in the period from approximately the 13th to 16th centuries. This site at Moray in the Cusco Sacred Valley area of Peru is located at an elevation of 3,500 metres. The circular depression is 30 metres deep, creating temperature differentials which are significant to the growth of different crop species within it. (22) (23)

However despite this rich history and the good work of many during the past century, as a tragic counterweight to it, the fate of small farmers in South America has been described in a well documented report published in 2014:

*"The single most important factor in the drive to push small farmers onto ever smaller parcels of land is the worldwide expansion of industrial commodity crop farms .... The land area occupied by just four crops – soybean, oil palm, rapeseed and sugar cane – has quadrupled over the past 50 years."* (24)

The area of land involved represents approximately the same area as all the farmland in the European Union. This process is continuing to occur in America on a vast scale as the second decade of the 21st century draws to a close and the invaluable forests of the Amazon burn in the ineffectual spotlight of mainstream media attention. (25)

Having suffered food shortages and decimation of the economy for decades, the government and urban residents of Havana in Cuba chose a different path. Relying upon community-organsied horticultural skills, innovative recycling and well respected teams of workers, the government provided initial support for people to become self sufficient in vegetables and livestock. (26)

In another positive 21st century example, Kris and Doug Tompkins began in the early 1990's to buy hundreds of thousands of acres in the wild Patagonia region of Chile. Their goal was to:

*" buy and restore as much land as they could, improve and protect it, and then return it to people as public, national parks."* (27)

After two decades they had acquired 2.2 million acres. In 2018 the Chilean government accepted a gift of one million acres of this land to be managed as National Park. Before the land was handed over, infrastructure such as paths and cabins had been built and regeneration of native ecosystems had been encouraged in both the new Parks and on adjoining lands. (28)

***Below*** Image credit 8.17 ***Cuban urban farming***

# Chapter 9 North America

Previous page Image credit 9.1

# Table of Contents Chapter 9

| | |
|---|---|
| Timeline for harvesting light | 9.4 |
| Map of North American sites | 9.5 |
| 10,000 BCE Native Americans | 9.6 |
| 1730 to the present day: the Amish in Pennsylvania | 9.8 |
| 1858: Central Park in New York and Frederick Law Olmstead | 9.10 |
| 1890: Yosemite National Park | 9.12 |
| 1904 Butchart Gardens | 9.13 |
| 1914 Longwood Gardens | 9.15 |
| 1914 – 2014: glass and light | 9.16 |
| 1935 *'Fallingwater'* and Falling Light capture the imagination | 9.17 |
| 1969 *'Design with Nature'* | 9.18 |
| 1970 *'Arcosanti'* | 9.19 |
| 21st century urban farms: Alabama and Brooklyn | 9.20 |
| 2012 Detroit and vertical gardens | 9.21 |
| 2016 Light Gardens in Orbit and the Quakers Light of God | 9.22 |
| Review: 1730 - 2030 | 9.23 |
| Chapter Summary | 9.24 |

# Timeline for harvesting light

*As indicated in the timeline below and described later in this chapter, the Amish are one example of a North American community that operates largely in accordance with 'Light Garden' principles to produce food, manage their culture and manage the environment.*

In this chapter I shall write from a historical perspective about the influence of light on the design of gardens and landscapes in North America. Firstly, I shall write about the perception and harvesting of light in the Native American culture and how this was supplanted by a culture that did not value light and other natural resources in the same way.

I shall then trace the historical process of rejuvenation of a nature-based culture with a conscious, sustainable management of light and other natural resources. I shall do this by referring to examples of work that I regard as milestones. The image below summarises these examples.

**Below:** Image credit 9.4.1 *One way of harvesting food in the 21$^{st}$ century*

## North American Milestones in the use of light

Image credit 9.4.2

- Circa 10,000 BCE Native American
- 1730's to the present day Amish in Pennsylvania
- 1858 *Central Park*, New York by Frederick Law Olmstead
- 1890 Yosemite National Park in California
- 1904 *Butchart Gardens*, Vancouver
- 1914 *Longwood Gardens*, Pennsylvania
- 1935 *Fallingwater* by Frank Lloyd Wright
- 1969 *Design with Nature* by Ian McHarg
- 1970's communities: *Arcosanti*
- 2012 Detroit urban renewal gardens
- 2016 Edible gardens in space

# Map of North American sites

*The map below shows the location of North American sites discussed in this chapter. There are many types of Light Garden subcultures in evidence on this continent. For example, The Amish could be considered one of these subcultures, due to factors which allow their community to disconnect*

> " *from the strings that bind most of us to modern-day corporate, capitalist society . . . The Amish communities live a sustainable life in large part because of their traditional agricultural practices, economic freedom and alternative healthcare practices.*" (1)

Butchart Gardens on Vancouver Island

Colorado River

Arcosanti in Arizona

Jones Valley Urban Farm in Alabama

Community Gardens, Detroit

Central Park, New York

Amish in Pennsylvania

Longwood Gardens, Philadelphia

Fallingwater, Pittsburgh

Space station at Cape Canaveral in Florida

*At right* Image 9.3.2 ***An Amish roadside stall, with a horse drawn black buggy in the background.***
This is an activity that falls within the Amish principles for living, which have been described as:

- Commitment to God and community
- Obedience to Amish rules
- Sense of purpose and independence
- Simplicity
- Work Ethic
- Tradition

The Amish are one of many community groups who live in North America. The Amish population is thought to be growing. It is estimate to be 200,000 people by the year 2020. (2)

# 10,000 BCE: Native American

*Native Americans have given a significant food and sunlight harvesting gift to the world because 60% of the current world's cultivated garden and farm food supply species originated in the Americas, including wild species of corn, rice, beans, nuts, berries, tomatoes and potatoes* (3)

**Patient** cultivation from the wild of the plants listed above over thousands of years was carried out by the Native American peoples. During the last ice age, around 10,000 BCE, these peoples migrated eastwards across the Bering Strait land bridge. As described by Park et al:

> *The people quickly adapted to local food sources and developed gardens where corn, beans and squash formed the three basic inter-planted food species. Gardens and food sources included many other cultivated and wild plant foods and medicines, plus fish, wild game, berries and nuts.* (4)

Multiple tribes of people developed and well over five hundred Native American Tribes are recognised in the United States alone. The territories of some of the well known tribes are illustrated on the map below. Fish formed a major part of the diet for many tribes. Food gardens were made typically but not exclusively of mounds of soil, raised about 300 mm above intervening irrigation channels.

Proximity to water sources and arable soil were thus common features of settlement patterns. Locally adapted varieties of corn were grown by hand at all latitudes from southern Canada to Central America. Nutrient rich organic fertilisers, including rotting fish, were used to meet the soil nutritional requirements for growing corn. (5)

**Below** Image credit: 9.6.1 **Corn**

**Above** Image credit: 9.6.2 *Map of USA depicting major Native American tribes*

**A** famous Native American by the name of Geronimo was born into a tribe in Arizona in the year 1829. He spoke of the significance of light in the gardens and landscape of North America when he said:

> *"I was born . . . Where the wind blew free and there was nothing to break the light of the sun . . ." (6)*

Painting a picture of Native American life in the early 19th century, Geronimo described how as a child, he started food growing with his parents. Fields were about two acres in size. They broke the ground with wooden hoes and planted corn in straight rows. Beans, melons and pumpkins were interplanted in the same fields and allowed to spread across the land. Various organic fertilisers were used.

Geronimo described how melons were eaten as soon as they were gathered but pumpkins, beans and corn were stored for use in winter. His tribe had ponies to help carry loads of corn from the fields but they had no cattle. Thus all the energy for the villages came from open access to sunlight. *(7)*

> *The fields were never fenced. It was common for many families to cultivate land in the same valley and share the burden of protecting the growing crops from destruction by the ponies of the tribe, or by deer and other wild animals. (8)*

His tribe thus had what would be described in the 21st century as a zero carbon economy, with free access to the energy of sunlight and shared access to other natural resources such as space, water, land and living organisms. They harvested the energy of the sun by converting it to food energy that humans could eat in the short term, or store away for winter. Thus we see a historical precedence for management of the natural resources of North America under the *'Light Garden'* concept.

As found in the Balinese *Tri Hita Karana* philosophy described in Chapter Two, the three realms of the *spirit, human and natural worlds* are present in Native American cultures as well as in Bali. There is also reference to sunlight. For example the following chant is attributed to the Sioux:

> *Kuate, leno leno, mahote.*
> *Hyano, hyano, hyano*
> *[We are one with the infinite sun.*
> *Forever and ever and ever]. (9)*

But the 21st century, this chant had been taken up by many other groups in North America and around the world, as these groups too felt and celebrated a connection with divine order.

Although most languages have a word for the concept of beauty, the traditional Navaho people of North America did not. To the Navaho, *Nizhoni* is their closest concept to beauty - and that word can refer to something that is both *good* and to something that is *attractive*. Beauty is a *sense of being* that must be felt as an internal harmony and balance.

Image credit: 9.7

That sense of being is as true for a whole person as it is for a whole garden, and for the whole natural world order. The essence of the Navaho philosophy - which encompasses beauty, harmony, order and balance – has quietly persisted in North American culture and indeed has much in common with the 21st Century principles of quantum biophysics. I will now consider this in more detail with reference to a series of historically significant examples.

# 1730 to the present day: the Amish in Pennsylvania

*"If you admire our faith -- strengthen yours. If you admire our sense of commitment -- deepen yours. If you admire our community spirit -- build your own. If you admire the simple life -- cut back. If you admire deep character and enduring values -- live them yourself."* (10)

The first Amish arrived in Pennsylvania in the 1730's, having departed Europe to escape persecution. As illustrated below, 21st century Amish gardens, farms and buildings have an air of being built in traditional styles that may well be very similar to those that were brought from Europe some 300 years ago.

In an interesting turn of events, the time honoured organic farming practices of the Amish have become profitable sources of off-farm income for the Amish in the 21st century. Knowledge of the benefits of organically grown food has spread far more widely through the North American community and the Amish religion permits interaction of the Amish with the wider community through the sale of home grown organic produce at road-side stalls.

The traditional farming practices used by the Amish are based on their understanding of Biblical scriptures. Tilling the soil has religious significance. A large proportion of the population, from children to the elderly, are engaged in working on the land, using horse drawn machinery and human labour.

Farming, stewardship of the Earth and food production are also vital means by which the Amish seek to live in accordance with their philosophy of local, self sufficient and sustainable communities. They choose to turn away from influences of the outside world that would lead them away from this philosophy.

For example, Amish largely use their own alternative health care practices, rather than purchase healthcare insurance, or use the mainstream health care system. However, if it is decided that a member of an Amish community does require mainstream healthcare treatment, members of the community will pool together and donate the funds required to obtain the treatment.

An impression of the Amish way of life is also stamped upon the public consciousness in North America by the image of their black horse-drawn carriages travelling along country roads. The Amish do not own cars but instead use horse drawn carriages with metal wheels. However the Amish will accept transport in cars and taxis owned by other people when the need arises. (11)

**Below** Photo credit 9.8 *a 21st century North American Amish farm*

# An Amish 'Light garden' event

*Notes 1 – 10 in the example below illustrate the extent to which the ten Light Garden parameters identified in Chapter 1 are present in a traditional Amish barn raising event*

**1. Energy.** The sun is the energy source for the Amish, as they live in self sufficient farming communities and only drive horse-drawn buggies.

**2. Space.** The bright red barn encloses a readily recognisable, purpose-built space.

**3. Waves and particles.** Waves of Amish men work together to place the roof tiles.

**4. Lines, Patterns and probabilities.** The design of the barn and the work clothes the men wear are highly probable to be the same as buildings and garments in other Amish settlements.

**5. Multiplication effects.** The recognisable style of Amish buildings when clustered together creates multiplication effects.

**6. Entanglement and Focal Points**
The peak of the roof is a focal point in the farm landscape, as illustrated more clearly in the photograph on the previous page. In addition, psychological entanglement within the community is demonstrated by the deep sense of security that the Amish have in knowing that the community they are part of will return such barn-building favours if they ever find themselves in need.

**7. Perception and Measurement** The people involved in this project applied careful measurements and human mindsets appreciative of the cultural significance of what was being built.

**8. Context.** The building materials in Amish settlements do not necessarily come from the surrounding landscape and are one example of the need for the Amish to interact with the wider community in order to obtain materials.

**9. Human use.** Barn raisings are an example of what the Amish term "frolics." They

"take pleasure from participating in joint cooperative work projects—both from the social aspect as well as from the deeper sense of satisfaction in seeing tangible results of one's labor". (12)

**10. Storage and sharing of information.** The design of this barn and the lives of the people who use it are based on information stored in the Biblical scriptures, the Amish traditions the minds of the people. Barn raisings are supervised and organsied by master Amish "engineers", who organise the free labour to build the barns and employ centuries old building traditions.

*Below* Image credit 9.9 *An Amish barn raising*

# 1858: Central Park, New York by Frederick Law Olmstead

**Although** is may be difficult to imagine in the 21st century, by the time the famous Native American Geronimo was thirty years of age, the design and construction of Central Park in New York was underway.

It is thus not so incongruous in the historical context that we find that Frederick Law Olmstead, the Landscape Architect who designed Central Park, had many values in common with Geronimo.

Olmstead is regarded as the father of Landscape Architectural profession in the United States and was the author of the term "landscape architect." This term was subsequently adopted by the profession all around the world.

As described below, Olmsted's philosophy was formed in his early years. Although he does not specifically refer to light, he does refer to *"cultivating susceptibility to the power of scenery"*.

*"The root of all my good work is an early respect for, regard and enjoyment of scenery… and extraordinary opportunities for cultivating susceptibility to the power of scenery."* (13)

Describing this influence in more detail, an observer noted:

*". . his father set him on a pillow in front of his saddle and took his son through the countryside around their home in Hartford, Connecticut. These short rides expanded to become annual tours in search of the picturesque that took Olmsted, by the age of sixteen, through the Connecticut Valley and White Mountains, up the Hudson River, and westward to the Adirondacks, Lake George and Niagara Falls."* (14)

Although Central Park is located in the densely populated CBD of New York City and probably rests beside the Statue of Liberty and the New York Public Library as one the city's three best known icons, Olmstead designed Central Park to heighten people's psychological sense of connection with nature.

He did this by including walkways between trees and lakes, whilst being aware of the strongest human response to the power of scenery that would prevail in particular places within the design. He insisted that design elements that would distract from the main purpose be not permitted.

> *He vigilantly guarded against distracting elements that would intrude on the consciousness of the observer. In the process, he simplified the scene, clearing and planting to clarify the "leading motive" of the natural site and heighten the effect of a particular quality of nature. (15)*

As described in Chapter Ten, Jorn Utzon included a similar stipulation in the design guidelines for the Sydney Opera House, where he insisted that white café umbrellas not be permitted on the harbour-side outdoor podium of the Opera House. This was because white umbrellas would detract from the white roof sails of the building as the dominant and uncluttered statement on the site, in contrast to the darker blues, browns and greys of the surrounding harbour-side setting.

Olmstead's philosophy, although profound, has rarely been allowed to prevail by clients with a lesser comprehension of the connection between nature, light, the human soul and

**society.** However there are some happy examples of this philosophy capturing the public imagination in subsequent projects by other North American designers. Not least among these are Ian McHarg and Frank Lloyd Wright.

Continuing the reference to the light and open spaces of the prairies that Geronimo cited as part of the Native American culture, it has been said that Frank Lloyd Wright too

> "liked the sense of shelter in the look of the building" yet he "loved the prairie by instinct as a great simplicity — the trees, flowers, sky itself, thrilling by contrast." (16)

Nearly eighty years after the construction of Central Park, in 1935 Frank Lloyd Wright designed one of his most famous projects, *Fallingwater*. As with all his projects, he designed the colours, forms, lines, massing and play of light and shade to reflect his philosophy of creating organic forms that blended with nature.

Although it may take some imagination, by referring to the photographs at right one can compare the towering cliffs, waters and forest of Yosemite to the towering buildings of Manhattan, with Central park in their midst. Through this process, one may come to some appreciation of the Western concept of bringing the rejuvenating qualities of Nature and "a green lung" into the city, through projects such as Central Park.

Illustrating the rapid development of the movement for the preservation of wilderness at the same time as urban development, *Yellowstone* was declared as North America's first National Park in 1870, only ten years after construction of Central Park. The world's first National Park had been declared almost a century earlier at Khan Uul by the Mongolian Government in 1783. (17)

*Below Top* Image credit 9.11.1 *Yosemite autumn foliage.*

*Below Centre* Image credit 9.11.2 *Central Park autumn foliage*

*Below Bottom* Image credit 9.11.3 *Central Park "green lung" in New York*

# 1890 Yosemite National Park

**Yoṣ ṣ e'meti** ( from the Central Miwok Native American language), originally referred to the Indian tribe that lived in Yosemite Valley. (18) Little did I know until recently that Yosemite means *"those who kill"*. (19)

However in 1851, some forty years prior to declaration of Yosemite National Park, they were killed themselves, or forced to relocate to a distant Indian reservation. Prior to this event, the local County Sherriff had been found *"unequal to the task"* (20) of eradicating the local Native American population. There are various accounts of whether it was the Sheriff, or Dr Bunnell, who wished to honour, rather than kill the tribe when noting in relation to the naming of Yosemite National Park:

> As I did not take a fancy to any of the names proposed, I remarked that "an American name would be the most Appropriate; . . . American scenery—the grandest that had ever yet been looked upon. That it would be better to give it an Indian name than to import a strange and inexpressive one; that the name of the tribe who had occupied it, would be more appropriate than any I had heard suggested." (21)

After California became a state in 1850, the US federal government tried to persuade or force tribes in the Sierra Nevada region, (including the Yosemite tribe), to move to reservations in California's Central Valley. Unconvinced, most tribes fought to stay where they were.

In 1851 a state-sanctioned militia, mostly made up of prospectors and miners calling themselves the Mariposa Battalion

> "invaded . . . the group razed and set fire to the village of the Ahwahneechee, forcing the tribespeople onto reservations down in the Central Valley and capturing their leader, Chief Tenaya."

However Chief Tenaya later escaped from the reservation and managed to spend his last days at Yosemite and thereabouts. (22)

**Above** Image credit 9.12.1 **Central Park.** **Left** Image credit 9.12.2 **Yosemite**: land set aside in 1864 by a bill that is claimed to be the first time in history that land was set aside purely for preservation and recreation for all.

# 1904 Butchart Gardens

*Although it is rated by visitors as one of the top ten most beautiful gardens in the world, (9.17) I doubt that Frederick Law Olmstead, Chief Tenaya, Frank Lloyd Wright or Ian McHarg would agree with all the principles behind the colourful floral displays that draw millions of visitors each year to Butchart Gardens in Canada.*

**The** golden yellow tulips depicted below at Butchart Gardens are part of the floral displays that draw one million visitors to these gardens each year. If you were to think: *I should learn more about what makes something beautiful, because there is money to be made in such things*, you would not be the first.

Before the boom and bust cycle of tulip mania in Holland ended in the 17th century, prized tulip bulbs were worth their weight in gold. The Butchart family, thinking to make a garden from a disused quarry on their property, certainly found another way of making money from tulips and flowers.

This garden is consistently rated as one of the ten most beautiful gardens in the world (23) and remains a family run business that must make a profit to survive. In 1907, while the quarry was still in operation, Japanese designer Isaburo Kishida of Yokohama was commissioned to design a garden. It was constructed thereafter but it is the garden that Jenny Butchart designed and planted once quarry operations ceased that has made Butchart Gardens famous.

Jenny had shown artistic talent from a young age and had intended to travel to Europe to study art before marrying Robert Butchart. After marriage, she became involved in his limestone quarry and cement plant business. The following extract from an article by Steve Whysall in the *Vancouver Sun* describes how the garden grew from this:

> *"It is not too big a reach to see the parallel between Jennie's restoration of the old limestone quarry with the reconciliation and renewal of her own personal passion for artistic expression".* (24)

Perhaps, like Olmstead, Jenny also had a passion for connecting people and nature. However she was not designing a park on public land, so she simply set about the work of planting the steep quarry banks, meanwhile planning the floral displays that now bloom in the rich soil in the base of the quarry below.

**Right** Image credit 9.13 ***Tulips under a tree at Butchart Gardens.***

# 1904 Butchart Gardens, cont.

**Olmstead** wanted his designs to remain true to the character of their natural surroundings, and not to clash with them. The failure of flower bedding and specimen-planting of hybrids to follow this basic rule was one of his chief reasons for seeking to differentiate his profession of landscape architecture from that of gardening.

In this respect, as in many others, he kept alive the teachings of eighteenth-century English writers on landscape design. The prevalence of conifer trees and shrubs in the foreground, middle ground and background of this view through the garden actually provides a subtle framework for the flowers in the centre of the garden. It was this type of flower beds and hybrids that Olmstead warned can clash with the natural character of a site - as much as poor site planning.

After a close look at the photograph below I think one could say, that as was Olmstead's wish, the trees *"remain true to the character of their natural surroundings and [do] not . . . clash with them"*. (25) People can enjoy moving through the garden with a much greater sense of connection to nature than for example, in a formal garden such as Versailles. (Refer Chapter 7).

***Below*** Image 9.14  ***Colourful flowers in the landscape setting of Butchart Gardens in Canada.***

# 1914 Longwood Gardens

*Unequivocally designed to harvest light and create delight, the conservatories at Longwood Gardens in Pennsylvania, USA attract over one million visitors per year.*

**21st** century revegetation projects seek to recreate natural plant communities but Butchart Gardens was not conceived of in that manner. Beginning in 1904, Jenny Butchart used her ideal of a grand and beautiful garden as her guiding light, even though the project involved revegetation of a quarry site. In order to keep Butchart Gardens as an economically viable, internationally renowned visitor destination, succeeding generations of the Butchart family have added to the original gardens with more attractions, such as a large fountain.

**Longwood Gardens** in the USA began as a private garden and it also has grown incrementally since construction of the first glasshouse in 1914. Its largest conservatory is regarded as one of the great glasshouses of the world. Continuing the discussion around Olmstead's concern about whether a garden can remain true to the character of its natural surroundings if flower bedding and specimen hybrids are the mainstay of it, the flowers of Longwood Gardens have been compared to Eastern style gardens, such as found in China and Japan.

Young North American gardeners James Rockwell and Timothy Heslop have observed that in the East, beauty is often seen as arising from unique details that give something its particular character. This is associated with what they described as the Japanese focus on the expression of the individual. They described Longwood Gardens as perhaps the epitome of the Western tendency to see beauty not as something that is individual but as something like a massed display of flowers. As they noted:

> 'There is something awe-inspiring in the large drifts of color strewn across a living canvas'. (26)

*Below* Photo credit 9.15.1
***A Longwood Gardens Conservatory***

*Below* Photo credit 9.15.2
***A conservatory at Longwood Gardens.***

# 1914 – 2014: glass and light

*Glasshouses are perhaps the epitome of designs intended to inspire awe through the beauty of space, light and plants but all gardens to a greater or lesser extent rely upon conscious use and control of light to create the growing conditions for plants and other creatures.*

**The** reflective flooring and arched shapes of conservatory windows at Longwood Gardens complement each other to create a light–filled, spacious and inspiring experience for visitors.

These glasshouses, constructed in the early 20th century in many ways were harbingers of the atriums and air-conditioned human dwellings that have proliferated since that time.

Paralleling the construction of the great glasshouses was the first modern electrical air conditioning unit, which was invented in 1902 by Willis Carrier in New York. By 1904, the public had been exposed to the concept of air-conditioned buildings at the St Louis World Fair. By the 1920's, air conditioning had become common, not in homes or offices, but in the newly constructed movie theatres of the USA. (27)

Returning to the story of glass walled, light filled, air-conditioned buildings that house plants, the first atrium in a modern building in the USA was constructed in 1957. (28) Indoor gardens started transmogrifying into Green Walls by the early 21st century. The Green Wall, (or Botanical Brick) concept had been patented in 1938 by Professor Stanley Hart White of the University of Illinois. However his work did not receive nearly as much public recognition as that of the Frenchman Patrick Blanc, who some 50 years later modernized, popularised and raised the aesthetic appeal of the concept. (29)

Unlike the light filled 21st century atrium depicted at left, the visual impact of Frank Lloyd Wright's design for his famous *Fallingwater* project relies heavily upon the central beam of sunlight that falls upon the structure, as depicted on the following page.

After an eventful but professionally unsatisfying life, Frank Lloyd Wright was 67 years old by the time he achieved a turning point in his career with the design of the country house *Fallingwater* in 1935.

> "Almost from the day of its completion, "Fallingwater" was celebrated around the world. The house and its architect were featured in major publications including the cover of Time Magazine. Over the years its fame has only increased." (31)

The apparent disparity between the espoused American dream of living in harmony with nature, versus the reality that the USA has virtually the largest ecological footprint of any nation on Earth, and is thus contributing disproportionately to the destruction of Earth natural resources, can be only party explained by reference to the historical examples given in this chapter.

**Below** Image 9.16 **Light through an atrium**

# 1935 *Fallingwater* and Falling light capture the imagination

*Probably the most remarkable feature of the design of "Fallingwater" is the juxtaposition of the structure against its forest setting. This project immediately captured the imagination of the American public and catapulted the Architect who designed it to international fame.*

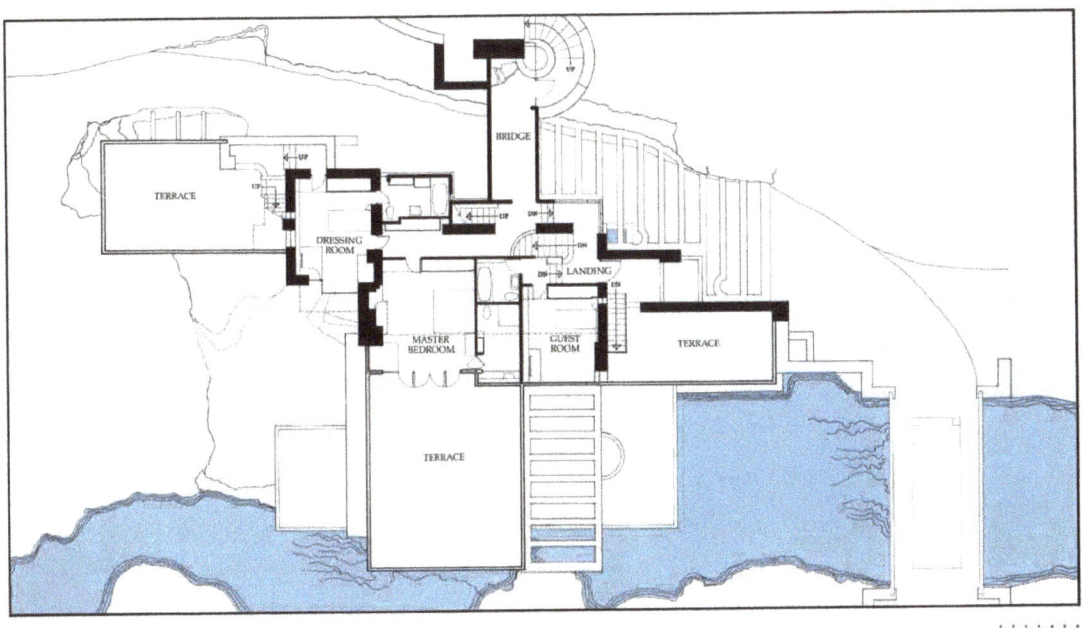

SECOND FLOOR PLAN

**Above** Image credit 9.17.1
***Plan of "Fallingwater"***

**Right** Image credit 9.17.2 The site includes a home built over a stream where a beam of light falls upon it through the forest.

# 1969 'Design with Nature'

*Let us now look at more examples of the American dream of living in harmony with nature. Although far less publicised in the media and much less well known to the general public than Frank Lloyd Wright, Ian McHarg, Professor and practitioner in Landscape Architecture, actually went into far greater detail towards making this dream a reality than did Frank Lloyd Wright.*

**Ian** McHarg's book *'Design with Nature',* set a wider agenda than anything before it in the field of environmental planning in the USA. Indeed it was acknowledged as a pioneer in the world wide movement towards sound environmental planning. (32)

Image credit 9.18

The book was published in 1969, just over a century after the design of Central Park. It set forth principles and practices for how to go about designing cities and whole regions in a systematic and ecologically sustainable process.

I was a young teenager at that time and had started reading books about society and the environment. By the time I was a university student, the principles of *Design with Nature* had been brought to my native country of Australia and there was excitement amongst the academic and student community when the opportunity arose to apply these principles.

In 1971, Mc Harg delivered an address to the North American Wildlife and Natural Resources Conference in Portland, Oregon. At that time he publicly warned that the human species may not survive if it continued on the economic globalisation, or Western cultural path of killing and plundering the living systems of the planet.

Almost forty years later in 2018, naturalist David Attenborough gave a similar address in the United Kingdom, with a focus on climate change and biodiversity conservation. Both these issues were encompassed within the broader Landscape Architectural and Planning processes that McHarg's team established.

Mc Harg used the term *biosphere* to refer to the living systems of the planet. Since the "Earth Summit" in 1972, the United Nations has also used this term. For example by the year 2020, a worldwide network of approximately five hundred biosphere reserves had been established where integrated management of economic, social, educational, environmental, cultural and aesthetic factors was encouraged.

The value of this integrated approach to management was briefly described in Chapter 2 of this book with reference to the World Heritage listing of the *'Cultural Landscape of Bali Province: the Subak System as a Manifestation of the Tri Hita Karana Philosophy'.'* The limited value of including a site on the World Heritage Register without adequate comprehensive planning of the type encouraged under the Biosphere reserve program has been apparent in Bali. However no doubt on-going efforts will seek to gradually address this problem. As with many things, time is of the essence with this process, before the older farmers die and with them, the opportunity to pass on their agricultural skills to the next generation.

# 1970 'Arcosanti'

To celebrate the 50th anniversary of "Design with Nature" a team of landscape architects and planners from the University of Pennsylvania Stuart Weitzman School of Design have showcased some of the most advanced ecological design projects in the world today. In many ways but not all, 'Arcosanti' was the antithesis of McHarg's work, as illustrated below.

**Established from 1970 as an artisans' community, Arcosanti proclaimed one of its goals was to be environmentally sustainable.**

**Below** Images 9.19.1 and 19.2 and 19.3 *Google Earth aerial view image of Arcosanti*

Image 9.19.1

Fifty years later, as illustrated below, although buildings and a swimming pool have been constructed, the revegetation and Light Garden principles have lagged behind.

**Image 1** illustrates the proximity of the site to urban development and the highway, whilst Image 3 illustrates the swimming pool. The blue pool is located in the broader site just to the left of the number 2 in Image 2 below.

Image 9.19.3

Image 9.19.2

# 21st century urban farms: Alabama and Brooklyn

*Helena Norberg-Hodge, writing of rural Chinese villages in the last years of the 20th century, said: "the people I encountered were able to meet most of their basic needs locally, using their own labor and ingenious small-scale technologies. We were greeted with spontaneous laughter and humor.* (33)

**Such** accounts of the value and happiness of cooperative village life have inspired many 21st century ventures in the USA. For example, **Jones Valley Urban Farm is located on a 5 acre property in the downtown area of Birmingham,** a city of just over 200,000 people in the state of Alabama, USA.

This not-for-profit organisation runs educational programs about healthy food and grows organic produce and flowers. These are marketed in the local community.

During the late 19th century, Birmingham had developed as an industrial city where relatively cheap, non-unionised labour could be sourced. However since the mid 20th century those enterprises have declined. In the city's post-industrial era, sizable inner city sites have become available for urban farms and gardens, attracting the attention of government support agencies with funding to support them. (34)

**Oko Farms** is the catchy name of an another local community project. **It is an aquaponic farming business set up in Brooklyn, New York.** It has brought affordable, healthy fresh food to people in the neighbourhood. Surprising additional benefits have also accrued, such as it's function as a safe place where people can meet or enjoy some passive outdoor recreation amidst gardens in their dense urban neighbourhood. (35)

**Just as Gandhi** knew that in India that he needed to promote small scale local businesses as an important part of empowering local communities to speak up for their rights in the larger democratic system, so too in Brooklyn, the Oko Farms project has begun to function in that way, under a capable leadership team that includes a nutritionist and mental health worker.

Image credit 9.20.1

Image credit 9.20.2

# 2012 Detroit & vertical gardens

**Moving** from New York to **Detroit,** we find that in 2012, Detroit was considered the most dangerous city in the USA, with a murder rate ten times that of New York City. In the 1950 census, the city of Detroit reached it's peak population of 1.5 million people. During the next 65 years, it has lost well over half its population, leaving vast areas of the inner city derelict. (36)

Rising out of this dereliction, urban farming has been one of the most successful ventures supporting urban renewal in Detroit. As of 2019, there were approximately 200 urban farming and community gardening enterprises in the city. Visitors book tours to see them and the city has announced its goal of becoming a food sovereign city for all fruits and vegetables consumed. (37)

**By 2012** vertical gardens for food production started to appear in high rise buildings in various countries around the world. Lighting for the gardens is an important factor in any cost-benefit analysis of these. Although lighting can be sourced from sunlight or LEDs, full spectrum light is not required. Red, blue or purple light can be used and generated at a lower cost with less electricity than full spectrum light. In 2018, commercial LEDs were about 28% energy efficient, but research has since demonstrated LEDs with a significantly increased efficiency of 68%.

The world's first commercial vertical farm was opened in Singapore in 2012. In 2018 the United States Department of Agriculture and the Department of Energy held a workshop focused on vertical agriculture and sustainable urban ecosystems, citing opportunities to address the food security of the nation. (38)

Around this same time a speaker from the Chinese Academy of Agricultural Sciences presented data about extensive research into vertical farms in China. One of the advantages he was reported as describing was that due to climate variabilities in China their vertical farms *need to be capable of producing food in winter in temperatures as low as -55ºC.* (39)

*Below* Image credit 9.21 *Detroit*

# 2016: Light Gardens in Orbit and the Quakers Light of God

*Although space stations and rockets are not built as glass houses or green walls, they do often contain solar panels and they can now house units for production of food plants grown under artificial lights, literally creating the first 'Light Gardens' in orbit around Earth.*

**By** the 21st century, gardens began to proliferate as hybrid offspring of initiatives aimed primarily at other things such as solar energy production, carbon sequestration, waste management, water conservation, biodiversity conservation, economic localisation, sustainability, organic farming, hydroponics, aquaculture and so on.

**As illustrated below, gardens can now be grown on board the International Space Station. In 2016, astronauts had their first taste of lettuce they had grown onboard during their flight. Specially designed red, green and blue LED lights were used to simulate Earth's natural lighting conditions for the growth of plants.** (40) This opens up the question of growing plants on Mars. Now that water has been found on Mars and we know there is light on Mars, how long will it be before plants are grown in special containers on Mars? Maybe plants will come from planet Earth, or from seeds found somewhere else but whatever the outcome, awareness of the value of access to life-giving sunlight will increase.

Taking a more low risk approach, when asked about how they share their lives together back on planet Earth, some North American Quakers replied:
*"We eat together at least once a week, we garden together, we delight in each other's children, and we care for this land and its non-human inhabitants together. We work together to care for and maintain our common house"* (41)

**Light** from the heavens is a common symbolic analogy in many of the religious groups that are found in contemporary North American society. In the past and going forward, these groups exercise considerable influence. For example, Quakers believe the light of God exists within each person. (9.32) Following on from this belief, Quakers were prominent and successful in the social movements in North America for both the abolition of slavery and the granting of equal voting rights for women.

***Above*** Image credits 9.22.1 and 9.22.2 ***Below*** Image credit 9.22.3
*Plants growing under LED lights in the International Space Station.*

# Review: 1730 - 2030

*In the 21st century the USA is acknowledged among Western, or globalized, non-indigenous cultures as placing a higher importance upon religion than many other comparable nations. To consider how this influences the prospect for a more pervasive 'Light Garden' culture in North America, a brief review is given below. Refer also to the Summary at the beginning of this chapter.*

**As** illustrated by recent survey data, when it comes to the importance of religion in daily life, the USA is unusual among nations with comparable post-industrial cultures. About 55% of American citizens said religion was very important in their lives. However this figure was much lower in comparable places such as Canada (27%), Germany (21%), Russia (19%), Australia (18%), Japan (5 %) and China (3 %). (42)

Among Western cultures, the prevalence of gardening does not correlate with this data about religion. In a 2015 survey it was found

> that *Australia has the highest level (45%) of daily or weekly gardening among all the countries measured. China came in second (36%), followed by Mexico, the US, and Germany – all of which had levels of over one-third.* (43)

How have these patterns of participation in religion and gardening influenced the gardening and farming movements in North America ? By looking at some of the oldest and some of the newest gardens in America we may find some answers to that question.

For example, as described earlier in this chapter, the Amish first settled in Pennsylvania in 1730. They brought with them a religion developed in Switzerland in the 17th century. Some three hundred years later, they still live by the original religious precepts in self-contained rural communities. Tilling the Earth through farming and gardening has religious significance to the Amish, as established in their biblical texts. In contrast to the longevity of the Amish communities, the community of Arcosanti in Arizona, USA, has struggled to survive during recent decades, after it was established by charismatic leader Paolo Soleri in 1970.

Soleri's vision was for an ecologically sound medium density urban settlement of artisans working together as a community. Revenue to support the Arcosanti building project has been generated from a bell-making business and visitor information services on the site. (9.39) However, religion was not part of the vision. Gardens have not blossomed on the site either. As of 2017, neither the terraced gardens nor the fields that were included on the original plans for the site had been constructed. (44)

**In contrast to Amish communities, who are intentionally self-reliant and self-contained, Arcosanti proactively seeks to attract up to 40,000 visitors annually.** It tends to have between fifty to one hundred and fifty residents at one time, many of whom are architectural students who stay for a while to assist with building work and learn about life on the ten hectare site.

**In contrast to this, Amish communities are based around families, the members of which work together from early childhood to old age**. Their farming principles are based on adherence to centuries old traditions, whereas Arcosanti was conceived as a bold new adventure to create a community on the edge of the desert, with easy vehicle access to a State Route highway only one kilometre away.

# Chapter Summary

*Each event identified on the timeline below has been assigned a rating based on the more detailed discussion in this chapter and the Light Garden model set out Chapter One. The ratings are somewhat arbitrary and space does not permit a full explanation of the reasons behind them. However consider how you would rate them yourself as Light Gardens!*

**For** example, the age old practices of the Amish are quite well aligned with the 'Light Garden' concept, so I have rated them as 4.5 out of 5 on the timeline diagram below.

Yosemite National Park and "Design with Nature" are also rated highly because of the comprehensive manner in which they address Light Garden principles. All the milestones on the time line are historically significant and are quite positive examples of the application of Light Garden principles but some such as Butchart Gardens and Arcosanti have been assigned three star ratings for various reasons.

These reasons include factors such as the energy use may not reflect best practice for sustainability; there may be few examples of quantum biophysics entanglement and multiplication effects in the designs, or human use may not be planned in a restrained manner that reflects a wider agenda to contribute towards rejuvenation of natural resources of the planet. These comments are not to be taken as failings of the projects but rather as a way of charting how the historical development of thought and priorities for such projects has occurred.

*Below* Image credit 9.24

# Chapter 10
# 21st Century

Previous page Image credit 10.1

# Chapter 10 Table of Contents

| | |
|---|---|
| Introduction | 10.4 |
| Collective Decision Making Needed | 10.5 |
| Applying the Light Garden model to make decisions about climate change | 10.6 |
| Some background data for the decision making model: climate change | 10.7 |
| Ten factors for the Light Garden | 10.8 |
| Ten criteria: Light Garden decision making | 10.9 |
| Ten components of the Light Garden | 10.10 |
| Testing how the light garden model can address climate change | 10.11 |
| Humanity can plan and achieve change! | 10.12 |
| Nexus: 21st century decision making | 10.13 |
| Summary of chapter findings, 2 - 9 | 10.14 |
| 21st century examples | 10.16 |
| Cities, light, sustainability | 10.17 |
| Light, shade and climate codes | 10.18 |
| Design sensitivity to light | 10.19 |
| Light and water in Chengdu | 10.20 |
| Walking into the future | 10.21 |
| Sunlight attracts visitors | 10.22 |
| Livable Cities in the 21st century | 10.23 |
| Paris, Singapore, Dubai | 10.24 |
| Translucent City Living | 10.25 |
| References and Image Credits | 10.27 |

# Introduction

*Before further considering the Light Garden model at the global scale, let us turn to what each of us can do individually, or in small groups. For example a simple thing that each of us can do to help draw carbon from the atmosphere and regenerate the planet's biodiversity is to hand weed and mulch around the edges of patches of remnant native trees, whether it be one tree beside the road, or an ancient grove of trees.*

**Above** Image credit 10.4 ***Managed regeneration of rainforest in Australia***

**As** can be seen above, the branches of the Australian native tree *Araucaria cunninghamii*, reach forth over the forest floor. This species can live to over 450 years of age. The *Araucaria* genus has been dated back to approximately 200 million years ago, well before the age of the dinosaurs. (1) As they grow, these trees drop small leaflets to the forest floor, where in the shade of the tree, few weed species grow. The regenerating rainforest slowly inches its way forward as the forest mulch accumulates.

We can help this process by selectively removing weed species by hand and keeping the forest litter mulch intact. Working this way, not only the trees but also the soil microorganisms continue to sequester carbon, (or store it away), rather than release it to the atmosphere.

Each person working in this manner is choosing be part of the movement towards application of quantum biophysics 'Light Garden" principles in the 21st century. For example, rainforest regeneration done in this way fosters quantum biophysics multiplier effects. As described above, these arise throughout the soil and ecosystem, when just the simple task of removing weeds is done.

This type of weeding and rainforest regeneration also illustrates other 'Light Garden principles. For example, Principle 9 acknowledges that *Human Use* is part of natural resource management under the Light Garden model. However, human use in the Light Garden is carried out with intelligent, radical *restraint* that is within the capacity of the planet's life systems to sustainably co-exist.

Another example of how this type of forest regeneration activity is in accordance with managing the Earth's resources as a Light Garden, is the manner in which it supports Principle 1. This is concerned with working with the energy flows of nature. In this case, careful hand weeding allows the energy and carbon trapped within the soil and vegetation to remain there, rather than being released to the atmosphere. More invasive vegetation removal techniques such as bulldozing release much energy and carbon to the atmosphere, as noted in Chapter 2.

Being mindful of the multiplier effects and opportunities for intelligent use of appropriate technologies, this simple human activity is one quantum leap forward towards managing the Earth as a Light Garden.

# Collective decision making needed

*The changing climate and changing economy of the 21st century has outpaced humanity's collective decision making capacity to act as fast and as effectively as is required for the common good. We need an upgrade to our system for collective decision making.*

**Examples** from each chapter in this book show that over the centuries, cultures on every continent have harnessed light in both practical and symbolic religious terms into their activities of daily living.

Wherever societies have developed, the human body and psyche have developed in conjunction with energy fields, including those of light. It is no wonder that light is such a consistent, cross cultural symbol.

However it is a wonder that to date light has not been adopted more widely into the 21st century global consciousness. The year 2015 was declared by the United Nations as the International Year of Light and Light-Based Technologies. Following that, an annual International Day of Light was declared to raise public awareness of the role light in fields such as the sciences, medicine, communications, culture and energy.

Harking back to the need for a responsible global approach to management of climate change and society, the Dalai Lama has said:

> " Ultimately, the decision to save the environment must come from the human heart. The key point is a call for a genuine sense of universal responsibility that is that is based on love, compassion and clear awareness." (2)

This book is written in that context, for the nature of the human heart is found at least partly within the realm of quantum biophysics. That is why I chose in the Introduction to this book to highlight the value of the human perception of beauty as a guiding light to follow towards what is balanced and appropriate in the natural ecosystems of the world and what resonates with the human heart, mind and energy fields.

This final chapter begins with a simple example of individual action that can be taken to manage the Earth's resources as a Light Garden. I will then revise and explain how the ten components of the Light Garden concept can be applied to decision making in the 21st century. A set of ten criteria for decision making in the 21st century is then proposed, on the basis that application of these criteria leads to multiple synergistic benefits in economic, social, scientific, governance and environmental spheres.

> I will then test the usefulness of this set of ten decision making criteria against a question that is prominent in the second decade of the 21st century: *How to stabilise ecosystems and rejuvenate life amidst climate change ?*

One fundamental question is: Can humanity's collective decision making capacity be improved through multiplier effects and other quantum biophysics effects in the Light Garden model. The answer should be Yes, but let us see what testing the model reveals.

Bearing in mind that 55% of the world's population lived in urban areas by the year 2018, the remainder of the chapter is devoted to examples of urban projects that demonstrate management of the Earth's natural light resources in accordance with *'Light Garden'* principles.

# Applying the Light Garden model to make decisions for managing climate change

*In the 21st century we continue to need the light energy from the sun to power the ecosystems of the Earth, ( which include human food production), but our atmosphere has changed. Too much heat energy and greenhouses gases are being retained now to continue to support the existing food chains of the planet. Species such as polar bears and corals on the Great Barrier Reef are dying. So the need for a decision has arisen:* **How to stabilise ecosystems and rejuvenate life in the context of climate change?**

## Background:

One response to the temperature rise that has occurred during the 21st century is that scientists in various countries have been conducting and are continuing to conduct large scale climate modelling and experiments. This work consists of trying to manipulate particles in the atmosphere and oceans to try to stop the sun's rays from overheating the Earth.

However, for example, the published results of a recent five billion pound UK study into climate geo-engineering were so alarmingly dangerous for life on Earth that the project has been abandoned. Billions of people in various regions on the Earth would be adversely affected by droughts, floods and other effects of climate engineering. (3)

There have been reports in books and the mainstream media about the predicted impact of climate change for the duration of my life. For example, in 1988 a NASA study modelled a scenario that has proved to be quite accurate thirty years later. (4) As the year 2020 draws near, the vast majority of citizens and scientists now acknowledge that the evidence has become overwhelming that the concentration of carbon dioxide in the atmosphere continues to rise and the effects of climate change are accelerating.

From now on, *drawdown* must be an imperative principle for all human activities, as we seek to maximise sequestration of greenhouse gases in plants, in the soil and through an array of other technologies.

Although there are thousands of valuable technological advances and projects underway to address climate change, the collective efforts of humanity have not yet produced results at the required scale, and in the necessary time frames to avoid changes that will be catastrophic for human life on Earth. In my native country of Australia, this need for collective international action has been cited by business and the ruling political parties for many years as a reason for not taking effective action at the national level.

However by 2018 – 19, with international business leaders solidly recognising the risks they are being held accountable for with regard to climate change (5), even in Australia the politics changed. As the Federal Government said: *" An effective response to climate change requires collective action by all countries and sectors."* (6) Let us now consider some of the supporting data behind this.

# Some background data
## for the Light Garden decision making model about climate change

In order to inform how the Light Garden model can be applied to answering the question raised on the previous page: *How to stabilise ecosystems and rejuvenate life in the context of climate change,* **some basic comparative** data from multiple sources is summarized in the table below and applied in the discussion that follows.

Below Image credit 10.7   Note: References for events (a) to (l) below are included in chapter references 10.7 – 10.18

| Events and Milestones | $CO_2$ in atmosphere (parts per million ppm) | Sea level | Temperature change (degrees C compared to year 1870) | Millions of years ago |
|---|---|---|---|---|
| Cretaceous period. The Gondwana land mass separating into continents of Antarctica, Africa, Australia, South American and Indian subcontinent (a) | 1,000 | ? | ? | 100 |
| Mass dinosaur extinction event (b) | Not known | ? | ? | 65 |
| Pliocene Epoch (c) Antarctic beech trees alive in Antarctica. | 400 | 20 metres higher | 20 degrees hotter | 5.3 – 2.6 |
| Homo sapiens species emerges (current human species) (d) | Similar to 280 | ? | ? | 0.8 - 0.3 |
| Zero million years ago | | (dates below this line are in current era years) | | |
| Pre-industrial revolution (e) | 280 | 0 (baseline in mm) | 0 | 1760 |
| Mid 20$^{th}$ century (f) | 310 | 90 mm | ? | 1948 |
| Paris Agreement signatories aim to limit global warming to 1.5 degree C (g) | 399 | 239 mm | ? | 2015 |
| Average annual global $CO_2$ above 400 ppm (h) | 400 | ? | ? | 2016 |
| Average national summer temperature 2°C above 30 year previous long term average in Australia (i) and (j) | 410 | 255 mm | 2 degrees | 2019 |
| Fossilised Antarctic beech tree *Nothofagus beardmorensi* leaves found in Antarctica. This announcement was made in the global public media. (k) and (l) | 410 | | | 2019 |

# 10 Factors for the Light Garden

*Ten parameters to apply for management of the Earth as a quantum light garden in the 21st century are illustrated below. These apply at both the broad scale and at the local scale. A mnemonic to help remember these in order of 1 - 10 is* **Every Summer We Love Matilda Eating Perfect, Crimson, Heavenly Strawberries.** *(E) for energy, (S) for space and time, (W) for waves and particles, (L) for lines and so on.*

***Below*** image credit 10.8

Image copyright
Anne Whittingham 2019

# 10 criteria to apply for decisions

**Applying** the ten Light Garden principles with the goal of managing and rejuvenating Earth's natural and cultural resources, the following criteria for decision making emerge. Application of these criteria potentially leads to multiple synergistic benefits in economic, social, scientific, governance and environmental spheres.

**Below** image credit 10.9

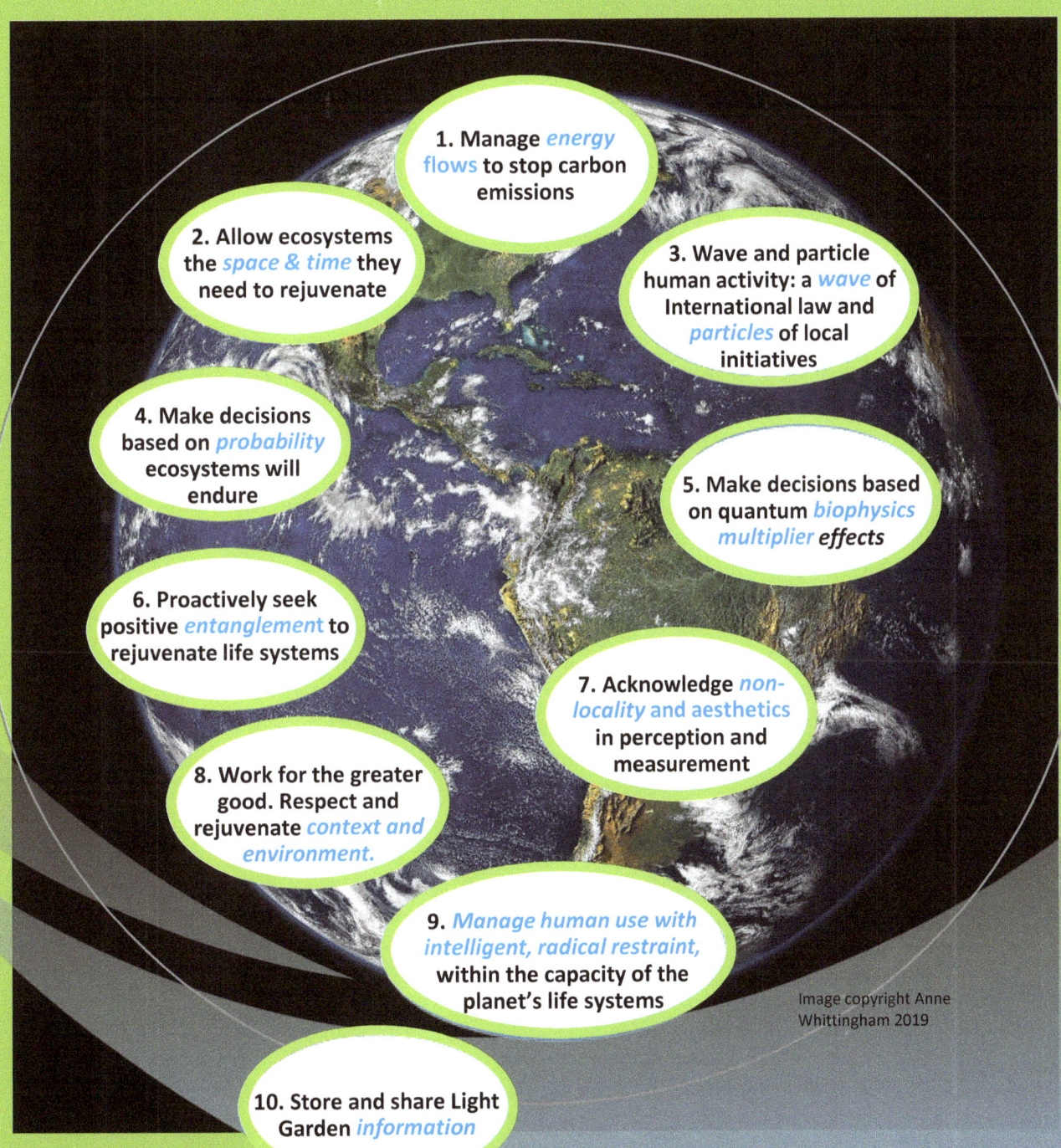

1. Manage *energy flows* to stop carbon emissions
2. Allow ecosystems the *space & time* they need to rejuvenate
3. Wave and particle human activity: a *wave* of International law and *particles* of local initiatives
4. Make decisions based on *probability* ecosystems will endure
5. Make decisions based on quantum *biophysics multiplier* effects
6. Proactively seek positive *entanglement* to rejuvenate life systems
7. Acknowledge *non-locality* and aesthetics in perception and measurement
8. Work for the greater good. Respect and rejuvenate *context and environment.*
9. *Manage human use with intelligent, radical restraint,* within the capacity of the planet's life systems
10. Store and share Light Garden *information*

Image copyright Anne Whittingham 2019

# Ten components of the Light Garden

*In Chapter 1 the ten basic components of the Earth as a 'Light Garden' concept were introduced. These reflect the principles of quantum biophysics in simple terms. To assist in explaining how these ten components can be applied to decision making in the 21st century, they are listed again below for ease of comparison with items one to ten on the following page.*

1. **ENERGY.** Enhance and work with the energy flows of nature that direct movement and determine the optimal relative placement of particles and waves.

2. **SPACE and TIME.** There is the space through which particles and wave move.

3. **WAVES and PARTICLES.** There are tiny waves and particles that move in energy fields

4. **LINES, PATTERNS and PROBABILITIES.** There are the lines of motion that we perceive and patterns of motion that form. In addition there are uncertainties and probabilities.

5. **MULTIPLICATION.** Multiplication effects arise due to clustering of similar entities into materials that we can feel and feel. For example, one group of carbon atoms might cluster together to form graphite, while another might form a brilliant pink diamond.

6. **ENTANGLEMENT and FOCAL POINTS.** There are points where energy paths intersect and where we perceive focal points to arise. In addition there is the related concept of Quantum entanglement, where particles cannot be perceived or described independently of each other.

7. **PERCEPTION and MEASURE.** There is humanity's measurement and perception.

8. **CONTECT and ENVIRONMENT.** There is the wider environment in which particular patterns form. For example, a labyrinth garden follows a repeatable basic plan but also is influenced by its wider setting and the intention of the people who plan and build it.

9. **HUMAN USE.** There may be restrained human intervention for particular purposes, such as food production, education, control of a parcel of land, water or space and so on.

10. **STORAGE and SHARING.** There is the storage of information, so that the patterns of nature and human use can replicate and evolve.

*Common patterns at different scales from the small to the large:*
*Below left* Image credit 10.6.1, **Curving patterns on a leaf.**
*Below centre* Image credit 10.6.2, **Labyrinth garden path and trees.**
*Far right* Image credit 10.6.3, **Ancient stone engraving of labyrinth pattern.**

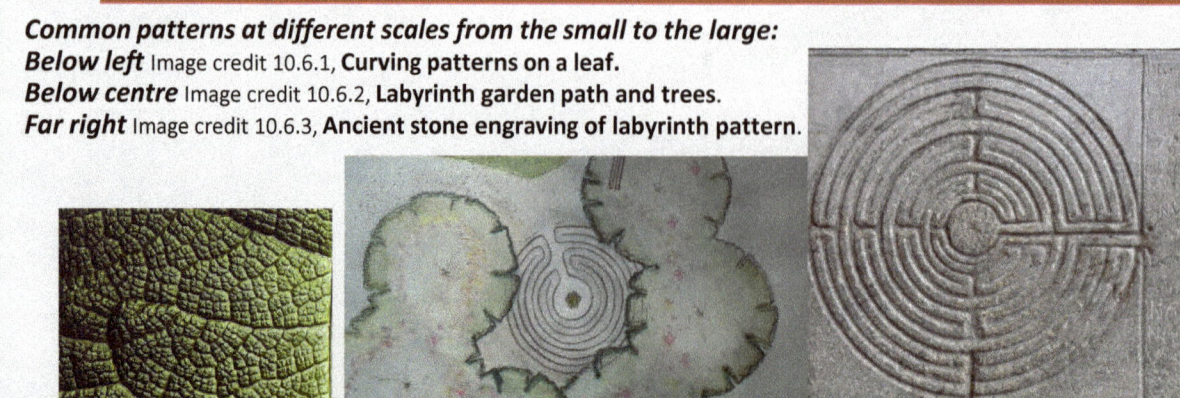

# Testing the Light Garden model: climate change

*Let us now test how the Light Garden model can be applied to answering the question raised on page 10.6: How to stabilise ecosystems and rejuvenate life in the context of climate change? Using data from the previous page, the results of testing with the ten criteria are shown below.*

**Column 2 scoring:** How relevant is this to stabilising ecosystems and rejuvenating life? (rate 1 – 5)
**Column 3 scoring:** To what extent is this happening already without the light garden model? (rate 1 – 5)

| Does the Light Garden model prompt more rapid and effective action? | Column 2 | Column 3 |
|---|---|---|
| **1 ENERGY.** Yes. Managing *energy flows* to stop carbon emissions prioritises stabilization of ecosystems and rejuvenation of life more rapidly and effectively than present planned reductions. | 5 | 2 |
| **2 SPACE and TIME.** Yes. Allowing ecosystems the *space & time* they need to stabilise and rejuvenate entails a radical curtailment of human resource use through international restraint and equitable access to resources. | 5 | 2 |
| **3. WAVES and PARTICLES.** Yes. The model of a *wave* of International law and *particles* of local initiatives is sorely needed and greatly lacking at present, so these features would greatly assist stabilization of life and climate. | 5 | 1 |
| **4. PATTERNS and PROBABILITIES.** Yes. Making decisions based on the *probability* that ecosystems will endure implies a reordering of priorities away from exploitation of resources towards rejuvenation of living systems. | 5 | 1 |
| **5. MULTIPLICATION.** Yes. Making decisions based on quantum *biophysics multiplier* effects has the potential to rapidly lead to a radical reordering of priorities away from exploitation of natural resources towards rejuvenation of living systems. | 5 | 1 |
| **6. FOCAL POINTS.** Yes. Proactively seeking positive *entanglement* to rejuvenate life systems has the potential to rapidly improve the effectiveness of action towards rejuvenation of living systems. | 5 | 1 |
| **7. MEASURE.** Acknowledging *non-locality* in Perception and measurement implies adopting existing systems such as quadruple bottom line accounting where social, environmental, economic and governance issues are all more comprehensively factored into measurements and decision making, thus greatly increasing opportunities for taking effective climate change action. | 5 | 1 |
| **8. CONTEXT.** Yes. Working for the greater good and respecting and rejuvenating *context and environment* set the framework for an equitable and just society capable of taking rapid and effective climate change action. | 5 | 1 |
| **9. HUMAN USE.** Yes. Applying intelligent, radical *restraint in human use, within the capacity of the planet's life systems* is a goal that is sorely lacking but could be rapidly achieved, as history has shown in cases of rationing. | 5 | 1 |
| **10. STORAGE.** No. Information *Storage & sharing of* may not lead to action | 5 | 1 |

Image credit 10.11

# Plan & achieve

As described on the previous page, testing of the Light Garden model for its usefulness in prompting effective action to address climate change indicates there is great potential for collection human action at the global scale. Let us now consider decision making at a more site-specific scale.

**Below top left** Image credit 10.12.1 **View to the flagpole on Parliament House Canberra, 2018.**
**Below top right** Imaged credit 10.12.2 **A wild kangaroo in the open space grasslands of Canberra.**

**Above Left and Above Centre** Image credit 10.12.3 **Watercolour illustrations** for the design of the new city of Canberra, prepared by Landscape Architect Walter Burley Griffin and his wife Marion Mahoney Griffin.
**Above right** Image credit 10.12.4 **Google Earth** images of Canberra in 2018.

# Nexus: 21ˢᵗC decision making

*In one of the contemporary, and not so accidental triumphs of environmental planning and legislation, kangaroos thrive in Australia's national capital, the city of Canberra.*

As illustrated on the previous page with the example of Canberra, humanity has great capacity to plan for and live in harmony with nature and share the sunlight, food, water and energy with other living creatures The water colour illustrations prepared in 1911 by the Griffins bear a striking resemblance to photographs of the city taken just over a century later in 2018.

For example, the proportions of the water colour illustration of Parliament House align almost perfectly with the current building that is set against the backdrop of forested hills. Construction of the city of Canberra commenced in 1914 but Lake Burley Griffin was not constructed until some fifty years later in 1957.

The Australian Prime Minster of the time, Sir Robert Menzies, named the lake *Lake Burley Griffin*. This was after declining proposals that the lake be named after himself. Although the Griffins were under-appreciated during their time in Australia, this gesture by the Prime Minister indicated that public recognition for the quality of their Landscape Architectural design has grown during the decades since it was originally chosen as the winning design for the nation of Australia's first capital city.

A century after construction of the city began, wild kangaroos are still frequently seen in the grasslands of public open space in Canberra. Retreating to the hillside bushland to rest, these protected, wild creatures forage freely in the road verges, in quieter parklands and on larger institutional sites such as the Australian War Memorial which adjoins the Mt Ainslie reserve.

One of the saving graces of the Australian culture has been that the nexus between the city and the bush has never been lost in the nation's mythology. Speaking of another nexus of relevance to many nations as they plan for how to best use their natural resource of sunlight, Andrew Noble, former director of the Water, Land and Ecosystems project in Sri Lanka, said when describing the nexus between water and solar power:

> *" Solar buyback provisions have tremendous potential to support aquifer health and address the 'energy-water nexus' in the developing world. "I feel this is potentially a 'game changer' in addressing the challenge of over-extraction of groundwater, a challenge that not only India is facing."*
> (19)

Over-extraction of groundwater is just one of multiple issues that can be better addressed by applying the combined set of decision making criteria in the quantum Light Garden model proposed in this book.

On that note, let us now review some of the main findings of each chapter in this book to bring together examples of how the Light Garden model is working in different cultures around the world.

**Below** Image credit 10.13 *Sculpture in Canberra.*

# Summary of chapter findings

Image credit 10.14

| Chapter | What is an example from this chapter showing the application of Quantum biophysics ? | How does this example fit with the concept of the Earth as a Quantum Light Garden ? |
|---|---|---|
| **2 South East Asia** *Image credit 10.17.1* | Thousands of shrines dot the landscape and villages of Bali, so the probability of being in proximity to the influence of at least one shrine within this network is high. This is an example of application of **quantum probability theory in society.** | Multiple shrines throughout the land is consistent with managing the natural resources of Light Garden Earth as a **network of many interconnected living systems**, so the probability is high for the survival of biological and cultural diversity in any particular location within the network. |
| **3 North East Asia** *Image credit 10.17.2* | The emphasis on Feng Shui and the energy of the Earth as vital design elements in these cultures is equivalent to application of **the quantum biophysics concept that energy fields influence movement, growth and patterns in life forms.** | This is consistent with managing **Light Garden Earth as a balanced, living energy system**. For example, if too much heat energy is entering the garden to support stabilisation and rejuvenation of living systems, then the flow needs to be reversed to regain balance and avoid loss of life. |
| **4 Islamic** *Image credit 10.17.3* | Light is used as a symbol to help people gain an understanding of God in Islamic texts and Paradise Gardens. It predates **quantum *entanglement* theory,** where everything is related through flow on- effects, (such as an understanding of God and humanity). | Managing the planet as a field for the making of Paradise Gardens parallels the Light Garden quantum entanglement concept that **results of measurements made at a particular location can depend on the properties and influences of distant objects,** (or religious beliefs in God). |
| **5 Africa** *Image credit 10.17.4* | Quantum biophysics is concerned with keeping a diverse range of inter-dependent life forms alive and the smallholder farmers of Africa support such biodiversity through the diversity inherent in their farming practices. | Supporting traditional farming practices in Africa, (which are being ravaged due to warfare, corruption, land and water grabs by foreign entities), is consistent with the aims of the Light Garden concept, that recognizes the need for a legally enforceable, cooperative international program for equitable access to resources. |

# Summary continued

Image credit 10.15

| Chapter | What is an example from this chapter showing the application of Quantum biophysics ? | How does this example fit with the concept of the Earth as a Quantum Light Garden ? |
|---|---|---|
| **6 India**<br>*Image credit 10.18.1* | The Indian state of Sikkim was declared the world's first fully organic state in 2018. This demonstrates the power of government to prioritise and support the life processes that are the focus of quantum biophysics. | **Quantum biophysics and the Light Garden concept focuses on life processes.** Quantum biophysics makes us more aware of the need for rejuvenation and connection between human society, biodiversity, organic gardening and farming. |
| **7 Europe**<br>*Image credit 10.18.2* | After the unabashed display of power by monarchs such as Louis XIV of France, the people in many European countries rebelled and established **cultures of restraint**, with more equitable, participatory systems of governance. Restraint is one of the quantum biophysics principles. | The Light Garden concept includes light energy as valuable resource to be used consciously within a *culture of restraint.* |
| **8 South and Central America**<br>*Image credit 10.18.3* | **The a**wareness of the role of light in the growth of crops and in the monitoring the calendar each year at sites such as Machu Pichu demonstrates application of the **Quantum concept that light travels in discrete packages of energy and in repeatable patterns.** | This is consistent with managing the Earth as a Light Garden, where **discrete parcels of light energy are equitably shared**, rather than garnered by powerful groups. Light is retained as available for absorption by all living ecosystems. This is necessary for food production and rejuvenation of biodiversity. It also avoids loss of life. |
| **9 North America**<br>*Image credit 10.18.4* | Through working for abolition of slavery, although often relatively few in number, religious groups such as the Quakers have had a strong influence in shaping the current culture of the USA. This is an example of applying **quantum multiplier effects** principles. | **Small but scalable.** Quakers believe the light of God exists within each person. The light of each person potentially affects the behaviour of larger groups of people. **Research in q**uantum biophysics is extending beyond small particles to larger networks. This is consistent with the Light Garden multiplier effect principles. |

# 21st century examples

*" Our vision is underpinned by the precinct's core values of delivering a welcoming and inclusive place that everyone can enjoy – one that is supported by excellent design and infrastructure; uniquely Queensland; innovative, creative and bold; ecologically and financially stable; collaborative; and balances community and commercial needs."* (20)

**Although** never envisaged in quite the same way as the *Gardens by the Bay* project in Singapore, the *Southbank* site in Brisbane fulfills some similar roles within the urban fabric of Brisbane. In Singapore, the aim was **to transform Singapore from a "Garden City" to a "City in a Garden."** The project was intended as a role model for others and was developed as a purpose built site that opened in 2012.

In contrast, *Southbank* has gradually evolved since 1988, when it began life as the *World Expo 88* site. It now includes large-scale public entertainment venues, public transport interchanges and a riverbank promenade that is popular with joggers, walkers, ferry passengers and cyclists. Scattered through the site there are gardens, lawns, picnic areas and a large, resort–style swimming pool fringed by palm trees. Located in this setting are approximately ninety restaurants, bars, cafes and boutiques; apartment and hotel buildings; public outdoor markets, heritage listed buildings and educational facilities.

Amidst the diversity of uses in this garden, the towering form of the floodlit bougainvillea arches depicted above left has an important way-finding and landmark function. It is not just a floral display: it assists people to find their way safely through the extensive and complex site by day and by night. The powerful floodlighting is an important part of the overall safety and success of this massive trellis garden, which is open to the public 24 hours a day.

**Above** Photo credit 10.16.1
***Southbank in Brisbane, Australia.***

**Above** Photo credit 10.16.2 ***Close up view of flowers trained upon the Southbank archway.***

# Cities, light and sustainability

*In comparison to the smaller numbers of visitors in Singapore and Brisbane, in New York City there are 35 million visitors annually to Central Park. (21) With a population of 8.6 million, New York has four times the number of residents than are found in Brisbane). (22)*

In contrast to Central Park, gardens such as the New York Botanic Gardens and Kew Gardens in London, each receive a much lower annual rate of visitation, at the rate of one to two million people. These statistics illustrate the global trend towards public gardens being managed as part of the urban landscape rather than as separate gardens per se. This trend has been driven to a large extent by international recognition of the need to implement a sustainability agenda.

Planting trees that will harness the energy of light and use it to store carbon is part of this agenda and many cities have legally enforceable codes that specify requirements for tree planting. An example from the Brisbane City Council Landscape Code is given overleaf. It highlights the importance of achieving minimum amounts of tree canopy cover.

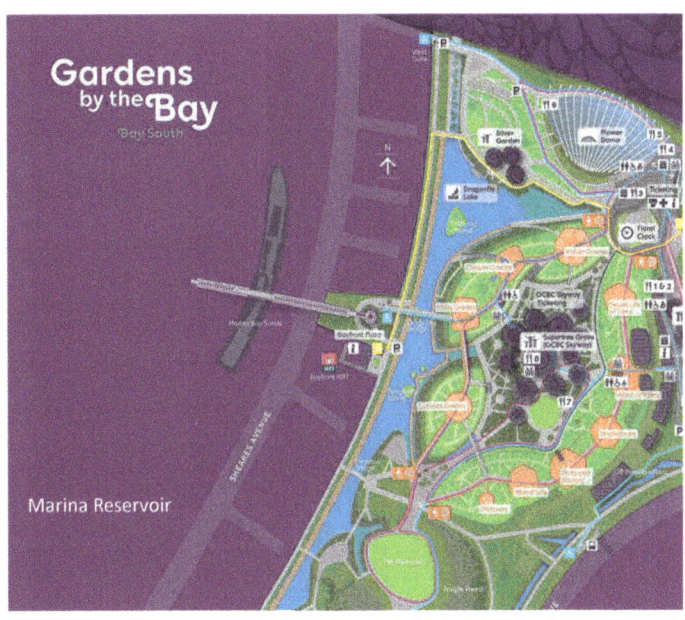

**Above** Image credit 10.17.1 **Gardens by the Bay, Singapore**

**Below** Image credit 10.17.2 **Central Park, New York**

**Number of visitors annually.**

Central Park, New York, USA – 35 million visitors commenced (c) in 1858

Southbank, Brisbane, Australia – 11 million visitors. (c) 1988

Disneyland USA – 9 million, Disneyland Hong Kong – 6.2 m. (c) 2005

Gardens by the Bay, Singapore, - 6.4 m. (c) 2012

# Light, shade & climate codes

*Above* Image credit 10.18.1 *Southbank*

**The** Brisbane City Council Landscaping Code requires that for all non-residential sites, landscaped areas along the frontage of the site include trees. These are not just trees but

" *large trees that achieve a canopy spread over a minimum of 50% of the frontage, within 10 years of planting.*" (23)

There is a similar requirement for planting on residential sites. As illustrated at left and below, the Southbank site in Brisbane provides an example of the type of urban environment that is achieved when the Landscaping Code is applied. Here we see a balanced, 50% mix of open lawn and paving, plus a 50% tree canopy cover. (24) Indeed the pleasant leafy environment is one of the main and enduring attractions on this intensively used site.

As noted in her 2016 – 2017 Annual Report, Dr Catherin Bull AM, (25) Landscape Architect and Chair of Southbank Corporation, reminded readers that the enduring popularity and viability of this site has been the outcome of twenty five years of committed professional teamwork.

*Below* Image credit 10.18.2 *Southbank (Google Earth)*

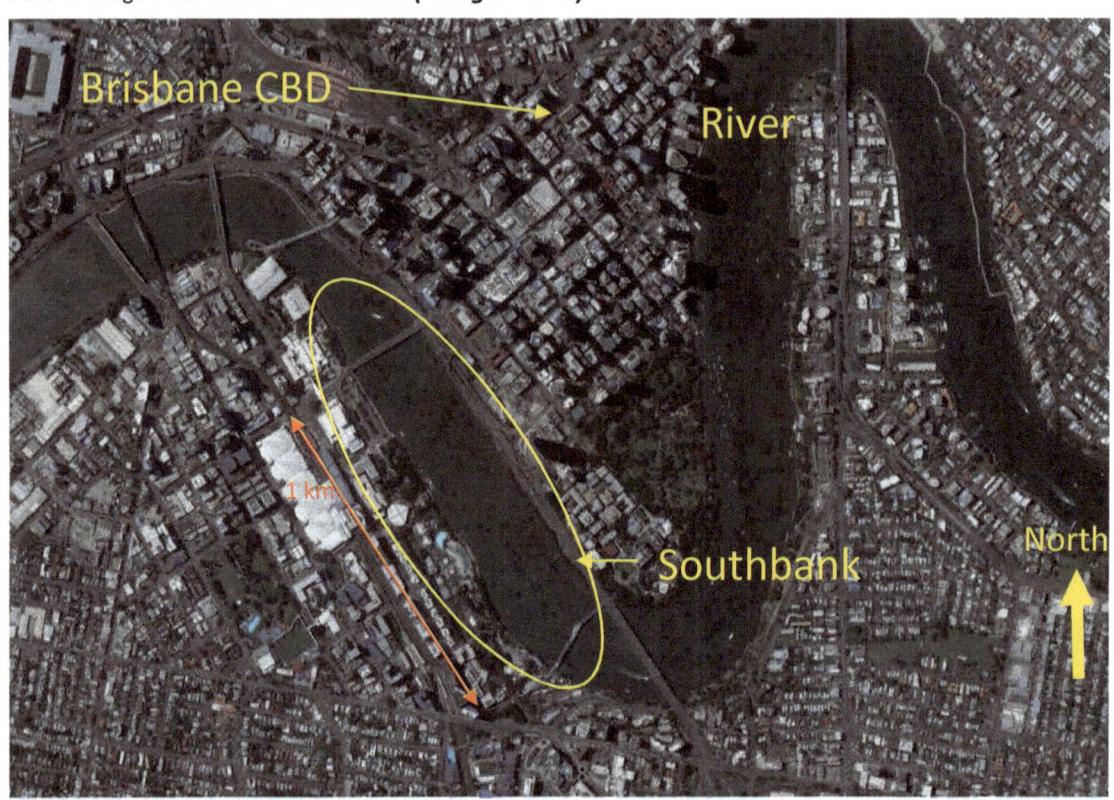

# Design sensitivity to light

*Unlike the concept for the domes at Singapore's "Gardens by the Bay", Danish Architect Jorn Utzon did not conceive of his 1957 winning design for the Sydney Opera House as a building in a garden but rather as a landmark on a spectacular peninsular of Sydney Harbour.* (26)

**Top right** Image credit 10.19.1
**Singapore's Gardens by the Bay project: the flower dome.**
**Centre right** Image credit 10.19.2 **Sydney Opera House** on the shores of Sydney Harbour.
**Lower right** Image credit 10.19.3
**Light reflecting off the roof tiles on the Sydney Opera House.**

**Forty** five years after his winning design was selected for the construction of the Sydney Opera House, in 2002 Jorn Utzon was invited to prepare a document setting out principles to safeguard the heritage significance of the site, which by then had been listed on the World Heritage Register in the intervening years.

The set of principles was to be a benchmark against which the validity of proposals for future work around the opera house could be assessed. One design principle that Utzon emphasized was that the roof sails of the building should be white and the surrounding base of the building should be dark.

The reason for this was to maintain the contrast of the white roof sails against the broader, darker, harbour setting. As part of this concept Jorn Utzon's team went into great design detail to achieve the durable, white, reflective finish of the purpose-made tiles that line the roof shells. (Refer to the image at right). In another example illustrating Utzon's sensitivity to light as part of the design, he said that white café umbrellas on the podium of the building were not appropriate, as they would detract from the huge roof sails as the main light-reflecting feature of the site. (27)

10.19

# Light and water in Chengdu

*The combination of light and water at the Symantec Chengdu Campus in the city of Chengdu, China is quite different from that at the Sydney Opera House. Workers who walk through this garden report a welcome sense of retreat as they pass though this patch of vegetation on the one hectare site that houses the company Symantec's Chinese office and research centre.* (28)

Surrounded by glass-walled buildings which give off myriads of reflected light, this garden was designed by Landscape Architects SWA and completed in 2009. The vegetation includes conifer and bamboo species, which were chosen because they are native woodland species from the south west region of China where Chengdu is located.

**Top Left** Image credit 10.20.1 Although this garden does not look like a traditional Chinese garden, it has some features in common with traditional designs, including the elements of water, stone, timber and plants. The stones in the garden are not natural looking stones but as depicted above left, they are large white sculpted forms that contrast with the grey gravel in which they are placed.

**Centre Left** Image credit 10.20.2 **The water** in this garden is not in the form of a pond or stream but flows as a "water mirror": a thin sheet of water only a few centimeters deep beside the path.

**Bottom Left** Image credit 10.20.3 **LED lights** set into the timber path through the garden are an appealing feature. The raised timber path has a practical purpose that could not be achieved by a ground level concrete path, as this garden forms part of the stormwater harvesting and dispersal system for the whole Symantec Campus.

# Walking into the future

*" Nice place to get exercise with lovely view. Keep walking and enjoying the various flowers and plants with various fragrance."* (29) This was a public website post in 2018 by a visitor *to Gardens by the Bay* in Singapore but it could equally well apply to walking at Southbank or many other places.

**The** allusion to fragrance in the website post quoted above echoes the ancient appeal of the Islamic Paradise Garden. It also highlights the continuing appeal of modern gardens as places to walk in safety for exercise and recreation amongst flowers, trees and sunlight.

As each of the three photographs at left illustrates, there is a trend for contemporary gardens to feature archways and constructed paths. At top left, arches covered with yellow orchids are the prime feature. At centre left, tall steel frames supporting purple bougainvillea are the main feature.

At bottom left, the timber planks of a boardwalk, winding with minimal intrusion through the mangroves, are the characteristic feature. In each case, the garden offers opportunities to relax, walk and be surrounded on all sides with flowers or trees.

**Above left** Image credit 10.21.1
**Singapore Botanic Gardens orchid arches**

**Centre Left** Image credit 10.21.2
**Southbank in Brisbane, Australia.**

**Bottom Left** Image credit 10.21.3
**Mangroves with boardwalk access across the tidal mud flats.**

# Sunlight attracts visitors

*As illustrated on the previous page, the simple pleasure of walking in safe, pleasant, even beautiful surrounds is a universal one. It also brings great health benefits. However, is humanity in the process of turning popular waterside sites the world over into theme parks, rather than opportunities to experience authentic local culture and landscape?*

**Above** Image credit 10.22 *Southbank, Brisbane, Australia*

## Southbank

in Brisbane, Australia is an example of the trend towards integration of gardens and landscape in multiple-use, high density, urban forms, where good quality public open space is provided. The warm sub-tropical climate with plenty of sunlight all year round encourages people to spend their recreational time outdoors. Southbank attracts 11 million visitors annually, (30) whilst the resident population of the city is 2.2 million. (31) The 17 hectare site occupies one kilometer of the inner city riverbank.

In comparison, Singapore's population is 5.6 million (32) and Singapore's *Gardens By the Bay* project covers an area of 101 hectares. It has two kilometres of water frontage to Marina Reservoir, which adjoins the central business district and connects to Singapore Harbour. The site was opened in 2012 and in 2017 received 6.4 million visitors (33). In comparison, Hong Kong Disneyland received 6.2 million visitors that year (34) whilst Universal Studios Disneyland theme park received 9 million visitors. (35)

Although theme parks such as Disneyland may spring to mind as the most popular visitor destinations in the world during the early 21$^{st}$ century, the multiple-use, diverse landscape settings of Central Park in New York, Southbank in Brisbane and West Lake in Hangzhou, China, actually attract many more visitors per year. What is the significance of this, as an ever larger percentage of the world's population lives in cities and the technology that underlies the form of cities keeps developing?

# 21ˢᵗ century liveable cities

*Whilst the Syantec courtyard in Chengdu may be an example of a stormwater harvesting garden that brings native plant species and a welcome respite into a dense urban area, the rapid urbanisation of China in the decades since the mid 20ᵗʰ century raises other issues.*

**Helena** Norberg-Hodge, writing of rural China in the last years of the 20ᵗʰ century, has said:

> "the people I encountered were able to meet most of their basic needs locally, using their own labor and ingenious small-scale technologies. In the villages, we were greeted with spontaneous laughter and humor, simple but delicious food . . . " (36)

Helena then compared the changes that she had seen in China and in Detroit during the fifteen year period preceding 2010. Whilst on the one hand many people in China had moved rapidly from village life to high rise city life, on the other side of the Pacific, the people of Detroit had moved in the opposite direction.

In Detroit, Helena found a grassroots revolution underway, as nearly two hundred community gardens had sprung up amidst the crumbling houses and factories of the inner city. These gardens provided a focal point for people to gather; work cooperatively on a worthwhile project and experience a link with the world of nature and plants. (37)

Branching out from this example to discussion of urban farms and gardens as part of the wider trend towards creating liveable cities and landscapes in the 21ˢᵗ century, Helena noted:

> " Around the world, two opposing forces are contending to define our future. On one side are those working for a new economy—one that is more equitable, decentralized, and attuned to the needs of people and nature. On the other are the forces behind corporate globalization and its consolidation of political and economic power. " (38)

Helena's comments raise the question of whether allowing rapid expansion of cities is the best way forward for the 21ˢᵗ century, rather than a policy of decentralisation, localisation and atunement to the local ecology and culture. For example, programs to manage climate change through labour intensive, employment generating, global scale vegetation regeneration and low ecological footprint lifestyles are would need participation through both international and locally decentralised models. However, by 2014, for the first time in human history), more than half the world's population lived in urban areas.

The proportion of the population living in urban areas increased more than exponentially between 1900 and 2014. In 1900, seven percent of the population lived in urban areas. Before 1600, the estimated percentage of people living in urban areas was less than five percent. (39),(40).

Although catering for an expanding, city based population, *Sustainability City* in Dubai provides an example of a purpose built 21ˢᵗ century settlement that in many ways supports decentralisation, localisation and atunement to the local ecology and culture. This is because it effectively offers state of the art technology in an intensively managed oasis where the role of trees is valued.

# Paris, Singapore, Dubai

*Throughout this book I have described examples of projects that are seeking to support Life on Earth by heading towards the post carbon era and I will now conclude with a review of trends to even more 'light conscious' structures. Since the golden age of large greenhouses during the 19th century, domes, pyramids and futuristic translucent structures have continued to be developed during the 20th and 21st centuries. Where is this trend headed?*

**Above** Image credit 10.24.1 **The Louvre Pyramid,** which forms the main entry to this museum in Paris. It was built in 1980.

**Centre Left** Image credit 10.24.2 *"Gardens by the Bay"* in Singapore, built in 2012.

**Bottom Left** Image credit 10.24.3 *"The Sustainable City"* project in Dubai. It was opened in 2018.

**As** can be seen by comparing the three images on this page, the positive trend progressing from the Louvre in 1980 to Dubai's *Sustainable City* in 2019, is for the inclusion of more plants and carbon sequestration, plus less reliance on fossil fuels for energy generation, transport and other purposes. The *Sustainable City* project is discussed in more detail in Chapter Four of this book.

# Translucent city living

***Singapore Gardens by the Bay*** *is an example of a modern free - form* project that has the aim of "raising the quality of life through enhancing greenery and flora in the city". This project was also announced as a major step towards "transforming Singapore from a Garden City to a City in a Garden." (41)

**The Sky Domes:**
**The Flower Dome (1)** and
**The Cloud Dome (2)** plus
**the Super Trees (3)**

These Sky Domes were designed as giant glasshouses to trap and control light; generate electricity and recycle water and nutrients. They also showcase to the public a new way forward for sustainable city living *amidst an urban forest.* This is not a techno dream but is firmly focused on harmonious living amongst an urban forest of real live trees. (42)

*Top right* Image credit 10.25.1
*Centre right* Image credit 10.25.2

*Below right* Image credit 10.25.3
**Trees, light, people and cities of the future.**

*'Super Tree' towers with an elevated walkway linking them above the canopy of tropical trees in Singapore.*

Illustrating the concept that photonics are to the 21st century what electronics was to the 20th century, the "Light Garden" Super Trees and Sky Domes have a translucent quality, reminiscent of the fabric of petals as they reach for the light. As illustrated at right, they also are built around a strong framework that can withstand tropical storms and the test of time.

# Chapter 1  References

*Note. The APA Style Blog is used as a reference for how to write "21$^{st}$ century".*
https://blog.apastyle.org/apastyle/2010/06/announcing-new-features-on-the-apa-style-blog.html
1. For a definition of this term, go to https://www.asiaglobalonline.hku.hk/anthropocene-climate-change/
2. https://www.un.org/sustainabledevelopment/blog/2019/05/nature-decline-unprecedented-report/
3. Wilson, E. O., *"Half Earth: Our Planet's Fight for Life,"*
4. https://www.climate-engineering.eu/single/the-telegraph-sir-david-attenborough-says-geo-engineering-solutions-to-climate-change-are-fascist.html
5. Vaughan, Adam, *Could geoengineering really help us solve the climate crisis* ? May 2019, https://www.newscientist.com/article/2203085-could-geoengineering-really-help-us-solve-the-climate-crisis/
6. Raworth, Kate, *"Doughnut Economics: Seven Ways to Think like a 21$^{st}$ Century Economist"*. 2017
7. https://www.awake-tech.com/about-us
8. https://imagine.gsfc.nasa.gov/educators/lessons/xray_spectra/background-atoms.html
9. https://soho.nascom.nasa.gov/classroom/glossary_middle.html
10. Talbott, David and Thornhill, Wallace, in *'Thunderbolts of the Gods'*, Mikamar Publishing, (2005), quoted by McKusick, Eileen Day in *'Tuning the Human Biofield: Healing with Vibrational Sound Therapy,'* Simon and Schuster, (2014).
11. Hubacher J. *"The phantom leaf effect: a replication, part 1,"* J Alternative Complement Med. 2015;21(2):83–90. [ PubMed]
12. https://www.ncbi.nlm.nih.gov/pmc/articles/PMC4654779/
13. Kafatos, Menas C., PhD, Chevalier, Gaetan, PhD, Chopra, Deepak, MD, Hubacher, John, MA, Kak, Subhash, PhD and Theise, Neil D., MD, *"Biofield Science: Current Physics Perspectives"* in Global Advanced Health, 2015 Nov; 4 (Suppl): 25 – 34. Published online 2015 Nov1.
14. Skinner, Brian, PhD, published online at https://www.ribbonfarm.com/2015/08/20/qft/
15 Skinner, B. Op. Cit,
16. https://en.Wikipedia.org.wiki/Journal of Photochemistry and Photobiology  * As part of the growing recognition of the importance of new quantum concepts of light the Journal *of Photochemistry and Photobiology* was established in 1972. This journal publishes the fundamental scientific studies on all aspects of chemical phenomena induced by interactions between light and molecules/matter of all kinds.
17. Skinner, B. Op. Cit
18. Jonsson, Melissa Joy, in the article *"Love, Creation and Morphic Resonance – The Formula for All Matters in The Love Hologram"*, published online at https://wakeup-world.com/2015/12/07/love-creation-morphic-resonance-formula-all-matters-in-love-hologram-universe/
19. https://www.bibliotecapleyades.net/ciencia/antigravityworldgrid/ciencia_antigravityworldgrid09.htm
20. https://www.donnafisher.net
21. Bawdon-Smith, Jason, Op. Cit., p-81 -82
22. Bordoni, Bruno, PhD DO, Marelli, Fabiola, PhD,  and Sacconi, Beatrice, MD, *Emission of Biophotons and Adjustable Sounds by the Fascial System: Review and Reflections for Manual Therapy,* Journal of Evidence Based Integrative Medicine, 2018; 23: 2515690X17750750. Published online 2018 Feb 1.
23. op. cit.
24. op. cit.
25. Cifra M, Pospíšil P. *Ultra-weak photon emission from biological samples: definition, mechanisms, properties, detection and applications*. Journal of Photochemisty and Photobiology, B. 2014;139:2–10. [PubMed]
26. https://en.wikipedia.org/wiki/Biophotonics

## Chapter 1 References continued

27. https://www.famousscientists.org/Democritus/  (page 22 quote by Bertrand Russell)
28. https://en.Wikipedia.org/wiki/Atomism
29. Reynolds, Garr, *"Presentation Zen"*, Pearson Education (US), 2011.
30. Norberg-Hodge, Helena, *"Localization; essential steps to an economics of Happiness,"* Local Futures/ International Society for Ecology and Culture, 2016.
31. Bawdon-Smith, Jason, "In The Dark", Op. Cit. page 8.
32. https://en.wikiquote.org/wiki/Greta_Thunberg

## Chapter 1 Image credits

Note images are numbered by chapter, page number and position on the page from top to bottom. Thus in chapter 1, on page 25, the third image from the top of the page will be numbered 1.25.3. All images used have no known copyright restrictions and all original sources are acknowledged

**Image 1.1** (front cover) Copyright Anne Whittingham 2019, with background image of globe adapted by A. Whittingham from CC0 image at  https://www.pexels.com/photo/sky-earth-galaxy-universe-2422/ and
Image of moons adapted by A. Whittingham from 4 moons zoltan-tasi-1346503-unsplash CC0 and image of landscape adapted by A. Whittingham from Va Manh Ti/ pixabay.com CC0

**Image credit 1.7** Copyright Anne Whittingham 2019, with inset image of globe adapted by A. Whittingham from CC0  image at https://www.pexels.com/photo/sky-earth-galaxy-universe-2422/ and inset image of child with strawberry cropped by A. Whittingham from image by moniquedsv/ pixabay.com CC0

**Image credit 1.9** Map "Daniel R. Strebe", uploaded 15 August 2011 to https://commons.wikimedia.org/wiki/File:Winkel_triple_projection_SW.jpg ,
Strebe [CC BY-SA 3.0 (https://creativecommons.org/licenses/by-sa/3.0)]

**Image 1.10** Copyright Anne Whittingham 2019

**Image 1.11** Photograph background copyright Anne Whittingham 2019, with use of blue grid image edited after sourcing from Brian Skinner, postdoctoral researcher at Massachusetts Institute of Technology (MIT). Image posted free for use at https://www.ribbonfarm.com/2015/08/20/qft

**Image  1.12** https://en.wikipedia.org/wiki/File: Doughnut-classic.jpg . This file is licensed under the Creative Commons Attribution-Share Alike 4.0 international  license. This image was designed for Kate Raworth in 2017.

**Image 1.13** *Free-Photos/ pixabay.com CC0*

**Image 1.14** J. Tyman b124s httpwww.johntyman.combali12.html

**Image 1.15** ArtTower/ pixabay.com CC0

**Image 1.16** cindygrundsten pixabay.com CC0

## Chapter 1 Image credits continued

**Image 1.17** Hubacher J. *"The phantom leaf effect: a replication, part 1,"* J Alternative Complement Med. 2015;21(2):83–90. [PubMed]

**Image credit 1.18 for table** copyright Anne Whittingham 2019 with three photo credits on the base of this same page as follows:

**Image 10.18.1** Photo credit couleur/ pixabay.com CC0 leaf-3504797__3 with editing by A. Whittingham

**Image 10.18.2** Design and photo copyright Anne Whittingham

**Image 10.18.3** Image credit www.Wikipedia.com/labyrint

**Image 1.19** ParentRap/ pixabay.com CC0

**Image 1.20** Graphic image my Eileen Mc Kusick, January 2013, Electric You, Electric Universe: the New Cosmology. https://www/slideshare.net/emckusick/electric-you-electric-universe

**Image 1.22** Ian Cuming Flickr CC-BY-2.0 on www.reference.com_science _d938dc34732015fb

**Image 1.24.1** DreamyArt/ pixabay.com CC0

**Image 1.24.2** benscherjon/ pixabay.com CC0

**Image 1.24.3** Atlantios/ pixabay.com CC0

**Image 1.25.1** jordan-mcqueen-14250-unsplash CC0

**Image 1.25.2** MBatty/ pixabay.com CC0

## Chapter 2  References

1. Estoque, R. C., Ooba, M., Avitabile, V., Hijioka, Y., DasGupta, Rajarshi, Togawa, T., Murayama, Y., [Nature Communications 10, Article number: 1829 (2019). *"The future of Southeast Asia's forests."*
2. Estoque et al, Op. Cit.
3. https://www.scientificamerican.com/article/deforestation-and-orangutans/
4. Wilson, E. O., *"Half Earth: Our Planet's Fight for Life,"* Liveright; 1 edition (April 4, 2017).
5. Pildes, Russell, University of Illinois – Urbana-Champaign, 5 Nov 2012, from table on http://en.Wikipedia.org.wiki/List_of_countries_by_forest_area. Datum WGS 1984, Robinson Projection,
6. Estoque et al, Op. Cit.
7. Teske, Sven (Ed.) *"Achieving the Paris Climate Agreement Goals, Global and Regional 100% Renewable Energy Scenarios with Non-energy GHG Pathways for +1.5°C and +2°C"*, Open Access publishing, 2019 at https://www.springer.com/gp/book/9783030058425, and quoted on https://www.leonardodicaprio.org/the-global-deal-for-nature
8. Estoque et al, Op. Cit.
9. Estoque et al, Op. Cit.
10. Schneider, A., C M Mertes[1], A J Tatem[2,3], B Tan[4], D Sulla-Menashe[5], S J Graves[6], N N Patel[7], J A Horton[1], A E Gaughan[8], J T Rollo, *"New urban landscape in East–Southeast Asia, 2000–2010"*, Published 3 March 2015 • © 2015 IOP Publishing Ltd, Environmental Research Letters, Volume 10, Number 3
11. Estoque et al, Op. Cit.
12. Estoque et al, Op. Cit.
13. Estoque et al, Op. Cit.
14. Estoque et al, Op. Cit
15. Estoque et al, Op. Cit
16. Zeng, Z., Estes, L., Ziegler, A. D., Chen, A., Searchinger, T., Hua, F., ... & Wood, E. F. (2018). Highland cropland expansion and forest loss in Southeast Asia in the twenty-first century. *Nature Geoscience*, https://news.mongabay.com/2018/07/southeast-asian-deforestation-more-extensive-than-thought-study-finds/
17. Salamanca, A.M., A. Nugroho, M. Osbeck, S. Bharwani and N. Dwisasanti (2015), *"Managing a living cultural landscape: Bali's subaks and the UNESCO World Heritage Site"*, SEI Project Report 2015-05. https://www.sei.org/publications/managing-a-living-cultural-landscape-balis-subaks-and-the-unesco-world-heritage-site/
18. Estoque et al, Op. Cit
19. Keys, Patrick & Wang-Erlandsson, Lan & Gordon, Line & Galaz, Victor & Ebbesson, Jonas. (2017). Approaching moisture recycling governance. Global Environmental Change. 45. 15-23. 10.1016/j.gloenvcha.2017.04.007.
20 Loc. Cit.
21. https://www.usc.edu.au/research-and-innovation/forests-for-the-future/tropical-forests-and-people-research-centre/research-projects/16-years-of-research-in-the-philippines-and-still-going#background , **Enhancing Livelihoods through Forest and Landscape Restoration,** 2017-2022, funded through Australian Centre for International Agricultural Research (ACIAR), Leaders: Professor John Herbohn and Dr Nestor Gregorio
22. Tyman J. www.johntyman.com bali

## Chapter 2 references continued

23. https://whc.unesco.org/en/list/1194
Cultural Landscape of Bali Province: the *Subak* System as a Manifestation of the *Tri Hita Karana* Philosophy
24. https://whc.unesco.org/en/list/1194
Cultural Landscape of Bali Province: the *Subak* System as a Manifestation of the *Tri Hita Karana* Philosophy
25. Op. Cit
26. http://lokhabalitours.com/Lempuyang-temple-sacred-bali-tour
27. https://whc.unesco.org/en/list/1194
Cultural Landscape of Bali Province: the *Subak* System as a Manifestation of the *Tri Hita Karana* Philosophy
*28.* http://lokhabalitours.com/Lempuyang-temple-sacred-bali-tour
29. Op. Cit.
30. https://theculturetrip.com/asia/Indonesia/articles/why-mount-agung-is-the-most-sacred-mountiain-in-bali/
31. Tyman J. www.johntyman.com bali
32. Op. Cit.
33. Op. Cit
34. Op. Cit.

## Chapter 2 Image credits

Note images are numbered by chapter, page number and position on the page from top to bottom. Thus in chapter 1, on page 25, the third image from the top of the page will be numbered 1.25.3. Unless otherwise noted, all images had no copyright restrictions when sourced for inclusion in this book. Images by Dr John Tyman have been reproduced with his written permission.

**Image credit 2.1** photo credit John Tyman httpwww.johntyman.combali04.html b040

**Image credit 2.4.1** Map image credit https://en.wikipedia.org/wiki/South_East_Asia, with labels added by Anne Whittingham

**Image credit 2.4.2** Artist unknown: Balinese artwork from the collection of Dr John Tyman.

**Image credit 2.5** photo credit z0man/ pixabay.com CC0 (photo of Orangutan)

**Image credit 2.8.1 - 2.8.2** Estoque, R. C., Ooba, M., Avitabile, V., Hijioka, Y., DasGupta, Rajarshi, Togawa, T., Murayama, Y., [Nature Communications 10, Article number: 1829 (2019). "The future of Southeast Asia's forests"

**Image credit 2.9** Information transposed from Map by Pildes, Russell, University of Illinois – Urbana-Champaign, 5 Nov 2012, from table on http://en.Wikipedia.org.wiki/list of countries by forest area. Datum WGS 1984, Robinson Projection onto world map by "Daniel R. Strebe", uploaded 15 August 2011 to https://commons.wikimedia.org/wiki/File:Winkel_triple_projection_SW.jpg ,
Strebe [CC BY-SA https://creativecommons.org/licenses/by-sa/3.0 Yellow circle graphics and notes added by Anne Whittingham

**Image credit 2.10**
http://www.johntyman.com/bali/b004.jpg

**Image credit 2.12** Google Earth map of Bali with graphics and labelling by Anne Whittingham.

**Image credit 2.13** all images used with written permission from http www.johntyman.com bali

**Image credit 2.14.1** Oleksandr Pidvalnyi Pexels.com CC0

**Image credit 2.14.2** Aron Visuals/ pexels.com CC0

**Image credit 2.15.1** www johntyman com bali

**Image credit 2.15.2** www johntyman com bali

**Image credit 2.16.1 – 2.16.4** www johntyman com bali

**Image credit 2.17** www johntyman com bali/08

**Image credit 2.18.1** www johntyman com bali/131

**Image credit 2.18.2** www johntyman com bali/41

**Image credit 2.18.3** christopher1710 pixabay.com CC0

**Image credit 2.18.4** Photoman/ pixabay.com CC0

**Image credit 2.19.1** http www.johntyman.com bali.html 133

**Image credit 2.19.2** http www.johntyman.com bali .html 036

**Image credit 2.19.3** christopher1710/ pixabay.com CC0

**Image credit 2.19.4** http www.johntyman.com bali 14.html b162s

## Chapter 3 References

1. https://en.wikipedia.org/wiki/Guo_Pu

2. http://www.fengshuigate.com/zangshu.html

3. http://ajofengshui.co.nf/wpcontent/uploads/2017/05/Rowe_Tyler_2017_Guo_Pu_s_Antique_School_FS_H

4. http://www.bluemountainfengshui.com/

5. Li, Min (2009). 30 Talks on the Chinese Classical Gardens. China Architecture & Building Press. Quoted in: https://stud.epsilon.slu.se/3875/7/pang at Swedish University of Agricultural Sciences Faculty of Landscape Planning, Horticulture and Agricultural Science Department of Landscape Architecture "Ideas and Tradition behind Chinese and Western Landscape Design - similarities and differences". Junying Pang quotes Min Li in a Degree project in landscape planning, 30 hp Masterprogramme Urban Landscape Dynamics Independent project at the LTJ Faculty, SLU Alnarp 2012

6. https://en.wikipedia.org/wiki/West_Lake

7. Loc. cit.

8. http://www.bluemountainfengshui.com/

9. https://en.wikipedia.org/wiki/West_Lake

10. Loc. Cit

11. http://whc.unesco.org/en/list/1334/gallery/

12. http:/whc. unesco.org.en/list

13. Loc. cit.

14. Loc. cit.

15. Loc. cit.

16. https://en.Wikipedia.org/wiki/Central Park

17. Report on the public use of Central Park assets.centralparknyc.org/pdfs/. . . /3.002 Report+on+the+Public+Use+of+Central+Park.pdf

18. https://en.Wikipedia.org/wiki/Changdeokgung

19. https://www.theguardian. com/cities/2017/may/19/seoul-skygarden-south-korea-london-garden-bridge

18. 20. https://en.Wikipedia.org/wiki/Changdeokgung

21. https://www.360cities.net/image/ongnyucheon-stream-changdeokgung-palace

22. https://en.Wikipedia.org/wiki/Changdeokgung

23. Loc. cit.

24. Loc. cit.

## Chapter 3 References  continued

25. Reynolds, Garr,  *Presentation Zen*, Pearson Education (US), 2011.

26.  Li, Min (2009), op. cit.

*27.* Hong, Sun-Kee, Song, In-Ju and Wu, Jianguo, *"Fengshui theory in urban landscape planning"*, in Urban Ecosystems, *Vol 10, 2006/08/08, p221 – 237,* DO  - 10.1007/s11252-006-3263-2

*28. Yanagi, Soetsu,* The Unknown Craftsman: A Japanese Insight Into Beauty, adapted by Bernard Leach, Kodansha International, Tokyo, New York, London, revised edition 1989.

*29. attributed to The Buddha, "Muryoju-kyo" ("Sutra of Eternal Life), cited in* "The Unknown Craftsman: a Japanese Insight into Beauty", *by* Yanagi, Soetsu, adapted by Leach, B., Kodansha International, Tokyo, New York, London. revised edition 1989 p130.

30. Op. cit.

# Chapter 3 Image credits

**Image 3.1.** Photo credit mitch altman flickr CC0 httpswww.flickr.comphotos maltman236948854386.jpg v2-1

**Image 3.5** Map credit Google Earth 2019, with graphics and labels added by A. Whittingham

**Image 3.6** http://www.equate.net.nz/nz-feng-shui-a-guide/ , with graphic adaptations by A. Whittingham

**Image 3.7** copyright Anne Whittingham, 2019

**Image 3.8.1** copyright Anne Whittingham, 1980
**Image 3.8.2** copyright Anne Whittingham, 2019
**Image 3.8.3** GarysLens/ pixabay.com CC0
**Image 3.8.4** pixel2013/ pixaby.com CC0
**Image 3.8.5** stux/ pixabay.com CC0
**Image 3.8.6** KlausHausmann/ pixabay.com CC0
**Image 3.8.7** dimitrisvetsikas 1969 13088/ pixabay.com CC0
**Image 3.8.8** MabelAmber/pixabay.com CC0
**Image 3.8.9** hamxx005/ pixabay.com CC0
**Image 3.8.10** Free-Photos/ pixabay.com CC0

**Image 3.9** Map credit http://www.orangesmile.com/common.img city maps/Hangzhou-map-0.jpg

**Image 3.10** Photo credit mitch altman flickr CC0 httpswww.flickr.comphotosmaltman236948854386.jpg v2-1

**Image 3.11.1** Wikimedia CC0 'unknown person'

**Image 3.11.2** illiterateDeng/ pixabay.com CC0

**Image 3.11.3** Photo # 5 by Mlq4296, https://lovethesepicture.wordpress.com/2011/03.04.21-stunning-superbly-serene-chinese-gardens

**Image 3.12** tampigns/ pixabay.com CC0

**Image 3.13.1** by Daderot Self-photographed CC BY-SA 3.0_https commons.wikimedia.org w index.php curid=11292110ngnyucheon_Changdeokgung_Seoul,_Korea

**Image 3.13.2** Hyangwonjeong_photo_d_ramey_logan at httpsupload.wikimedia.orgwikipediacommons00fHyangwonjeong_photo_d_ramey_logan.jpg

**Image 3.13.3** HeungSoon/ pixabay.com CC0 temple-2557075 . The location of this temple is not know but is likely to be in South Korea.

**Image 3.14** Donggwol-do Changdokang httpsupload.wikimedia.orgwikipediacommonsee6Donggwol-do.jpg

**Image 3.15.1** Photo credit: Ossip van Duivenbode at httpswww.theguardian.comcities2017may19seoul-skygarden-south-korea-london-garden-bri

**Image 3.15.2** Photo credit: Ossip van Duivenbode at httpswww.theguardian.comcities2017may19seoul-skygarden-south-korea-london-garden-bri

**Image 3.15.3** Map prepared by Anne Whittingham, using basemap of Seoul from https://upload.Wikimedia.org/Wikipedia/commons/thumb/2/21/01-0.svg.png with overlay graphics added to show green and water open space networks from Seoul Green Network Plan for major green-spaces and its potential network in Seoul, Seoul Metropolitan Government, 1997.
Sourced from Figure 6, p 234 in Hong, Sun-Kee, Song, In-Ju and Wu, Jianguo, *"Fengshui theory in urban landscape planning"*, in Urban Ecosystems, *Vol 10, 2006/08/08, p221 – 237,*
DO - 10.1007/s11252-006-3263-2

**Image 3.16** copyright Anne Whittingham

**Image 3.17.1** copyright Anne Whittingham

**Image 3.17.2** copyright Anne Whittingham

**Image 3.18** fotoerich/ pixabay.com/ CC0

## Chapter 3 Image credits continued

**Image 3.19.1** Photo with two before and after images sourced from
http://www.metro.seoul.kr/kor2000/chungaehome/en/seoul/main.htm

Uploaded by Sun-Kee Hong to https://www.researchgate.net/figure/Cheonggyecheon-Stream-restoration-project-in-urban-Seoul-2004-This-large-restoration_fig6_225482289

From source publication by Hong, Sun-Kee, Song, In-Ju and Wu, Jianguo, *"Fengshui theory in urban landscape planning"*, in Urban Ecosystems, *Vol 10, 2006/08/08, p221 – 237,* DO - 10.1007/s11252-006-3263-2

**Image 3.19.2** Loc.cit.

**Image 3.19.3** Photo credit Jack Malipan Travel PhotographyAlamy at httpswww.theguardian.comcities2017may19seoul-skygarden-south-ko

**Image 3.20.1** https://en.wikipedia.org/wiki/File:Ryoan-ji-Garden-2018.jpg This file is licensed under the Creative Commons Attribution-Share Alike 4.0 International license.

**Image 3.20.2** copyright Anne Whittingham

**Image 3.20.3** http://www.bluemountainfengshui.com/gallery/feng-shui-tour-and-activities/feng-shui-tour-chinese-garden-hangzhou/.

**Image 3.21** CharlesRondeau/ pixabay.com CCO

## Chapter 4 References

1. The Qu'ran 24: 35-6 which was translated to English by Andul Haleem at http://www.vam.ac.uk/content/articles/f/festivals-of-light-islam

2. Multiple sources are available for this, for example https://worldloveflowers.com/events/taj-mahal-garden

3. The Qu'ran 24: 35-6 which was translated to English by Andul Haleem at http://www.vam.ac.uk/content/articles/f/festivals-of-light-islam

4. Multiple sources, for example http://www.vam.ac.uk/content/articles/f/festivals-of-light-islam

5. For example https://www.westernunion.com/blog/beautiful-Islamic-site

6. https://whc.unesco.org/en/list

7. http://www.bbc.co.uk/religion/religions/islam/practices/salat.shtml

8. https://en.wikipedia.org/wiki/Shalimar_Bagh,_Srinagar, citing the following two references:
   - *Sajjad Kausar (July 2005). "Meaning of Mughal Landscape" (PDF). p. 1. Archived from the original (pdf) on 2011-07-23. Retrieved 2009-12-31.*
   - *Blake, Stephen P. (2002). Shahjahanabad: The Sovereign City in Mughal India (1639-1739) Cambridge University Press. p. 44. ISBN 0-521-52299-4. Retrieved 2009-12-31*

9. https://en.wikipedia.org/wiki/Shalimar_Bagh,_Srinagar

10. https://whc.unesco.org /en/tentativelists/5580

11. Loc. Cit.

12. https://en.wikipedia.org/wiki/Shalimar_Bagh,_Sringar

13. The Qu'ran 24: 35-6 which was translated to English by Andul Haleem at http://www.vam.ac.uk/content/articles/f/festivals-of-light-islam

14. https://en.wikipedia.org/wiki/Shalimar_Bagh,_Sringar

15. Loc. Cit.

16. http://en.Wikipedia.org/wiki/Gardens of Versailles

17. http://en.Wikipedia.org/wiki/Gardens of Versailles

18. Loc. Cit.

19. https://worldloveflowers.com/events/taj-mahal-garden/

## Chapter 4 References continued

20. Nash, Elizabeth, at https://www.independent.co.uk/news/world/europe/after-650-years-the-wisdom-of-the-alhambra-is-revealed-1658050.html

21. Loc. Cit.

22. https://www.piccavey.com/granada-alhambra-walls/

23. Loc. Cit.

24. http://www.traveller.com.au/burhanpur

25 - 27. Loc. Cit.

28. https://whc.unesco.org/en/list/

29. https://www.tripadvisor.com.au/Attraction_Review-g187441-d191078-Reviews-The_Alhambra-Granada_Province_of_Granada_Andalucia.html

30. https://en.wikipedia.org/wiki/Alhambra

31. https://en.wikipedia.org/wiki/Shalimar_Bagh,_Srinagar, citing the following two references:
    - *Sajjad Kausar (July 2005). "Meaning of Mughal Landscape" (PDF). p. 1. Archived from the original (pdf) on 2011-07-23. Retrieved 2009-12-31.*
    - *Blake, Stephen P. (2002). Shahjahanabad: The Sovereign City in Mughal India (1639-1739) Cambridge University Press. p. 44. ISBN 0-521-52299-4. Retrieved 2009-12-31*

32. https://en.Wikipedia.org/wiki/Tetracty *special-about-the-golden-ratio*

33. Loc. Cit.

34. Leet, Leonora, "The Secret Doctrine of the Kabbalah: Recovering the Key to Hebraic Sacred Science", Inner Traditions, Rochester, Vermont, 1999, page 85.

35. Abdullahi, Yahya and Emb, Mohamed Rashid Bin, "Evolution of Islamic geometric patterns" in Frontiers of Architectural Research, Vol 2, Issue 2, June 2013, Pages 243-25 and at https://www.sciencedirect.com/science/article/pii/S2095263513000216

36. Petruccioli Attilio, "Rethinking the Islamic Garden", page 3, Islamic Environmental Design Research Centre, Como, Italy, and at https://environment.yale.edu/publication-series/documents/downloads/0-9/103petruccioli.pdf

37. Emirates News Agency, 2018. http://wam.ae/en/details/1395302665808

38. Birkeland, Janis, "Development: From Vicious Circles to Virtuous Cycles through Built Environment Design", Routledge, 2008.

## Chapter 4 References continued

39. https://www.nationalgeographic.com/environment/urban-expeditions/green-buildings/dubai-ecological-footprint-sustainable-urban-city

40. Emirates News Agency, 2018. http://wam.ae/en/details/1395302665808

41. https://www.nationalgeographic.com/environment/urban-expeditions/green-buildings/dubai-ecological-footprint-sustainable-urban-city

42. Emirates News Agency, 2018. http://wam.ae/en/details/1395302665808

43. https://diamond-developers.ae/

44. https://www.nationalgeographic.com/environment/urban-expeditions/green-buildings/dubai-ecological-footprint-sustainable-urban-city

45. https://www.insydo.com/things-to-do/sustainable-city-dubai-sustainable-development/

46. https://www.oxfam.org.au/oxfamliving/2017/08/21/5-essential-features-of-sustainable-cities-and-eco-cities/

47. https://www.thesustainablecity.ae/myhive-2/

48. Damluji, Salma Samar, *The Architecture of the U.A.E.*, Reading, UK, 2006.

49. https://trove.nla.gov.au/work/21039291?selectedversion=NBD40508234

# Chapter 4 image credits

**Image credit 4.1** mcvalosborne pixabay.com CC0

**Map image credit 4.5.1** : Google Earth 2019, with labels added by Anne Whittingham

**Image credit 4.5.2** Mohamed_Hassan/ pixabay.com CC0 , with text overlay by Anne Whittingham

**Image credit 4.6** https://indiaheritagesites.wordpress.com/category/jammu-kashmir-heritage-sites/, reproduced with permission.

**Image credit 4.7** originally posted to Flickr as India – Srinagar – 03r2 – sunset at Nishat Bagh Mughal Gardens HDR Author McKay Savage. Note Wikipedia credits this photo as being from the site of Shalimar Bagh, not Nishat Bagh.

**Image credit 4.8.1** Google Earth image of Shalimar Bagh and surrounds, May 2019. Labels and graphics added by A. Whittingham

**Image credit 4.8.2** sumulee/ pixabay.com CC0 (image of Versailles)

**Image credit 4.8.3** Depositphotos_199944122_xl-2015

**Image credit 4.9.1** Heidelbergerin/ pixabay.com CC0

**Image credit 4.9.2** Sarangib/ pixabay.com (image of the Taj Mahal

**Image credit 4.10** Image credit 4.10 free for use from httpwww.1zoom.me en wallpaperTaj_Mahal_India_Evening_Agra_Uttar_Pradesh_512710

**Image credit 4.11.1** buraka7/ pixabay.com CC0 (Italian garden)

**Image credit 4.11.2** Shrutimkrishnam/ pixabay.com CC0

**Image credit 4.11.3** Barthwo/ pixabay.com CC0

**Image credit 4.11.4** Gonzolive/ pixabay.com CC0 (image of The Alhambra)

**Image credit 4.12** Gonzolive/ pixabay.com CC0

**Image credit 4.13** photo credit by Gonzolive/ pixabay.com CC0, with phi ratio linework added by A. Whittingham

**Image credit 4.14.1** Image copyright Anne Whittingham. The Tetractys symbol that is depicted is thought to have been developed in the Greek culture during the period $6^{th}$ to $5^{th}$ century BCE. https://en.Wikipedia.org Tetractys

**Image credit 4.14.2** lonepige pixabay.com CC0

**Image credit 4.15** background photograph image credit to Gonzolive/ pixabay.com CC0 Overall image with added notes and graphics copyright Anne Whittingham

**Image credit 4.16** mcvalosborne pixabay.com CC0

**Image credit 4.17** copyright Anne Whittingham

**Image credit 4.18.1** Image credit 4.10 free for use from httpwww.1zoom.me en wallpaperTaj_Mahal_India_Evening_Agra_Uttar_Pradesh_512710

**Image credit 4.18.2** david-rodrigo-472557-unsplash CC0 Dubai mosque

**Image credit 4.18.3** http://wam.ae/en/details/1395302665808

# Chapter 4 image credits continued

**Image credit 4.19** elenajonesinbox/ pixabay.com CC0

**Image credit 4.20** https://upload.wikimedia.org/wikipedia/commons/thumb/5/5b/International_Center_for_Biosaline_Agriculture_Headquarters.jpg/1280px-International_Center_for_Biosaline_Agriculture_Headquarters.jpg

**Image credit 4.21.1** annegordon/ pixabay.com CC0 (The Burj Al Arab in Dubai)

**Image credit 4.21.2** Charly_G/ pixabay.com CC0

# Chapter 5 References

(5.1) https://www.treehugger.com /corporate-responsibility/fracking-water-rights-how-foreign-interests-are- cleaning-out-africa.html
(5.2) attributed to Milton Friedman at https://quoteinvestigator.com/2014/12/09/sand/
(5.3) This quote is commonly attributed to Tacitus, who lived in period approximately 55 AD – 120 AD. He was a Roman Lawyer and Senator. Historical controversy exists around the source of this quote.
(5.4) https://phys.org/news/2018-03-sahara-expandingworld-largest-grew-percent.html Deserts are typically defined as land where the annual rainfall is less than four inches.
(5.5) Tyman, J. at http://www.johntyman. com/africa/37 - 45.html
(5.6) Tyman, J. http://www.johntyman.com/africa/08
(5.7) https://www.one.org/us/2015/05/13/how-the-artisan-sector-can-change-the-world/
(5.8) John Tyman at http://www.johntyman.com/africa/07.html
(5.9) Dr John Tyman, at http://www.johntyman.com/africa/07.html
(5.10) http://www.unhcr.org/en-au/africa.html
(5.11) http://www.johntyman.com/africa/37.html
(5.12) Connie Nielsen, https://www.nation.co.ke/lifestyle/buzz/Connie-Nielsen-in-Kenya/441235-2413788-2ygxty/index.html
(5.13) http://www.johntyman.com/africa/45.html
(5.14) https://www.un.org/en/universal-declaration-human-rights/index.html
(5.15) https://www.quora.com/How-did-the-Nubias-come-to-Kenya
(5.16) https://www.kibera.org.uk/facts-info
(5.17) https://www.treehugger.com/corporate-responsibility/fracking-water-rights-how-foreign-interests-are-cleaning-out-africa.html
(5.18) https://www.historyonthenet.com/ancient-egyptian-food
(5.19) https://en.Wikipedia.org.wiki/Nymphaea caerulea
(5.20) ) https://www.treehugger.com/corporate-responsibility/fracking-water-rights-how-foreign-interests-are-cleaning-out-africa.html
(5.21) loc. cit.
(5.22) loc. cit.
(5.23) http://www.fao.org/cfs/home/activities/smallholders/en/ (as of 2018)
(5.24) loc. Cit.
(5.25) Loc. Cit.
(5.26) http://www.fao.org/fileadmin/templates/nr/sustainability_pathways/docs/Factsheet_SMALLHOLDERS.pdf
(5.27) loc. cit.
(5.28) loc. cit.

# Chapter 5 Image Credits

**Chapter cover page** Image 5.1 This photo occurs on multiple websites, including httpwww.africadevelopmentpromise.org

**Image 5.5** Image credit: https://commons.wikimedia.org/wiki/File:Africa-asia-america-to-scale.jpg, with yellow line added by A. Whittingham. This image is in the public domain because it is in a screenshot from NASA's globe software World Wind using a public domain layer.

**Image 5.6.1** Photo credit: by Dr John Tyman at http://www.johntyman.com/africa/37 - 45.html

**Image 5.6.2** Photo credit: by Dr John Tyman at http://www.johntyman.com/africa/37 - 45.html

**Image 5.6.3** Photo credit Edward2016/ pixabay.com CC0

**Image 5.7.1** Plan drawing credit http://www.johntyman.com/africa/08 with additional labelling by A. Whittingham,

**Image 5.7.2** Photo credit Dr John Tyman at http://www.johntyman.com/africa/08.html

**Image 5.8.1** Photo credit Dr John Tyman at http://www.johntyman.com/africa/07.html

**Image 5.8.2** Photo credit Dr John Tyman at http://www.johntyman.com/africa/07.html

**Image 5.8.3** Photo credit Dr John Tyman at http://www.johntyman.com/africa/07.html

**Image 5.9.1** Plan drawing credit Dr John Tyman, with added labels by A. Whittingham, http://www.johntyman.com/africa/07.html

**Image 5.9.2** Photo credit Dr John Tyman, at http://www.johntyman.com/africa/07.html

**Image 5.10.1** Photo credit Olita Ogonjo at http://www.johntyman.com/africa/37-45.html

**Image 5.10.2** Photo credit Olita Ogonjo at http://www.johntyman.com/africa/37-45.html

**Image 5.10.3** Photo credit Olita Ogonjo at http://www.johntyman.com/africa/37-45.html

**Image 5.10.4** Photo credit Olita Ogonjo at http://www.johntyman.com/africa/37-45.html

**Image 5.11.1** Photo credit Dr John Tyman and Olita Ogonjo at http://www.johntyman.com/africa/37.html

**Image 5.11.2** Photo credit Dr John Tyman and Olita Ogonjo at http://www.johntyman.com/africa/37.html

**Image 5.11.3** Photo credit Dr John Tyman and Olita Ogonjo at http://www.johntyman.com/africa/37.html

**Image 5.12.1** Photo credit: Olita Ogonjo athttp://www.johntyman.com/africa/37-45.html

**Image 5.12.2** Photo credit Olita Ogonjo athttp://www.johntyman.com/africa/37-45.html

**Image 5.12.3** Photo credit: Olita Ogonjo at http://www.johntyman.com/africa/37-45.html

**Image 5.13.1** Photo credit This image was originally posted to **Flickr** by Kingkongphoto & www.celebrity-photos.com at https://flickr.com/photos/36277035@N06/5113177708 It was reviewed on 30 November 2018 by FlickreviewR 2 and was confirmed to be licensed under the terms of the cc-by-sa-2.0.
Image was accessed in 2019 via https://commons.Wikimedia.org/wiki/File:Desmond Tutu 1997.jpg Words added to cropped photograph by A. Whittingham. Source of words attributed to Desmond Tutu is
https://www.brainyquote.com/quotes/desmond_tutu_454129

**Image 5.13.2** https://www.azquotes.com/quote/792571

**Image 5.13.3** Photo credit: 1351457973 httpwww.africadevelopmentpromise.orgblog previous2

# Chapter 5 Image Credits continued

**Image 5.14.1**
http://www.johntyman.com/africa/37.html

**Image 5.15.1** Photo credit: toodlingstudio/ pixabay.com CCO
**Image 5.15.2** kapa65/ pixabay.com CCO
**Image 5.15.3** DEZALB/ pixabay.com CCO – image cropped by A. Whittingham.
**Image 5.15.4** cocoparieienne pixabay.com CCO

**Image 5.16.1** Photo credit wjgomes/ pixabay.com CCO

**Image 5.17.1** (map) Map of Africa from Google Earth with labels added by A. Whittingham, using information from similar map at https://www.treehugger.com/corporate-responsibility/fracking-water-rights-how-foreign-interests-are-cleaning-out-africa.html. This image was credited to Friends of the Earth International on the above website but the link to the FOE website was no longer functioning as of 13/04/2019.
**Image 5.17.2** Numbercfoto pixabay.com CCO farmer-2008002
**Image** 5.17.3 (Ugandan National flag) https://www.countryflags.com/en/uganda-flag-image.html

**Image 5.18.1** https://www.the-scientist.com/daily-news/bees-molecular-responses-to-neonicotinoids-determined-29922

**Image 5.18.2**
http://www.africadevelopmentpromise.org/blog/previous/2ummy texts.

**Image 5.19.1** stweye/ pixabay.com CCO
**Image 5.19.2** Google Earth Africa, 2019 with labels added by Anne Whittingham

**Image credit 5.19.3** This image appears in several websites such as https://www.albawaba.com/ar/ but in one website the Photo is credited to Deng Mach, Kampala in https://paanluelwel2011.wordpress.com/category/featuredarticles/page/51/?iframe=true&preview=true%2Ffeed%2F
**Image 5.19.4** pietertz/ pixabay.com CCO
**Image 5.19.5** FotoshopTofs/ pixabay.com CCO
**Image 5.19.6** Google Earth Africa, 2019 with overlay of geographic zones added by A. Whittingham usingn information from a map included on over 40 websites including https://als.m.wikipedia.org/wiki/Datei:East_and_southern_africa_early_iron_age.png **Image 5.19.7** Image credit (flowers) fynbos TITLE-1080x575 httpthefynbosguy.comfynbos-easy-introduction

**Image 5.20.1** jeanvdmeulen/ pixabay.com CCO
**Image 5.20.2** Photo credit Jerome K/ pexels.com CCO
**Image 5.20.3** jeanvdmeulen/ pixabay.com CCO
**Image 5.20.4** franz160/ pixabay.com CCO

## Chapter 6 , Part 1 References

1. https://en.wikipedia.org/wiki/Sacred_groves_of_India
2. http://www.fao.org/docrep/008/ae537e/ae537e0k.htm
3. http://www.bsienvis.nic.in/Database/Status_of_Plant_Diversity_in_India_17566.aspx#
4. https://www.venerabletrees.org/how-many-tree-species/
5. https://www.bbc.com/news/science-environment-39492977
6. https://www.venerabletrees.org/how-many-tree-species
7. *https://www.dovepress.com/plant-wealth-of-a-sacred-grove-mallur-gutta-telangana-state-india-peer-reviewed-fulltext-article-IJGM*
8. Loc.cit.
9. Loc.cit.
10. *https://www.daytranslations.com/blog/2016/09/closer-look-indias-languages-7831/*
11. http://www.envfor.nic.in/soer/2001/ind_bio.pdf
12. https://en.wikipedia.org/wiki/Rigveda
13. op. cit.
14. *https://worldloveflowers.com/events/taj-mahal-garden/. (14*
15. https://www.thehindu.com/sci-tech/energy-and-environment/sacred-groves-of-the-western-ghats-are-shrinking-and-their-deities-being-sanskritised/article22260107.ece
16. Loc.cit.
17. Loc.cit.

## Ch 6, Image credits for Introduction and Part 1

**Image 6.1** (cover page for chapter) JungR/ pixabay.com CC0

**Image 6.4** (Map legend table) Copyright Anne Whittingham

**Image 6. 5** https://commons.wikimedia.org/wiki/File:India_Geographic_Map.jpg, with added labels and graphics by Anne Whittingham

**Image 6.6 (**Map credit) Google Earth Pro 2019 India

**Image 6.8.1** Photo copyright Michael Copeland, reproduced with permission
**Image 6.8.2** photo credit suketdedhia/ pixabay.com CC0 Shancaryacharya forest grove at Shrinagar_ mountains-2915350_1920

**Image 6.9** sarangib/ pixabay.com CC0

**Image 6.10.1** Google Earth 2018, Shankaracharya
**Image 6.10.2** Google Earth 2018, Shrinagar

**Image 6.11** Photo credit: H Vibhu in the Hindu Times, https://www.thehindu.com/sci-tech/energy-and-environment/sacred-groves-of-the-western-ghats-are-shrinking-and-their-deities-being-sanskritised/article22260107.ece

.

## Chapter 6, Part 2 References

1. https://www.mkgandhi.org/articles/swaraj.htm
2. https://www.onthegotours.com/au/India/guide-to-diwali-festival-of-lights
3. http://www.navdanya.org/site
4. http://www.navdanya.org/site
5. Loc. Cit.
6. Loc. Cit.
7. https://www.facebook.com/gretathunbergsweden/posts/688530981544236/
8. https://www.localfutures.org/planet-local-bhaskar-save-the-gandhi-of-natural-farming/
9. Loc. Cit.
10. Loc. Cit.
11. Loc. Cit.
12. https://www.onthegotours.com/au/India/guide-to-diwali-festival-of-lights
13. http://www.navdanya.org/site
14. http://www.navdanya.org/site
15. http://www.navdanya.org/site
16. https://www.facebook.com/gretathunbergsweden/posts/688530981544236/
17. https://www.localfutures.org/planet-local-bhaskar-save-the-gandhi-of-natural-farming/
18. Loc. Cit.
19. Loc. Cit.
20. Loc. Cit.

## Ch6, Part 2 Image Credits

**Image credit 6.13.1** Dr Vandana-Shiva at www.greenamerica .org

**Image credit 6.15.1** Image is a screenshot used with written permission from the film *"The Economics of Happiness", which* was released in 2011 by Helena Norberg-Hodge, Stephen Gorlick and John Page. Refer https://www.localfutures.org/
**Image credit 6.15.3** as for 6.15.1
**Image credit 6.15.3** as for 6.15.1

**Image credit 6.16.1** Timeline credit:
https://screenshots.firefox.com/yJ8PIseHP8re1zmJ/philosophy.lander.eduwhere, with text edits by A. Whittingham

**Image credit 6.17** Photo credit of Gandhi from  httpswww.azquotes.comquote867893 quote-in-the-midst-of-darkness-light-persists-mahatma-gandhi-86-78-93, with graphics and text added by A. Whittingham

**Image credit 6.19** Photo credit: sarangib/ pixabay.com CC0

## Chapter 6, Part 3 References

1. http://www.mapsofindia.com/india
2. https://en.Wikipedia.org/wiki/Yarlung Tsangpo
3. https://en.Wikipedia.org/wiki/Donyi-Polo
4. Mibang, Tamo and Chaudhuri, Sarit Kumar, "Understanding Tribal Religion". Mittal Publications, 2004. Sourced via https://en.Wikipedia.org/wiki/Donyi-Polo
5. Chaudhuri, Sarit Kumar, "The Institutionalization of Tribal Religion. Recasting the Donyi-Polo Movement in Arunachal Pradesh", in: *Asian Ethnology*, Volume 72, Number 2, Nanzan Institute for Religion and Culture • 2013, 259–277. Sourced from https://en.wikipedia.org/wiki/Donyi-Polo
6. https://whc.unesco.org/en/tentativelists/5893/
7. loc. cit.
8. https://www.soas.ac.uk/tribaltransitions/publications/file32488.pdf
9. https://www.researchgate.net/publication/242335346_A_sustainable_mountain_paddy-fish_farming_of_the_Apatani_tribes_of_Arunachal_Pradesh_India
10. https://whc.unesco.org/en/tentativelists/5893
11. https://www.thehindu.com/news/national/other-states/causes-behind-brahmaputra-turning-black-could-be-natural-union-minister/article21258572.ece
12. https://timesofindia.indiatimes.com/city/ itanagar/arunachal-river-turns-black-officials-blame-china/article

## Ch 6, Part 3 Image Credits

**Image credit 6.21** Google Earth 2018, The Himalayas

**Image credit 6.22** : https://commons.wikimedia.org/wiki/File:Ganges-Brahmaputra-Meghna_basins.jpgple/

**Image credit 6.23** Isaac Turay/ pixabay.com CCO

**Image credit 6.24** Trevor Cole/ unsplash.com CCO (woman with tattoos)

## Chapter 6, Part 4 References

1. https://commons.wikimedia.org.wiki/File:Taj_site_plan.png
2. https://en.wikipedia.org/wiki/List_of_World_Heritage_Sites_in_Indiahttps://worldloveflowers.com/events/taj-mahal-garden/
3. https://en.wikipedia.org/wiki/india
4. https://www.worldheritagesite.org/connection/Chahar+Bagh+Gardens
5. https://worldloveflowers.com/events/taj-mahal-garden/.
6. https://en.wikipedia.org/wiki/Vastu_shastra
7. https://www.vaastu-shastra.com/taj-mahal-vastu-analysis.html
8. Op. cit.
9. Translation by Sri Aurobindo from Book 1, Canto 1 (The symbol Dawn), in the *Rigveda*, quoted in *http://savitri.in/1/1/1* . The *Rigveda* is a collection of over 1,000 Hindu Sanskrit hymns. It is the oldest of the Hindu Scriptures, dating back some thousands of years.
10. Kumar, Rewar, (PhD in Vastua Shatra), at http://www.rewakumar.org/meet-rewa-kumar.html
11. https://en.wikipedia.org/wiki/Vastu_shastra
12. https://pdfs.semanticscholar.org/e19d/d80dae67f0f6bdeb32a4a96eac1cef53d342.pdf
13. https://www.nativeplanet.com/travel-guide/all-about-kandariya-mahadev-temple-in-khajuraho-002269.html

## Ch 6, Part 4 Image credits

**Image credit 6.26.1**  Google Earth, Taj Mahal 2019
**Image credit 6.26.2** mailanmaik/ pixabay.com CC0
**Image credit 6.26.3** Simon/ pixabay.com CC0

**Image credit 6.27.1**  JungR/ pixabay.com CC0
**Image credit 6.27.2** Suffix/ pixabay.com CC0
**Image credit 6.27.3** SuzyT/ pixabay.com CC0

**Image credit 6.29** hari_mangayil/ pixabay.com CC0

## Chapter 6, Part 5 References

1. Kramrisch, Stella, The Hindu Temples, (1946) quoted at https://www.gardenvisit.com/history theory/garden landscape articles/sacred gardens/hindu gardens lotus ponds
2. https://www.onthegotours.com/au/India/guide-to-Diwali-festival-of-lights
3. Loc. Cit. Loc. Cit.
4. https://asiasociety.org/education/origins-buddhism https://www.tripadvisor.com.au/Attraction Review-g424922-d3619160-Reviews-Bodhi Tree-Bodh Gaya Gaya District Bihar.html
5. https://indiaheritagesites.wordpress.com/tag/Bodhi-tree/  Harman, William P., The Sacred Marriage of a Hindu Goddess, Motilal Banarsidass, 1992, p 24. ISBN 978-81-208-0810-2. Bayly, Susan Saints, Goddesses and Kings: Muslims and Christians in South Indian Society, 1700-1900, 1989. Cambridge University Press. pp. 29–30. ISBN 978-0-521-89103-5.
6. Lewandowski, Susan J. (1977). "Changing Form and Function in the Ceremonial and the Colonial Port City in India: An Historical Analysis of Madurai and Madras". Modern Asian Studies. Cambridge University Press. 11 (02): 183–212.
7. King, Anthony D. (2005), Buildings and Society: Essaygs on the Social Development of the Built Environment, Taylor & Francis e-library, ISBN 0-203-48075-9.
8. Lewandowski, Op. Cit.
9. G. Venkatramana (2013). Alayam - The Hindu temple - An epitome of Hindu Culture. Mylapore, Chennai: Sri Ramakrishna Math. p. 31. ISBN 978-81-7823-542-4. quoted in https://www.revolvy.com/page/Meenakshi-Temple
10. Bayly, Op. Cit..
11. Harman, Op. Cit
12. Harman, Op. Cit.
13. https://www.revolvy.com/page/Meenakshi-Temple
14. https://iskconeducationalservices.org/HoH/practice/worship/mandir-the-temple/
19. https://en.Wikipedia.org/wiki/Meenakshi Temple

## Ch 6, Part 5 Temple gardens image credits

**Image credit 6.31.1** javieriborra/ pixabay.com CCO
**Image credit 6.31.2** This image is present without the photographer being named on at least four different French language websites. One of those websites is https://www.voyageinindia.fr/fete-lumieres-inde-diwali/
**Image credit 6.31.3** dMz/ pixabay.com CCO
**Image credit 6.32.1** https://www.wikihow.com/Make-Rangoli
**Image credit 6.32.2** Photo credit: ParagKini/ pixabaycom CCO
**Image credit 6.33.1** juemi/ pixabay.com CCO
**Image credit 6.34.1** Google Earth 2019, with linework overlay to street pattern by Anne Whittingham. Line work reference was wikipedia. org 600px-Madurai_Map_OSM002 Author in 2011
**Image credit 6.35.1** Google Earth 2019
**Image credit 6.35.2** https://commons.wikimedia.org/wiki/File:An_aerial_view_of_Madurai_city_from_atop_of_Me enakshi_Amman_temple.jpg

## Chapter 6 , Part 6 References

1. United Nations High Commission for Refugees
2. https://news.mongabay.com/2018/01/bangladeshi-forests-stripped-bare-as-rohingya-refugees-battle-to-survive/
3. Google Earth imagery copyright 2018
4. https://en.wikipedia.org/wiki/List_of_ cities_by_population_density
5. https://www.statista.com/statistics/ 279040/population-density-in-urban-areas-of-china-by-region/
6. United Nations High Commission for Refugees
7. United Nations High Commission for Refugees
8. *httpswww.rfa.orgenglishnewsmyanmarrefugees-jobs-11012017172548.htm*
9. http://worldpopulationreview.com/countries/india-population/
10. https://en.wikipedia.org/wiki/Islam_in_Bangladesh
11. *httpswww.rfa.orgenglishnewsmyanmarrefugees-jobs-11012017172548.htm*
12. IOM, the UN Migration Agency at https://www.iom.int/news/micro-gardening-scheme-help-feed-rohingya-refugees-bangladeshi-local-communities
13. United Nations Food and Agricultural Organisation's website: *Floating Garden Agricultural Practices in Bangladesh,* Ministry of Agriculture, People's Republic of Bangladesh. http://www.fao.org/3/a-bp777e.pdf
14. Loc. Cit.
15. https://www.downtoearth.org.in/news/agriculture/resort-to-heritage-53346
16. United Nations Food and Agricultural Organisation's website: *Floating Garden Agricultural Practices in Bangladesh,* Ministry of Agriculture, People's Republic of Bangladesh. http://www.fao.org/3/a-bp777e.pdf
17. thelivinggreens.com
18. Loc. Cit.
19. Loc. Cit.
20. http://www.navdanya.org/site
21. Loc. Cit.

### Ch 6, Part 6 image credits

**Image credit 6.37.1** hawkarena/ pixabay.com CCO
**Image credit 6.38.1 Google Earth** copyright
**Image credit 6.38.2** wikimedia commons 120px-Cox's_Bazaar_Refugee_Camp_(8539828824)_cropped from original
**Image credit 6.39** IOM, the UN Migration Agency at https://www.iom.int/news/micro-gardening-scheme-help-feed-Rohingya-refugees-Bangladeshi-local-communities
**Image credit 6.40**.1 http://www.arakanmedia.com/human-right/bangladesh-thousands-of-rohingya-escape-refugee-camps-in-search-of-jobs.html
**Image credit 6.41.1** https://www.downtoearth.org.in/news/agriculture/resort-to-heritage-53346
**Image credit 6.41.2** Loc. Cit.
**Image credit 6.42.1** *http://thelivinggreens.com/gallery.html*
**Image credit 6.42.2** *http://thelivinggreens.com/gallery.html*
**Image credit 6.42.3** A newspaper article published in Bangalore, India, and sourced from *http://thelivinggreens.com/gallery.html*
**Image credit 6.43.1** Dr Vandana Shiva, http://www.navdanya.org/site

## Chapter 7 References

1. https://www.wttc.org/-/media/files/reports/economic-impact-research/regions-2018/europelcu2018.pdfIn Europe it

2. https://ec.Europa.eu/Eurostat/statistics

3. https://newhavenurbanism.org/european-urbanism/paris/

4. https://en.wikipedia.org/wiki/Eiffel Tower

5. https://newhavenurbanism.org/european-urbanism/paris/

6. https://nca2009.globalchange.gov/corn-and-soybean-temperature-response/index.html

7. http://www.massey.ac.nz/massey/learning/colleges.colleye-of-sciences/clinics-and-services/weeds-database/wild-turnip.cfm

8. https://www.statista.com/statistics/264065/global-production-of-vegetables-by-type/

9. I estimated the weight of tulip bulb production. Statistics about how many tons of tulip bulbs are produced annually at the global scale are not available. The average weight of a tulip bulb varies with size, quality, variety, etc and no average statistics are available. When I looked at tulip sales on www.Amazon.com, a packet of 10 tulip bulbs produced in China weighed 7 ounces. So the weight of one tulip bulb from that packet was less than one ounce. I assumed a weight of one ounce for the calculation that I did for the weight in tons, of annual tulip bulb production.

10. https://earthobservatory.nasa.gov/images/92148/flower-power-in-the-Netherlands

11. https://psmag.com/news/stories-you-might-have-missed-this-week-October-19-2018

12. https://www.abc.net.au/news/2018-10-11/can-we-quit-coal-in-time/10361552

13. https://www.hollandtradeandinvest.com/key-sectors/horticulture-and-starting-materials/horticulture-facts-and-figures

14. https://www.ipcc.ch/2018/10/08/summary-for-policymakers-of-ipcc-special-report-on-global-warming-of-1-5c-approved-by-governments/

15. http://www.bom.gov.au/climate/updates/articles/a032.shtml

16. https://en.Wikipedia.org/wiki/Keukenhof

17. https://en.wikipedia.org/wiki/Daylight

18. http://www.rsc.org/learn-chemistry/content/filerepository/CMP/00/001/068/Rate%20of%20photosynthesis%20limiting%20factors.pdf

19. https://www.abc.net.au/news/2017-03-02/short-sightedness-epidemic-as-people-spend-less-time-outside/8318882

20. *https://en.wikipedia.org/wiki/Vaux-le-Vicomte*

21. Op. cit.

# Image credits Chapter 7

**Image 7.1** Copyright Pirotehcik purchased image from Depositphotos high res_94205026_l-2015

**Image 7.4** Photo credit: Dino Reichmuth at Unsplash, CC0 (vineyard)

**Image 7.5.1** map https://en.wikipedia.org/wiki/Europe , with labels added by Anne Whittingham

**Image 7.5.2** alehidalgo/ pixabay.com CC0

**Image 7.5.3** CC0 at https://www.kisspng.com/ png-europe-travel-tourism-vacation-business-people-tra-302304

**Image 7.6.1** walkerssk @pixabay.com CC0

**Image 7.6.2** 27707 @ pixabay.com CC0

**Image 7.6.3** 12019 @ pixabay.com CC0

**Image 7.7** Photo of Paris. There are literally dozens of websites that use this photo. One example is http://gytanalytics.com/france-announces-5g-roadmap/. No specific original source of this photo has been found.

**Image 7.8** Photo credit of flowers at Keukenhof gardens to Ellen26/ pixabay.com CC0, with Figure 7.8 copyright Anne Whittingham

**Image 7.9** Soorelis/ pixabay.com CC0

**Image 7.10.1** Free-Photos/ pixabay.com CC0

**Image 7.10.2** Depositphotos_205719644_l-2015 (with slight cropping by A. Whittingham)

**Image 7.10.3** Turnip Depositphotos_36230995_s-2019

**Image 7.10.4** Tulip bulb Depositphotos 15749829 l-2015

**Image credit 7.13** : Copyright Pirotehcik purchased image from Deposit photos high res_94205026_l-2015

**Image 7.14** Copyright Pirotehcik purchased image from Depositphotos high res_94205026_l-2015 with stark contrast editing added by Anne Whittingham

**Image 7.15.1** *Ellen26/ pixabay.com CC0*

**Image 7.15.2** plan freely available at www.tulipsinholland.com

**Image 7.16** original plan image by www.tulipsinholland.com, with amendments and notes added by Anne Whittingham.

**Image 7.17.1** Luis Enrique Carvajal pixabay.com CC0 daylight-park-people-1179075 (crop from original image)

**Image 7.17.2** Brett Sayles crop from pexels.com CC0 adults-bench-couple-977967

**Image 7.17.3** Brett Sayles pexels.com CC0 cropped image adults-bench-couple-977967

**Image 7.17.4** Plans and photograph copyright Anne Whittingham

**Image 7.18.1** Depositphotos_3487701_l-2015

**Image 7.18.2** Copyright Julietart_purchased photo from Depositphotos_11378063_l-2015

**Image 7.19.1** MabelAmber/ pixabay.com CC0

**Image 7.19.2** https://www.thesustainablecity.ae

**Image 7.19.3** Google Earth aerial photograph 2019, Keukenhof CC0

**Image 7.19.4** MabelAmber/ pixabay.com CC0

**Image 7.20.1** MrsBrown/ pixabay.com CC0

**Image 7.20.2** sumulee/ pixabay.com CC0

**Image 7.20.3** fancycrave1/ pixabay.com CC0

**Image 7.21** copyright Anne Whittingham

# Chapter 8 References

(8.1) https://en.wikipedia.org/wiki/Ceviche. Although this origin of the word is cited here, there is controversy over the origin of the term, which it has been noted can be traced back to various origins such as the Middle East or Spain.

(8.2) https://en.wikipedia.org/wiki/Via_Campesina

(8.3) viacampesina.org/en/struggles-la-via-campesina-agrarian-reform-defense-life-land-territories/

(8.4) https://en.wikipedia.org/wiki/Via_Campesina

(8.5) https://www.theguardian.com/environment/2014/may/28/farmland-food-security-small-farmers

(8.6) www.fao.org/fileadmin/templates/nr/sustainability pathways/docs/Coping with food and agriculture challenge Smallholders agenda Final.pdf

(8.7) https://en.wikipedia.org/wiki/Illuminance

(8.8) https://en.wikipedia.org/wiki/Lux

(8.9) https://en.wikipedia.org/wiki/Inti

(8.10) Loc. Cit.

(8.11) http://www.mofga.org/Publications/The-Maine-Organic-Farmer-Gardener/Spring-2012/Moray

(8.12) http: en.wikipedia.org wiki Brazilian cuisine

(8.13) http://www.fao.org/3/a-i5251e.pdf)

(8.14) https://en.wikipedia.org/wiki/Solidaridad

(8.15) https://whc.unesco.org/en/list/274

(8.16) https://www.bbc.com/news/world-latin-america-49460022

(8.17) http://www.bbc.com/ travel/story/20120606-
(8.18) https://en.wikipedia.org wiki Land of poets

(8.19) https://www.poetsofmodernity.xyz/POMBR/Spanish/Neruda.htm

(8.20) https://www.smithsonianmag.com/smart-news/chile-adding-11-million-acres-national-parks-

(8.21) Loc. Cit.

## Chapter 8 References continued

(8.22) https://en.wikipedia.org/wiki/Moray_(Inca_ruin) and

(23) http://www.mofga.org/Publications/The-Maine-Organic-Farmer-Gardener/Spring-2012/Moray

(8.24) https://ourworld.unu.edu/en/growing-corporate-hold-on-farmland-risky-for-world-food-security

(8.25) Loc. Cit.

(8.26) https://sustainablefoodtrust.org/articles/viva-la-produccion-urban-farming-in-cuba/

(8.27) https://www.smithsonianmag.com/smart-news/chile-adding-11-million-acres-national-parks-180962592/

(8.28) Loc. Cit.

## Chapter 8 Image credits

**Image 8.1** Photo credit: skeeze/ pixabay.com CC0, with inset image top right of main photo of La Via Campesina graphic at https://viacampesina.org/en/struggles-la-via-campesina-agrarian-reform-defense-life-land-territories/

**Image 8.4.1** Map by KVDP on Wikimedia Commons, Creative Commons Share –Alike 3.0. Map based on File: World map torrid.svg, now indicating subtropics, with labels added by A. Whittingham.

**Image 8.4.2** https mapcruzin.com free-world-maps south_america1080x1418.jpg south_america1080x1418

**Image 8.4.3** ciclaar/ pixabay.com CC0

**Image 8.4.4** photograph by Kaufdex/ pixabay.com CC0, edited by A. Whittingham

**Image 8.4.5** Photoman pixabay.com CC0 trout-953012_1920

**Image 8.5** Photo credit http://stories.coop/stories/organoponico-vivero-alamar-cuba

**Image 8.6.1** http://anzasca.net/wp-content/uploads/2015/12/ANZAScA_2009_Ibrahim_Hayman_Hyde.pdf

**Image 8.6.2** Photo credit Soorelis/ pixabay.com CC0

**Image 8.6.3** graph https://upload.wikimedia.org/wikipedia/commons/e/ee/Projected_changes_in_crop_yields_at_different_latitudes_with_global_warming.png

**Image credit 8.6.4** CLM-bv pixabay.com CC0

**Image 8.7.1** Image by Anne Whittingham. information obtained from https://en.wikipedia.org/wiki/Lux

**Image 8.7.2** Photo credit for sun image Jonathan Petersson at pexels.com CC0, with editing by A. Whittingham. Image credit for Illuminance Table: Anne Whittingham

**Image 8.8** Photo credit http://annualreport.solidaridadnetwork.org/2014/en/cotton

**Image 8.9** copyright Anne Whittingham

**Image 8.10** copyright Anne Whittingham

**Image 8.11.1** map credit Hobe/Map credit Hobe/ Holger Behr own work CC0, public domain, viewed at https://en.Wikipedia.org/wiki/Machu Pichu #/media/File:  Karta_MachuPicchu.PNG, with added label and graphic by A. Whittingham

**Image 8.11.2** photo credit: skeeze/ pixabay.com CC0

**Image 8.12** copyright Anne Whittingham

**Image 8.13** Written permission obtained for reproduction of photograph by Renzo Delpino. / Fotografo. httpjuangrimm.retazo.clenbahia-azul group

**Image 9.14.1** Written permission obtained for reproduction of photograph by Renzo Delpino. / Fotografo. httpjuangrimm.retazo.clenbahia-azul group

**Image 9.14.2** photo credit https://landscapeaustralia.com/articles/horse-island-a-garden-of-grandeur/

**Image 9.14.3** Written permission obtained for reproduction of photograph by Renzo Delpino. / Fotografo. httpjuangrimm.retazo.clenbahia-azul group

**Image 9.15.1 -9.15.** Written permission obtained for reproduction of photograph by Renzo Delpino. / Fotografo. Urubamba Garden at httpjuangrimm.retazo.clenjardines

**Image 8.16.1** https://depositphotos.com/stock-photos/moray-inca-cusco.html?filter=all

**Image** 8.16.2 Written permission obtained for reproduction of photograph by Renzo Delpino. / Fotografo. httpjuangrimm.retazo.clenbahia-azul group-13

**Image 8.17** this image is included without attribution on multiple websites, including https://free.myownemail.info/pics/cubas-sustainable-agricultural-success-story

## Chapter 9 References

*(9.1)* https://medium.com/thrive-global/how-amish-people-live-a-sustainable-life-53e977d24abd

*(9.2) http://www.bbc.co.uk/religion/religions/christianity/subdivisions/amish_1.shtml*

(9.3) Park, S., Hongu, N., Daily, J.W. III, *Native American foods: History, culture, and influence on modern diets,* in Journal of Ethnic Foods, http://hournalofethnicfoods.net (an open access article under CC BY-NC-ND license)

(9.4) loc.cit

(9.5) loc.cit. and http://factsheets.okstate.edu/documents/fapc-194-growing-north-american-indigenous-corn/

(9.6) https://www.brainyquote.com/ authors/geronimo

*(9.7) Geronimo's Story of his Life,* taken down and edited by S. M Barrett, published by Duffield & Company , New York, 2006 and available at https://www.ibiblio.org/ebooks/Geronimo/GerStory.htm

(9.8) op.cit.

(9.9) https://healingdelight.bandcamp.com/track/infinite-sun-kuate

(9.10) https://www.businessinsider.com.au/money-secrets-of-the-amish-2013-4?r=US&IR=T#they-eat-like-kings-but-they-grow-most-of-their-meals-themselves-12

(9.11) op.cit.

(9.12) http://amishamerica.com/what-happens-at-an-amish-barn-raising

*(9.13)* FLO to Mariana Griswold Van Rensselaer (draft, [June 1893]), Frederick Law Olmsted Papers, Library of Congress, quoted in an article by Charles Beveridge in the Twenty-fifth Anniversary issue of Nineteenth Century, the journal of the Victorian Society in America (Volume 20, no. 2, pp. 32–37, Fall 2000) and included at http://www.olmsted.org/the-olmsted-legacy/olmsted-theory-and-design-principles/olmsted-his-essential-theory

*(9.14) op.cit.*

*(9.15) http://www.olmsted.org/the-olmsted-legacy/olmsted-theory-and-design-principles/olmsted-his-essential-theory*

(9.16) https://www.thoughtco.com/frank-lloyd-wright-famous-american-architect-177881

(9.17 https://theculturetrip.com/north-America/articles/the-10-oldest-national-parks-in-the-world

(9.18) http://www.yosemite.ca.us/library/origin_of_word_yosemite.html

(9.19) op.cit.

(9.20) – (9.22) https://en.Wikipedia.org/wiki/Mariposa Battalion and https://www.myyosemitepark.com/park/miners-and-mariposa-battalion

## Chapter 9 References   continued

(9.23) youtube – top ten most beautiful gardens in the world

(9.24) Whysall, S., https://vancouversun.com/news/staff-blogs/2011-04-04/beautiful-Butchart-gardens

(9.25) http://www.olmsted.org/the-olmsted-legacy/olmsted-theory-and-design-principles/olmsted-his-essental-theory

(9.26) Rockwell, J., Heslop, T., 'Cultures of Beauty', https://longwoodgardens.org/blog/2015-11-16/cultures-beauty

(9.27) https://www.energy.gov/articles/history-air-conditioning

(9.28) https://www.bloomberg.com/ opinion/articles/2018-01-02/the-first-atrium-wasn-t-in-a-hyatt

(9.29) https://en.wikipedia.org/wiki/Patrick_ Blanc#/media/File:Patrick_Blanc_Puteaux.jpg

(9.30) https://www.thoughtco.com/frank-lloyd-wright-famous-american-architect-177881

(9.31) Essay by Charles **Wiebe on** https://www.khanacademy.org/humanities/ap-art-history/later-europe-and-americas/modernity-ap/a/frank-lloyd-wright-fallingwater

(9.32) https://mcharg.upenn.edu/book

(9.33)  https://www.localfutures.org/a-tale-of-two-cities-Beijing-and-detroit

(9.34) https://jvtf.org/

(9.35) www.okofarms.com/

(9.36) https://en.m.Wikipedia.org/wiki/Decline of Detroit

(9.37) https://theculturetrip.com/north-America/usa/Michigan/articles/the-best-urban-farms-in-Detroit-mi/

(9.38) https://www.usda.gov/media/blog/2018/08/14/vertical-farming-future

(9.39) https://www.smartcitiesdive.com/ex/sustainablecitiescollective/chinas-indoor-farming-research-feed-cities-leads-world/409606

(9.40) https://www.space.com/38723-astronauts-farm-plants-install-garden-instrument.html

(9.41) http://www.qivc.org/faq-qivc

(9.42) http://www.pewresearch.org/fact-tank/2015/12/23/americans-are-in-the-middle-of-the-pack-globally-when-it-comes-to-importance-of-religion/

(9.43) https://www.gfk.com/insights/press-release/us-ranks-among-top-three-countries-for-gardening-every-day-or-most-days/

(9.44) https://en.wikipedia.org/wiki/Arcosanti

# Chapter 9 Image credits

**Image 9.1** Photo credit: lacrimae/ pixabay.com CC0

**Image 9.4.1** Photo credit: lylafoggia/ pixabay.com CC0

**Image 9.4.2** Timeline diagram Copyright Anne Whittingham 2019

**Image 9.5.1** Free for use map image credit: https://en.wikipedia.org/wiki/North_America , with labels added by Anne Whittingham

**Image 9.5.2** Photo credit: skeeze pixabay.com CC0

**Image 9.6.1** ulleo/ pixabay.com CC0

**Image 9.6.2** Map Image credit: Park, S., Hongu, N., Daily, J.W. III, *Native American foods: History, culture, and influence on modern diets*, in Journal of Ethnic Foods, http://hournalofethnicfoods.net (an open access article under CC BY-NC-ND license)

**Image 9.7** Kermit frog image in yellow field. Dozens of websites feature this image. The original source of the image has not been located but it is attributed here to Jim Henson, creator of *The Muppets*. Kermit was also a central character in *Sesame Street* and served as the logo of The Jim Henson Company. This image is also claimed by LoggerWiggla/ pixabay.com CC0_oilseed-rape-383279__340

**Image 9.8** 12019/ pixabay.com CC0 (Amish)

**Image 9.9** randy fath/ unsplash.com CC0

**Image 9.11.1** 12019/ pixabay.com CC0

**Image 9.11.2** 12019/ pixabay.com CC0 (central park)

**Image 9.11.3** dariasophia/ pixabay.com CC0

**Image 9.12.1** 12019/ pixabay.com CC0

**Image 9.12.2** Faaike/ pixabay.com CC0

**Image 9.13** Purchased image from *shutterstock.com,* edited by A. Whittingham

**Image 9.14** skeeze/ Pixabay.com CC0, edited for use by A. Whittingham

**Image 9.15.1** Geraldshields11 own work_wikimedia_800px-Longwood_Garden_002

**Image 9.15.2** lacrimae/ pixabay.com CC0

**Image 9.16** christianpackenius/ pixabay.com CC0

**Image 9.17.1** httpswww.khanacademy.orghumanitiesap-art-historylater-europe-and-americasmodernity-apafrank-lloyd-wright-fallingwater

**Image 9.17.2** 12019/ pixabay.com

**Image 9.18** Hagertal/ pixabay.com CC0

**Images 9.19.1, 9.19.2, 9.19.3,** all , images from same source of Google Earth 2019, aerial views of Arcosanti.

**Image 9.20.1** wikiImages pixabay.com CC0

**Image 9.20.2** Free-Photos pixabay.com CC0

**Image 9.21** puzzleboxrecords pixabay.com CC0 (Detroit)

**Image 9.22.1** MichaelGaida/ pixabay.com CC0, edited by A. Whittingham

**Image 9.22.2** wikiImages/ pixabay.com CC0 moon-walk-60616_1920, edited by A. Whittingham

**Image 9.22.3** International Space Station plants photocredit By NASA - httpswww.nasa.govfeaturehow-does-your-space-gar 1024px-Veggie_plants

# Chapter 10 References

(10.1) https://www.anbg.gov.au/gnp/interns-2014/araucaria-cunninghamii.html

(10.2) H.H. the Fourteenth Dalai Lama, "A Policy of Kindness: An Anthology of Writings by and about the Dalai Lama", Snow Lion Publications, New York, 1990, page 107.

(10.3) https://www.bbc.com/news/science-environment-30197085

(10.4) https://www.theguardian.com/environment/climate-consensus-97-per-cent/2018/jun/25/30-years-later-deniers-are-still-lying-about-hansens-amazing-global-warming-prediction

(10.5) https://aicd.companydirectors.com.au/advocacy/governance-leadership-centre/external-environment/climate-change-a-growing-focus-for-boards

(10.6) Australian Government Department of Foreign Affairs and Trade, *"Climate Change"* website post downloaded April 2019

Page 7 (references 10.7 (a) – 10.18 ( l)

(10.7) ()a) https://thebulletin.org/2019/04/a-climate-change-preview-trees-at-the-south-pole-60-feet-of-sea-level-rise/

(10.8 )(b) https://www.nationalgeographic.com/science/prehistoric-world/mass-extinction/

(10.9) (c) https://www.sciencealert.com/there-were-trees-at-the-south-pole-the-last-time-there-was-this-much-co2-in-the-air

(10.10) (d) https://en.m.Wikipedia.org/wiki/Timeline of human evolution

(10.11) (e) https://climate.nasa.gov/vital-signs/sea-level/

(10.12) (f) https://www.climate.gov/news-features/featured-images/2015-state-climate-carbon-dioxide

10.13) (g) https://www.climate.gov/news-features/featured-images/2015-state-climate-carbondioxide

(10.14) (h) https://www.climate.gov/news-features/featured-images/2015-state-climate-carbon-dioxide

(10.15) (i) https://climate.nasa.gov/vital-signs/sea-level/

(10.16) (j) http://www.bom.gov.au/climate/updates/articles/a032.shtml

(10.17) (k) https://abcmedia.akamaized.net/rn/podcast/2019/04/ssw_20190413_1229.mp3

(10.18) (l) https://www.theguardian.com/science/2019/apr/03/south-pole-tree-fossils-indicate-impact-of-climate-change

## Chapter 10 References  continued

(10.19) Noble, Andrew, former director of the Water, Land and Ecosystems project in Sri Lanka, quoted in the article by Jeff Smith, " Sunshine: India's new cash crop", at
https://wle.cgiar.org/sunshine-india-new-cash-crop

(10.20) Bull, Catherin, Southbank Corporation, annual report 2016 – 17.

(10.21) https://en.Wikipedia.org/wiki/Central Park

(10.22) worldpopulationreview.com/us-cities/new-York-city-population

(10. 23) https://www.Brisbane.qld.gov.au/sites/dehault/files/ chapte5_landscaping code.pdf

(10.24) op. cit.

(10.25) Bull, Catherin, Southbank Corporation, annual report 2016 – 17.

(10.26) Utzon, Jorn, *"Sydney Opera House Design Principles*, 2002.

(10.27) op. cit.

(10.28) http://www.landezine.com/index.php/2015/06/symantec-chengdu-campus-by-swa/

(10.29) https://www.tripadvisor.com.au/Attraction_Review-g294265-d2149128-Reviews-Gardens_by_the_Bay-Singapore.html

(10.31) *www.population.net.au/brisbane-population/*

(10.32) *www.worldometers.info/world-population/singapore-population/*

(10.33) https://www.todayonline.com/singapore/gardens-bay-received-64m-visitors-last-year

(10.34) https://www.statista.com › Sports & Recreation › Parks & Outdoors

(10. 35) universal https://www.statista.com/statistics/236190/atte

(10.36) https://www.localfutures.org/a-tale-of-two-cities-beijing-and-detroit/

(10.37) Loc. Cit.

(10.38) Loc. Cit.

(10.39) https://en.wikipedia.org/wiki/World_population

10.40) https://www.un.org/development/desa/en/news/population/2018-revision-of-world-urbanization-prospects.html

(10.41) *https://en.wikipedia.org/wiki/Gardens_ by_the_Bay*

(10.41) op.cit.

## Chapter 10 Image credits

**Image 10.1** adam derwicki/ pixabay.com CC0

**Image 10.4** Copyright Anne Whittingham 2019

**Image 10.7** Copyright Anne Whittingham 2019, with inset image of globe adapted by A. Whittingham from CC0 image at https://www.pexels.com/photo/sky-earth-galaxy-universe-2422/

**Image 10.8** Copyright Anne Whittingham 2019 with background image of globe adapted by A. Whittingham from CC0 image at https://www.pexels.com/photo/sky-earth-galaxy-universe-2422/ and inset image of child with strawberry cropped by A. Whittingham from image by moniquedsv/ pixabay.com CC0

**Image 10.9** Copyright Anne Whittingham 2019 with background image of globe adapted by A. Whittingham from CC0 image at https://www.pexels.com/photo/sky-earth-galaxy-universe-2422/

**Image 10.10** copyright Anne Whittingham 2019 with three photo credits on this same page as follows:

> **Image 10.6.1** Photo credit couleur/ pixabay.com CC0 leaf-3504797__3 with editing by A. Whittingham
>
> **Image 10.6.2** Design and photo copyright Anne Whittingham
>
> **Image 10.6.3** Image credit www.Wikipedia.com/labyrint

**Image 10.11** Copyright Anne Whittingham 2019

**Image 10.12.1** copyright Anne Whittingham

**Image 10.12.2** copyright Anne Whittingham

**Image 10.12.3** Watercolour illustrations for the design of the new city of Canberra, prepared by Landscape Architect Walter Burley Griffin and his Architect wife Marion Mahoney Griffin. Reproduced with written permission from the National Archives of Australia.

**Image 10.12.4** *Google Earth* images of Canberra in 2018.

**Image 10.25.1** Photo copyright Anne Whittingham

**Image 10.13** Photo copyright: Anne Whittingham. Sculpture "Arches" by Henry Moore 1972 – 73 in the Sculpture Garden at the National Gallery of Australia, Canberra.

**Image 10.14** Summary Image copyright Anne Whittingham, with small icon photo credits given in relevant chapters where images are reproduced at larger sizes.

**Image 10.15** Summary Image copyright Anne Whittingham, with small icon photo credits given in relevant chapters where images are reproduced at larger sizes.

**Image 10.16.1** Photo credit: KWANSOON /pixabay.com CC0 (photo cropped A. Whittingham)

**Image 10.16.2** Photo credit: Mworldtraveller – own work CC0

**Image 10.17.1** http://www.gardensbythebay.com.sg/en/plan-your-visit/gardens-map

**Image 10.17.2** Photo credit: dariasophia/ pixabay.com CImage CC0

**Image 10.18.1** Photo copyright: Anne Whittingham

## Chapter 10 Image credits continued

**Image 10.18.2:** Google Earth, Southbank, Australia, with labelling added by A. Whittingham

**Image 10.19.1:** Arulonline/ pixabay.com CC0

**Image 10.19.2** Photo credit: www.abc.net.au news 2016opera house gold light at Diwali 7971964-3x2-940x627

**Image 10.19.3** Futuregirl/ pixabay.com CC0

**Image 10.20.1.** Photo credit Tom Fox. Photos were included in an article by Radenka Kolarov at https://land8.com/how-to-create-a-stunning-modern-design-that-respects-cultural-legacy Permission requested to use photos via landezine.

**Image 10.20.2** loc. cit.

**Image 10.20.3** loc. cit.

**Image 10.21.1** LittleMouse/ pixabay.com CC0

**Image 10.21.2** Photo copyright: Anne Whittingham

**Image 10.21.3** Photo copyright: Anne Whittingham

**Image 10.22** Photo copyright Anne Whittingham

**Image 10.24.1**
https://upload.wikimedia.org/wikipedia/en/thumb/4/42/Louvre_Pyramid.jpg/1200px-Louvre_Pyramid.jpg_Paris_July_2011-27a

**Image 10.24.2** LittleMouse/ pixabay.com CC0

**Image 10.24.3** Emirates New Agency, http://wam.ae/en/details/1395302665808

**Image 10.25.1** kamodayz/ pixabay.com CC0

**Image 10.25.2** MonicaVolpin/ pixabay.com CC0

**Image 10.25.3** Arulonline/ pixabay.com CC0

www.ingramcontent.com/pod-product-compliance
Lightning Source LLC
Chambersburg PA
CBHW061131010526
44107CB00068B/2909